Art Changes Lives
Pat Leclerc

I would like to thank my wife, Marisol, for
all her support. I also wish to thank David
Hambling for editing and typesetting my
books and to thank Lia Scandariato for her
proofreading skills.

Contents

ART CHANGES LIVES

Pat Leclerc

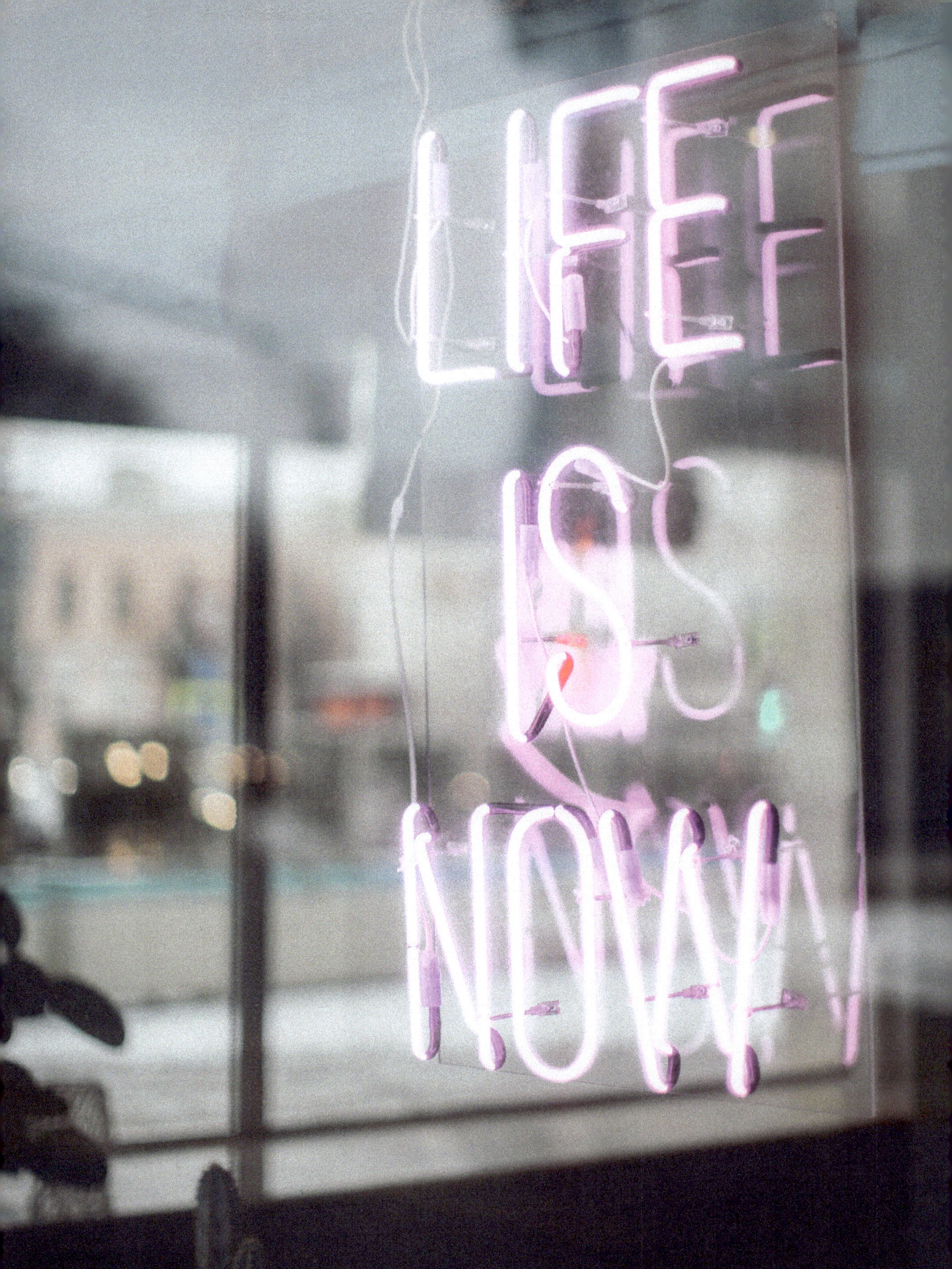

LIFE
IS
NOW

Tooth in Sincerity

What is the truth?
The truth is in your roots
In a life happening at this moment
Conceived of small segments
Flashes of lights
Appreciating nature's right
Renewing your sense of wonder
Looking forward to ponder
What's the truth
Do you really need proof
Or would you prefer
Living life, like it matters
Tomorrow's gone
The wind has blown
Old age will set on
The illusion will proclaim
The dream, the oration
Of this spoken dimension
In theory, only fantasy
Fabulous mountains
Immense emotional rains
Like tears of joy
Carrying messages
Of fraternity
Of unity
Of acceptance
Of true resonance
Reverberating

Celebrating
Life's simplicity
In all its beauty
Away from commotion
Bad news and their intentions
Refresh, de-stress
Relax take a deep breath
Admire the plan, its ambition
Nature and His passion
It's all there, now
Waiting for you
Needing all your attention
Open your eyes, heart
In this symphony play your part
Celebrate, admire the simple truth
The Universe holds you,
Remembering you're the smile
 of your youth...

Photo by Elly Fairytale

Dreamed Reality

If I offered you peace
Would you receive it with ease
Carry on, in the face
Of all our disgrace
If I offered you Love
Could you embrace it
If it came from above
Support it, elevate it to mountain top
Scream it, everywhere in every clock
If I offered you faith, for free
Would you take it, from me
This reality imagined, lived and dreamed
Only gets better when trust is esteemed
Love, to be loved
Be beautiful, to see beauty
Choose carefully what enters your mind
The light in your eyes
Can't make you blind

Darkness, could be, your demise
Money with blasphemy
Could destroy your divine entity
Humbleness with empathy
Could form you, peacefully
Are we part of the same family?
Or egos and individuality
If I offered you a dream
Would you wake up to redeem
This reality and your power
To shape and perceive this, Our
Into a brighter enlightened unity
A better world of human destiny
There is no need to wait
No reason, no force, without faith
Reality, stars and energy
Are defined, by your conscience purity
Form and shape your hearts

Photo by Nadi Lindsay

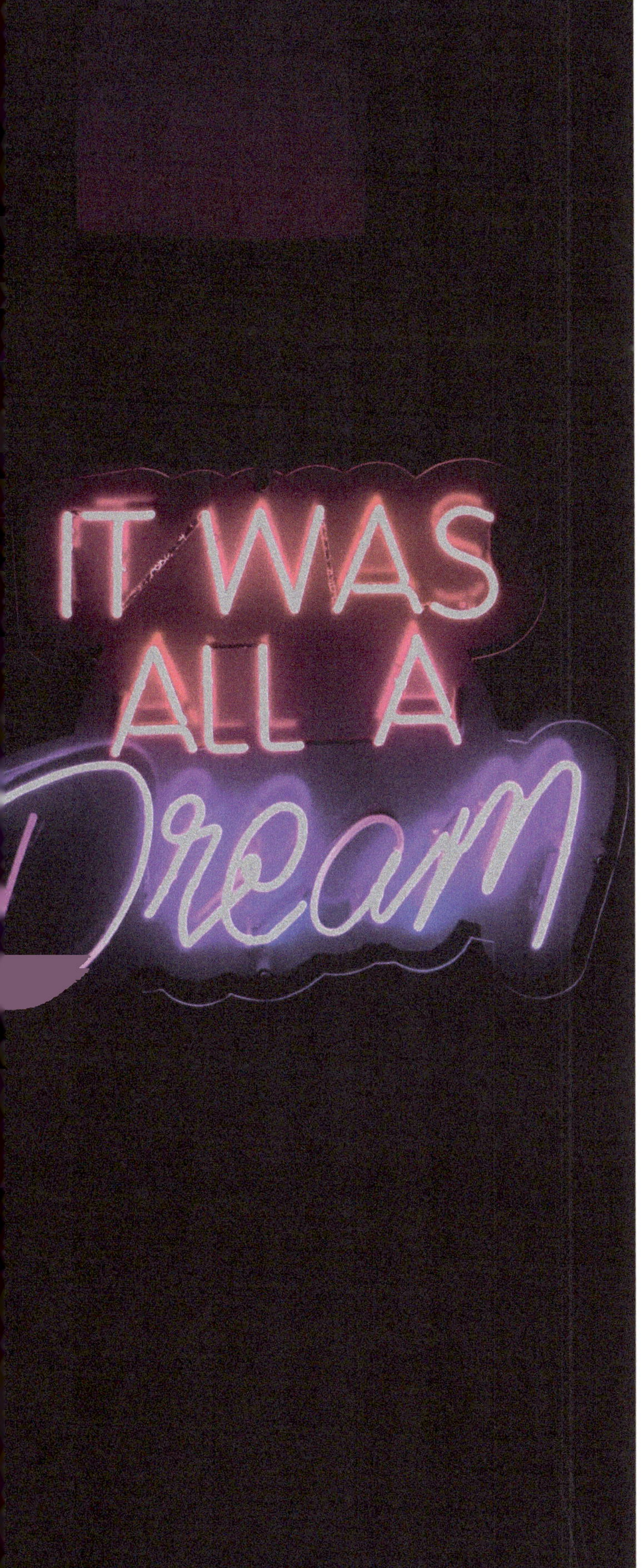

Your thoughts with magical art
It's there, it was already given
Their is no need for me to riven
Our bestial instincts
In our conscience, peace
Hate is very distinct
Choose wisely
Love abundantly
You can be, who ever, you want to be
Dream your reality
Open your eyes to see
It's all here, now, for you and me
I love you, I hope your soul can see...

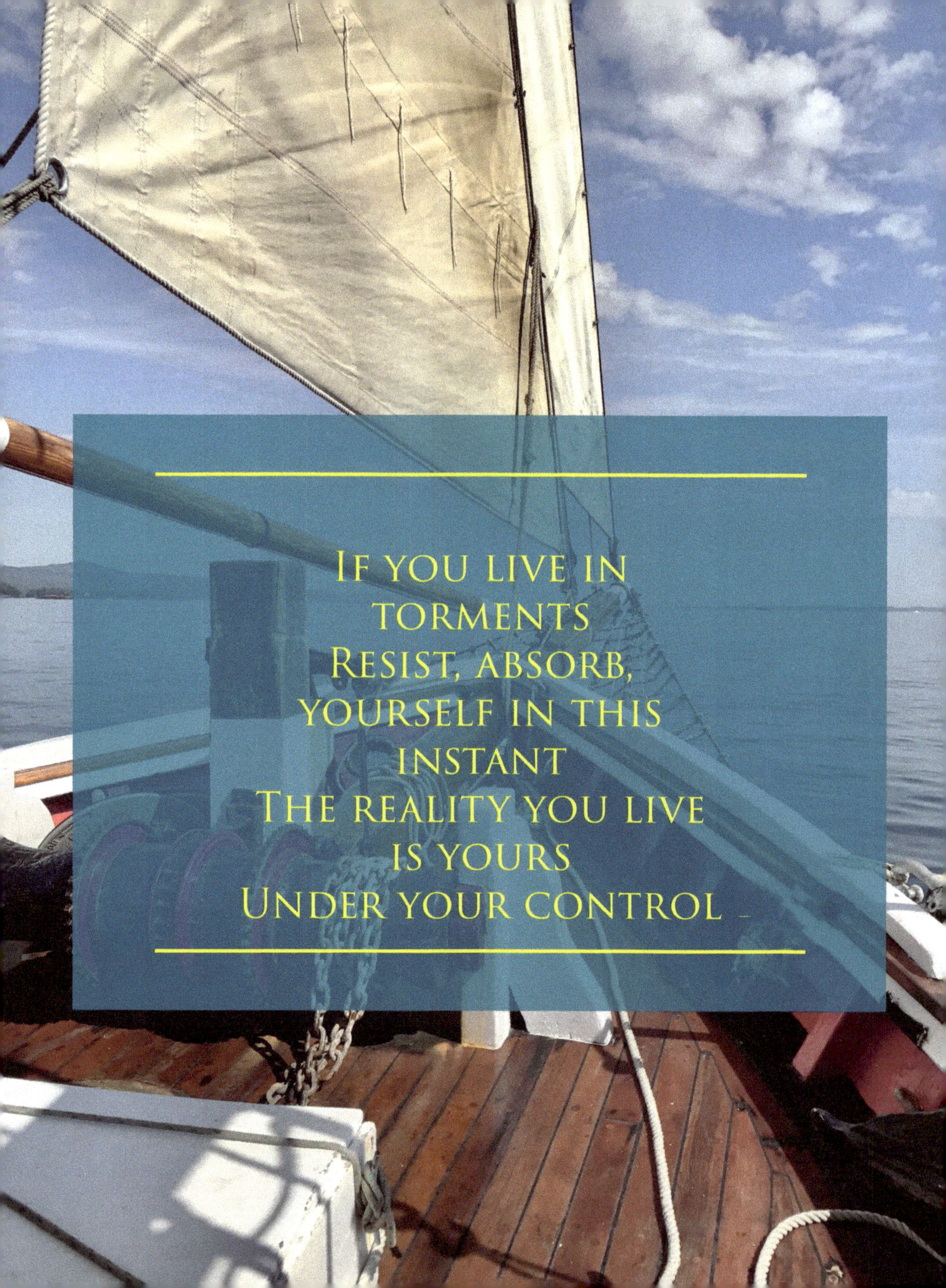
If you live in
torments
Resist, absorb,
yourself in this
instant
The reality you live
is yours
Under your control

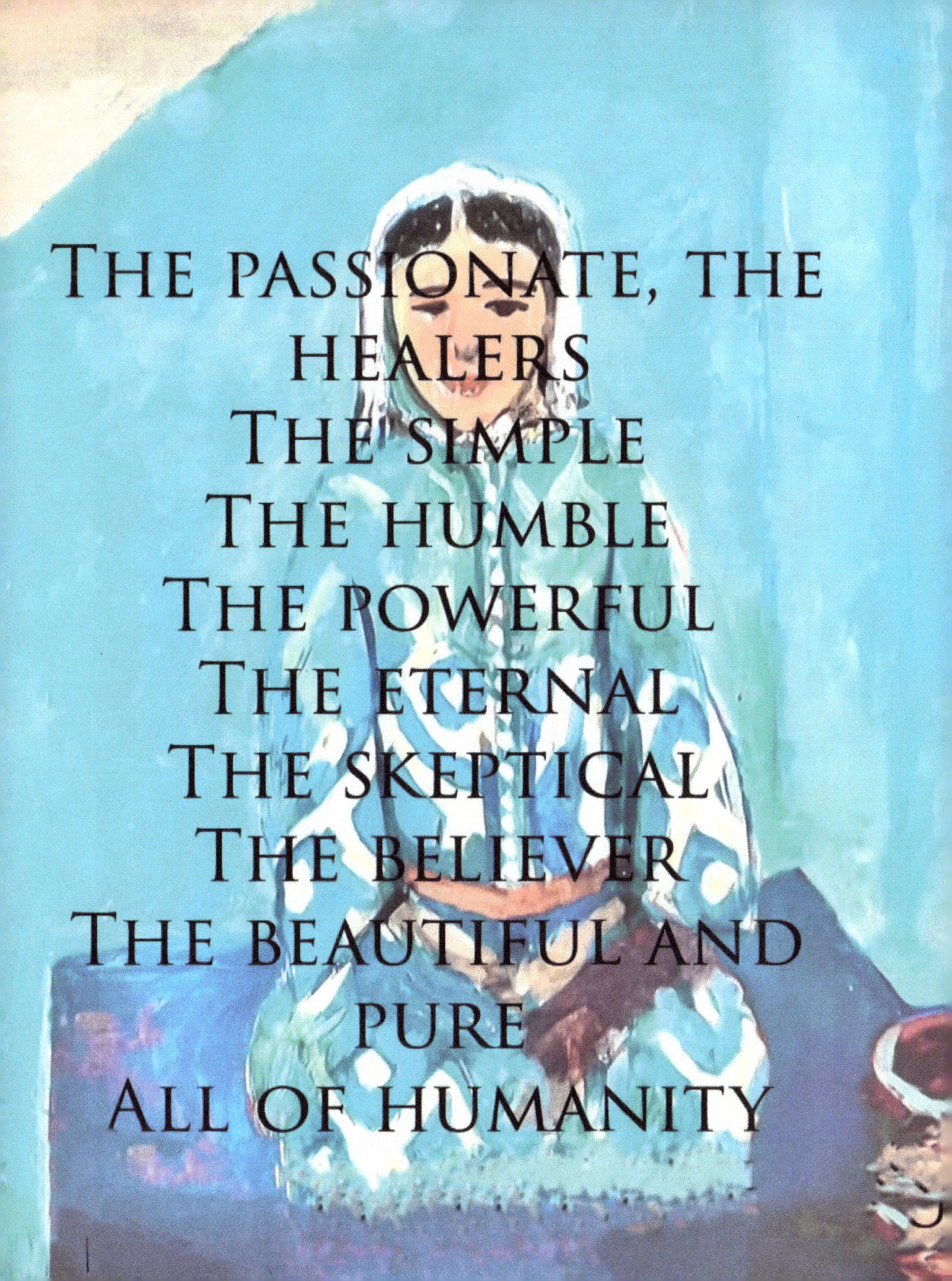

The passionate, the
healers
The simple
The humble
The powerful
The eternal
The skeptical
The believer
The beautiful and
pure
All of humanity

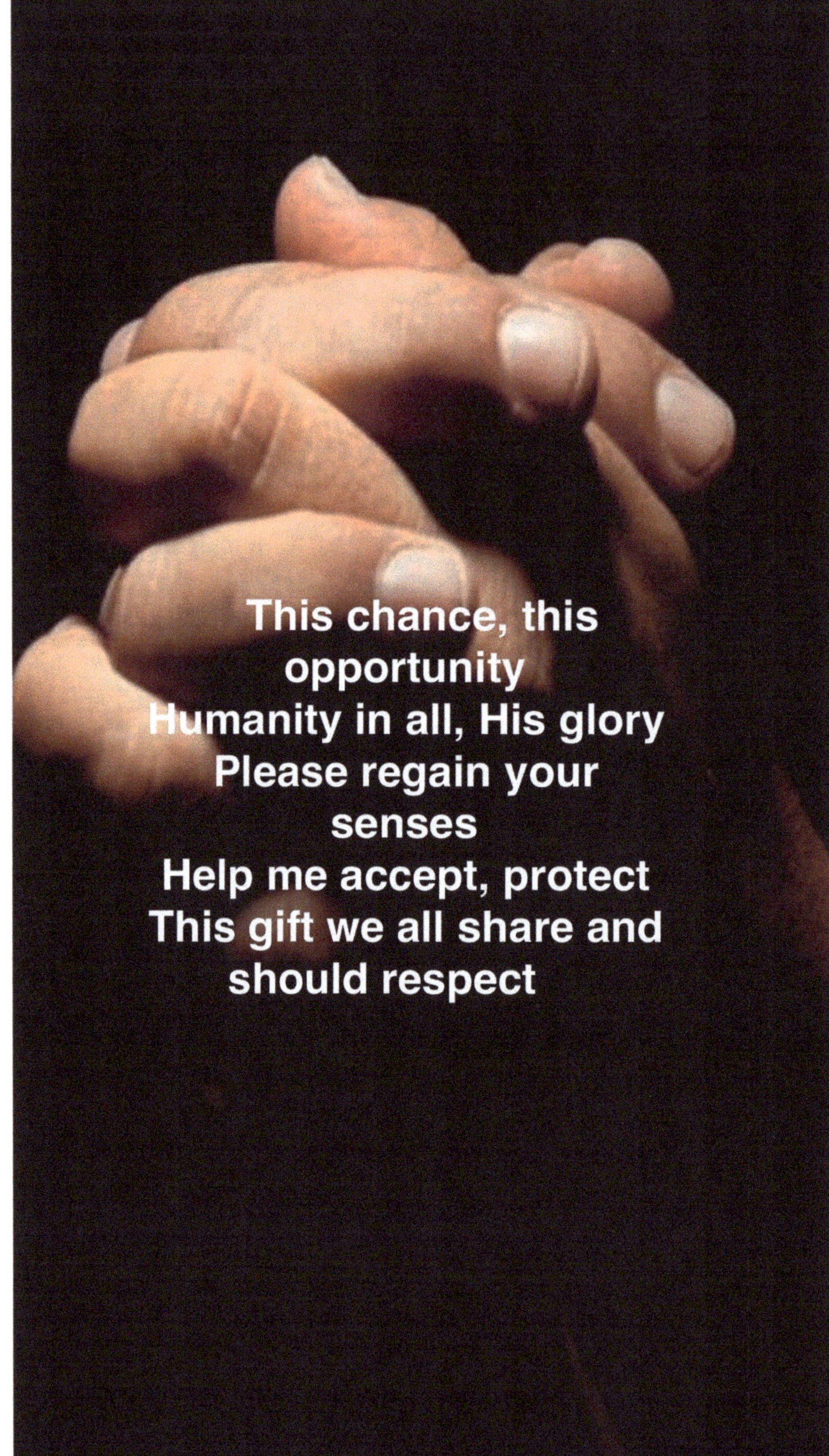

This chance, this opportunity
Humanity in all, His glory
Please regain your senses
Help me accept, protect
This gift we all share and should respect

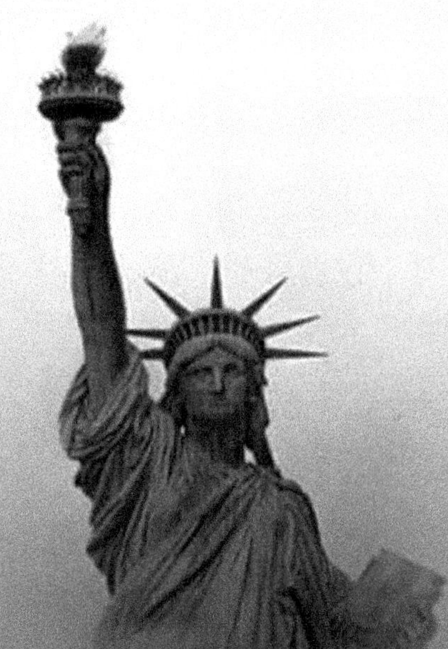

Protect your health importantly
Your good, clean conscience
Trust in the knowledge of
science
Respect in the vague
evidences

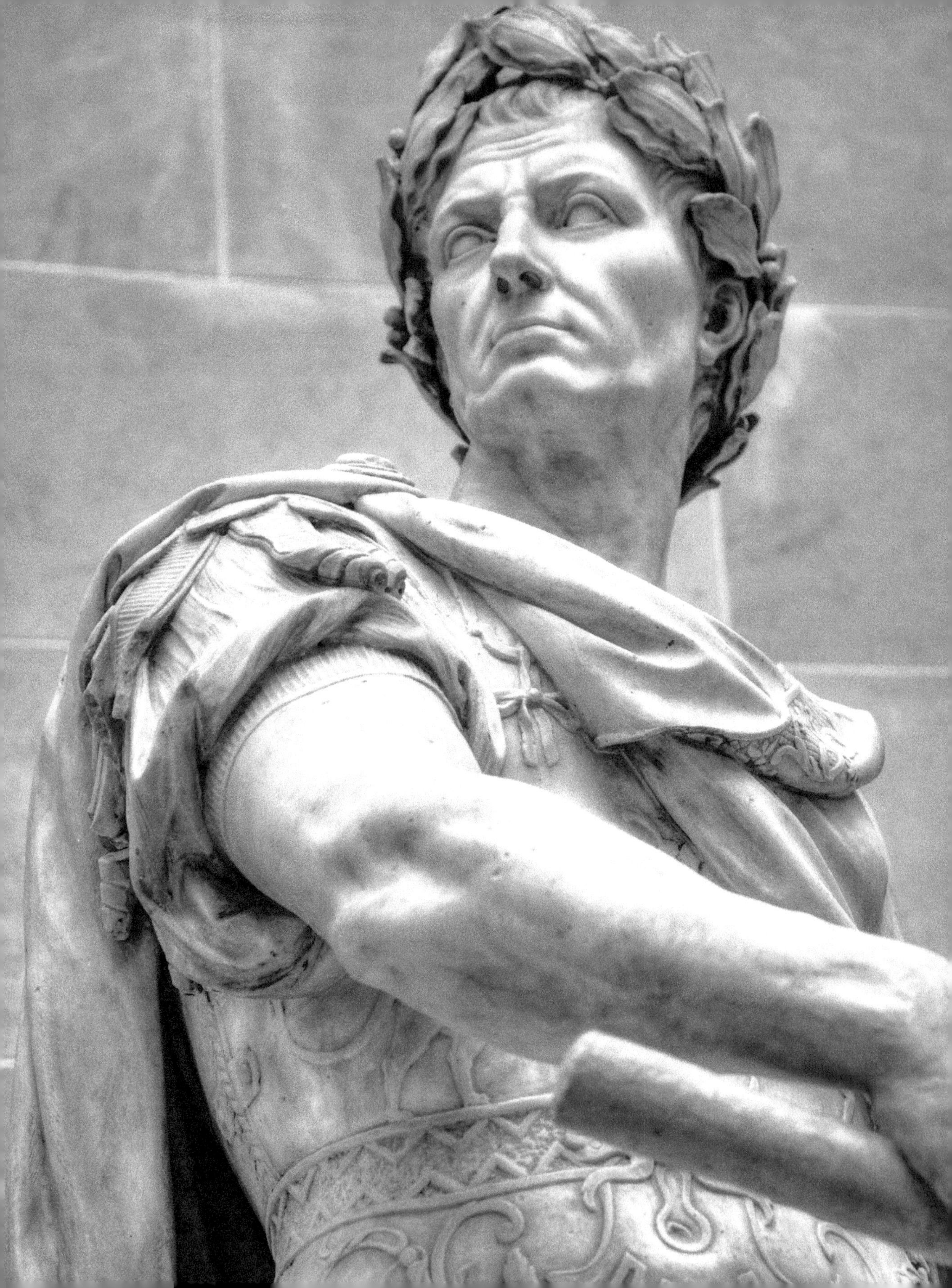

Leaders

What are we looking for in a leader?
Strength, wisdom, charisma
Truth, to make us cheerful
Intelligence, guidance, no enigma
Humbled, to be powerful
Lifting souls, with a sense of wonder
The kind of characteristics
Keeping amen, within the critics
Not bossy, a dignified commander
Someone looking up at the ladder
With good intentions
No moral aggressions
Sturdy, yet soft and adaptable
Kind and really knowledgeable
Respectful of genders
Transparency renders
Would be more than acceptable
Globalizing
Not dividing
In this twenty-first century
Peace given for glory
Love, acceptance, not hate
Pass through the gate
Encouragement for individuality
Hands in hands, total unity
Problematic, symptomatic
For the searching egocentric
There is power in wisdom

In chanting our anthems
While smiling at the neighbors
Appreciating many facets and colors
Transgressing not oppressing
Our mind to its fullest
Laughing, enjoying, the praise of the sun
Admiring their awareness, should be fun
Listen with your hearts
Let's play our parts
This utopia, the garden
The rivers flow, to Eden
Together, we live, apply the dream
Swim, breathe against the stream
Elevated by knowledge
Helped by kindness
Walking away from the ledge
To the center of humanity
Reaching our own purity
Free of darkness contaminants
At last... sunshine's on all continents

Photo by Skitterphoto

Rêver

Les rêves du passé
Désirent créer
Besoin inné
D'illusions brisées
Rêves d'une vie
Remplis d'objets inédits
Inutile, juste, maybe
Cœur vide, oublie
L'importance d'aimer
La seule vérité
Pour tout combler
Cervelle, inhabitée
Pour toi, comme pour moi
La tendresse, la loi
Seulement, donne droit
À qui veut être roi
D'un domaine inédit
Certainement interdit
Aux simples d'esprit
Si simple maudit
Pourquoi pas moi
S'ils me laissent froid
I might loose ma foi
Je pense y avoir droit
Désir d'un futur
Autre que ma nature
Laisse-moi être mature
Protège-moi for sûr

Mon futur incertain
Pourtant pas si lointain
Ne désirant rien de moins
Qu'un amour certain
Rêver d'aimer
Pire parfois rêver
D'être aimé
Peut parfois diminuer
Le besoin interdit
Par l'hypocrisie
De dire merci
Pourquoi inédit
Les rêves du passé
N'aiment que présenter
Un instant sans insister
Sur un futur filtré
Ne soyons pas bambins
L'avenir lointain
Trop souvent plein
De moments anodins
Vous voulez être purs
Oubliez la culture
Retournez à la nature
On sera tous matures
Personne n'aura moins
L'avarice sera loin
J'aimerais faire le point
L'humanité sera en plein

La paix pour tous
L'abondance surtout
L'amour avant tout
Pour l'avenir de nous

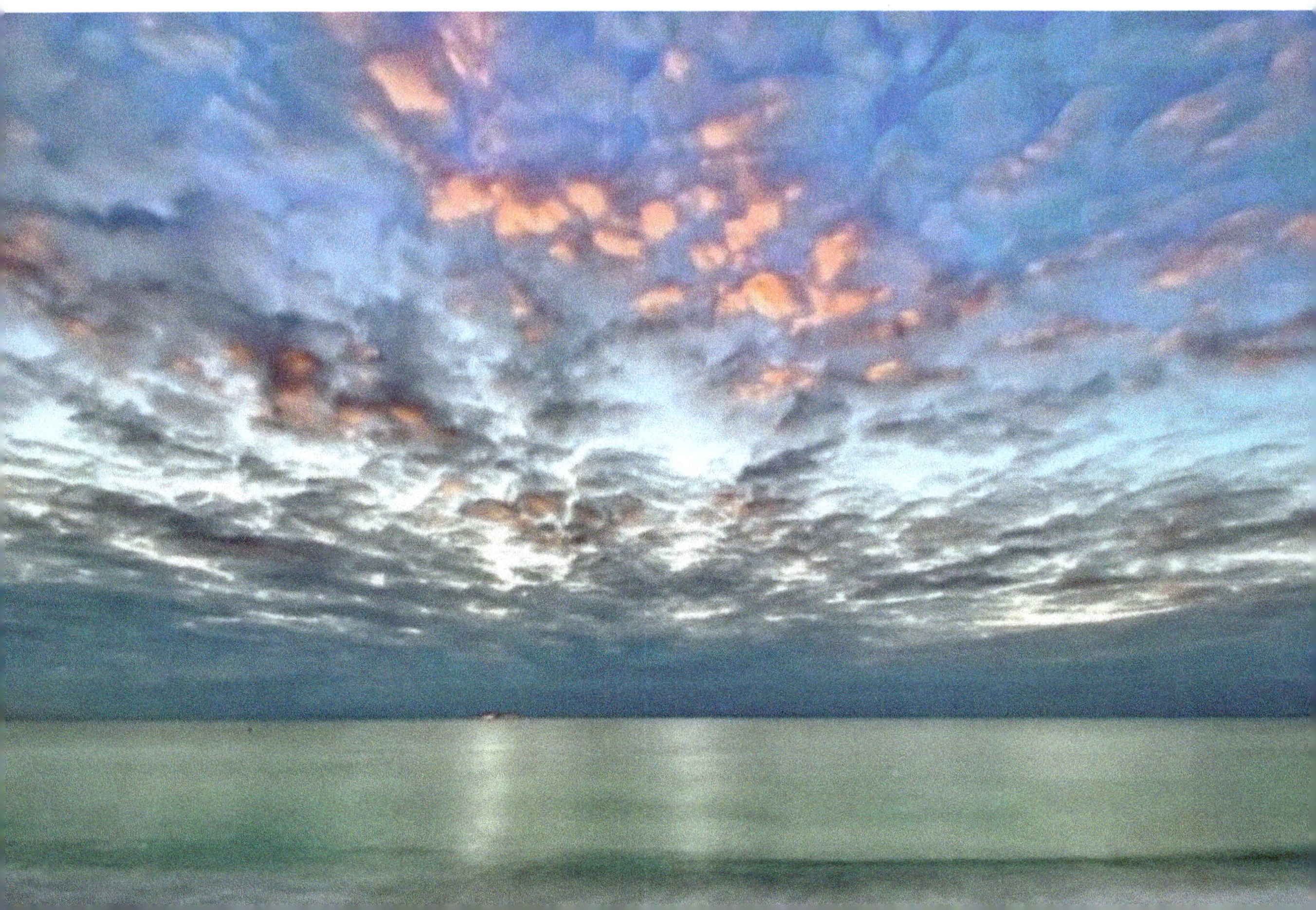

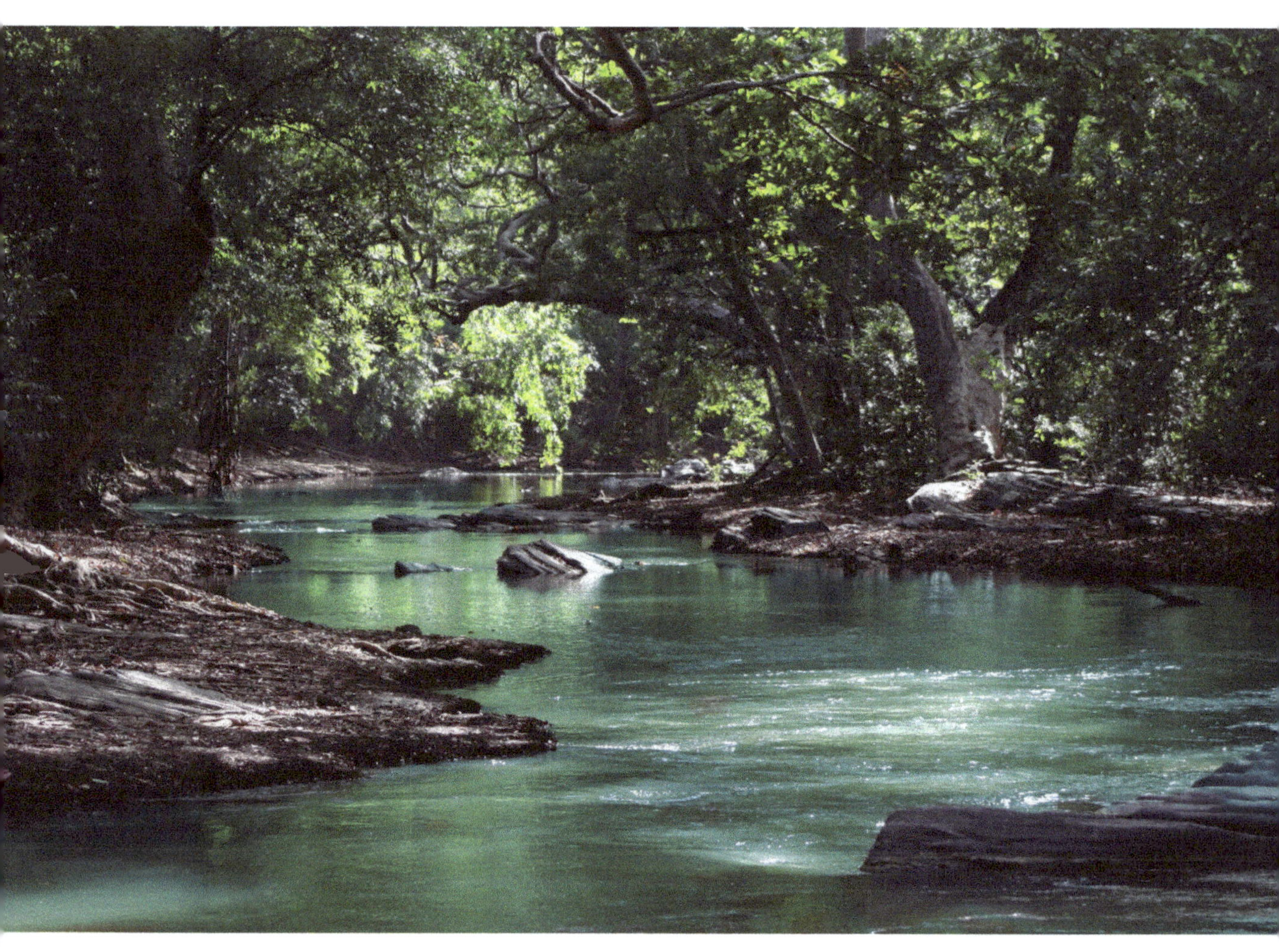

Photo by Ian Turnell

Relax, Read, Breathe

There is the need, within me
To write, to tell you, about He
Beautiful, majestic, humble
Strong, powerful, I stumble
In His wake, I am left in awe
By His faithfulness, ah
Deliverance, comfort
In satisfying the urge
To share, with you, my soul
The world needs more love
More, forgiveness
More, politeness
Maybe we could just for an instant
Go back imagining our infants
Sparkling minds awaken to beauty
Unaware of our folly
Innocent, pure, with the only goal
To discover, take a new look
Reopen the magical book
Of colors, smells and wonders
Of persistence in all mothers
His creation dreamed
In perpetuation of streams
Soft rivers of lights
Majestical swimming universe
Like words in a poetic verse
Touching, curing, the one's, crying
Enveloping, caressing the observing

Can I tell you, what's inside of me
The secret, behooved to me
He loves you, She lives, in you
Listen as you read
Breathe as He pleads
Slow down, find calm
Place your hands, in His palm
Rest, admire the simplicity
Of all this beauty
Enjoy and applaud
Remember to look beyond
To say thank you
Simply, appreciate the sun
Laugh in the rain
Transform your reality
To match His glory
Don't take life for granted
Accept
Recognize
This amazing... magical journey

There is power in
wisdom
In chanting our anthems
While smiling at the
neighbors
Appreciating many facets
and colors

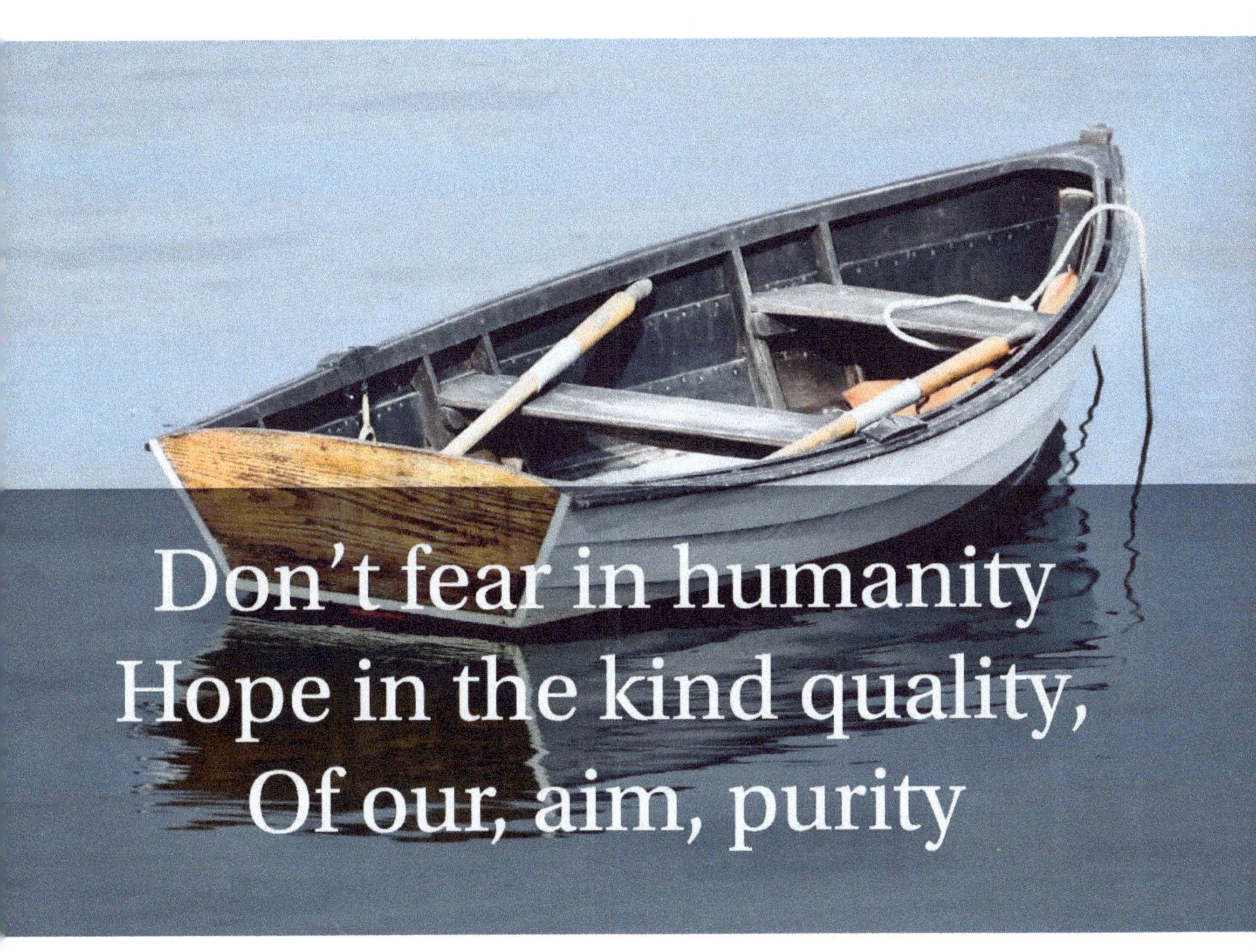

Don't fear in humanity
Hope in the kind quality,
Of our, aim, purity

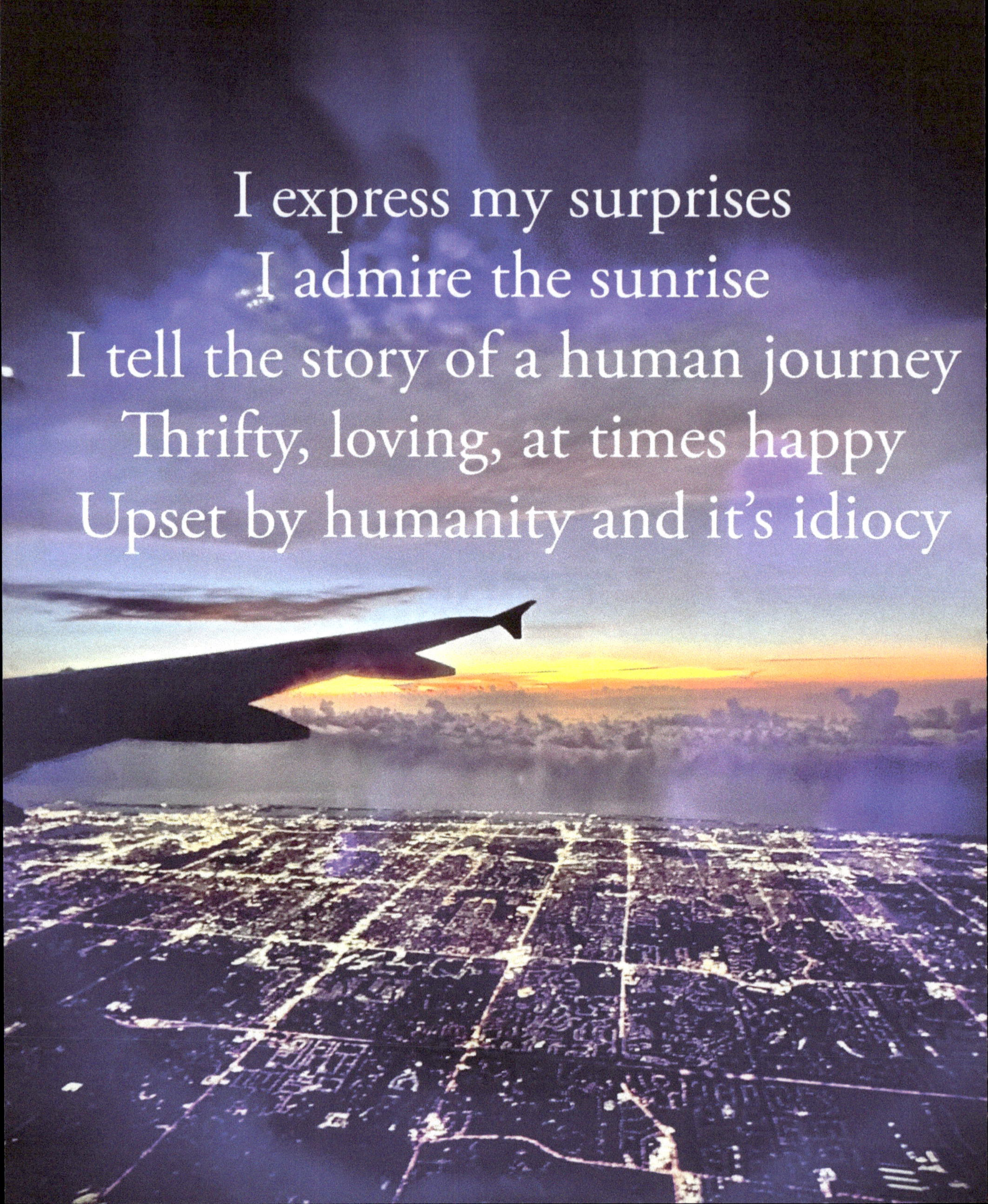

I express my surprises
I admire the sunrise
I tell the story of a human journey
Thrifty, loving, at times happy
Upset by humanity and it's idiocy

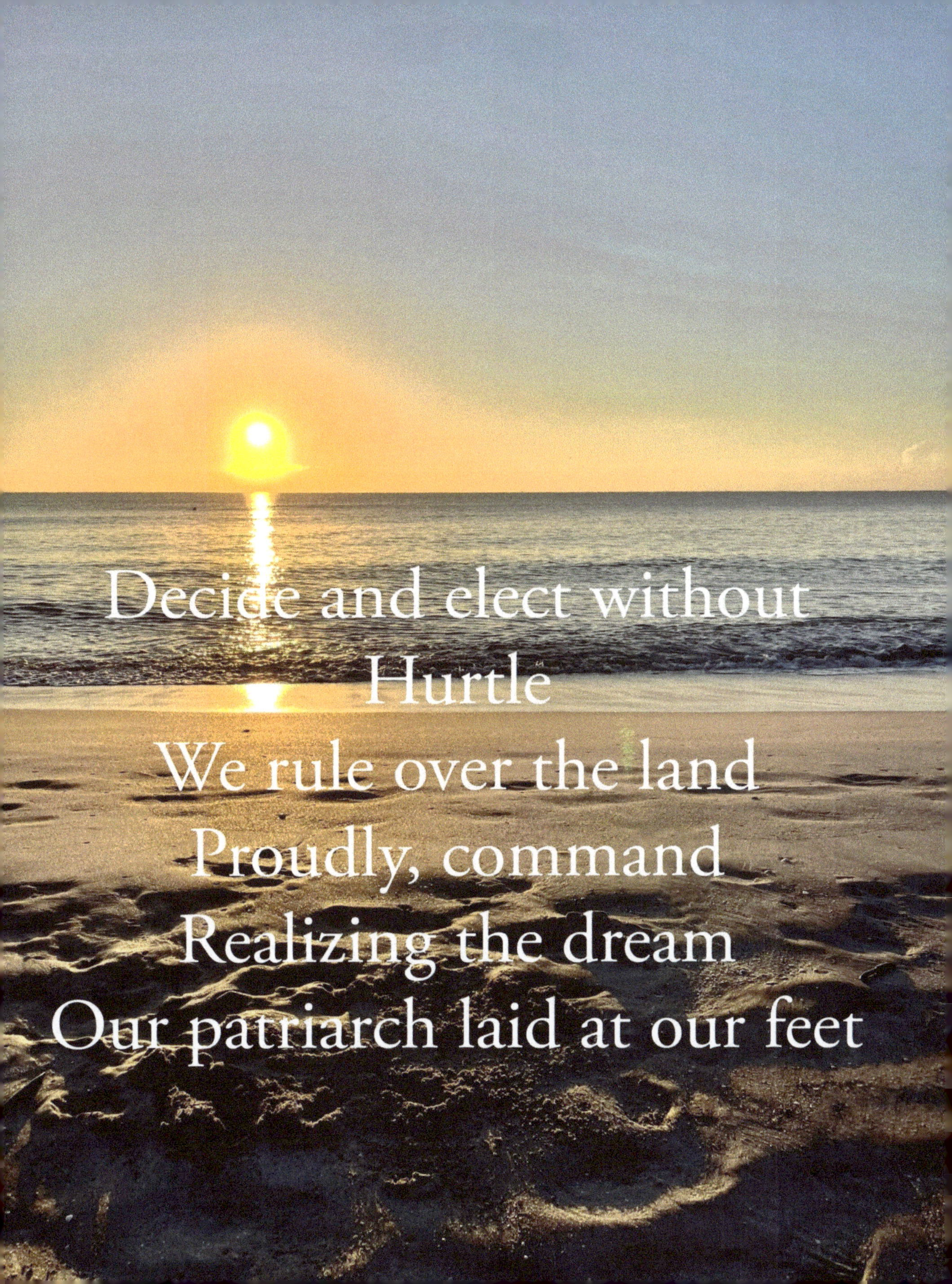

Decide and elect without
Hurtle
We rule over the land
Proudly, command
Realizing the dream
Our patriarch laid at our feet

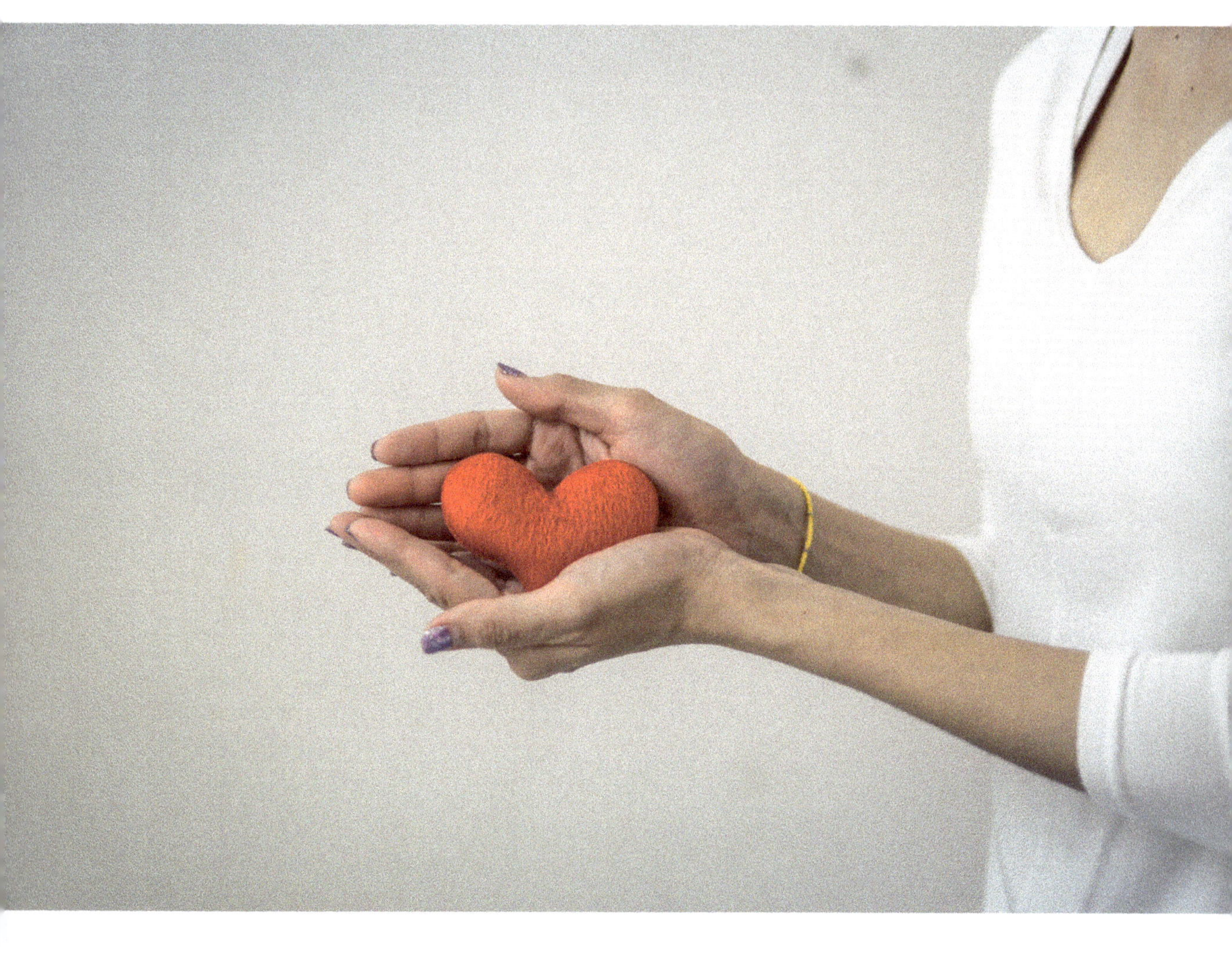

Healing

Greatness, I speak
Inspired indeed
From above
Only of love
What is the question
Where is our attention
Could we be unaware
Of the reasons
Really needing
Us all to look,
Interrogative
Don't let it be representative
Of a society
Nobody, seems to worry
Of what we could be
In a world
A place, where we would be
More intelligent
Maybe more diligent
Where everyone could be
More accomplished, happy
Our animal instinct
The basics restrained
Of our humanity
Perhaps bestial
Most times impartial
To a way
Indeed, we may

Or will we
Will you, and me
Carry society
Into a new world
Where peace
Love, ease
The suffering
Of every being
Animal and primal
Feelings are present
In every living, intent
For their ailing
Should be applied, inspiring
To those vital
Healers and lovers
What is the question
Our attention
The answer
In our prayers
Affection, respect
Let's all protect
Each other
Ask without regrets
Help, mostly, love...
...And live of the above

Photo by Puwandon Sang-ngernon

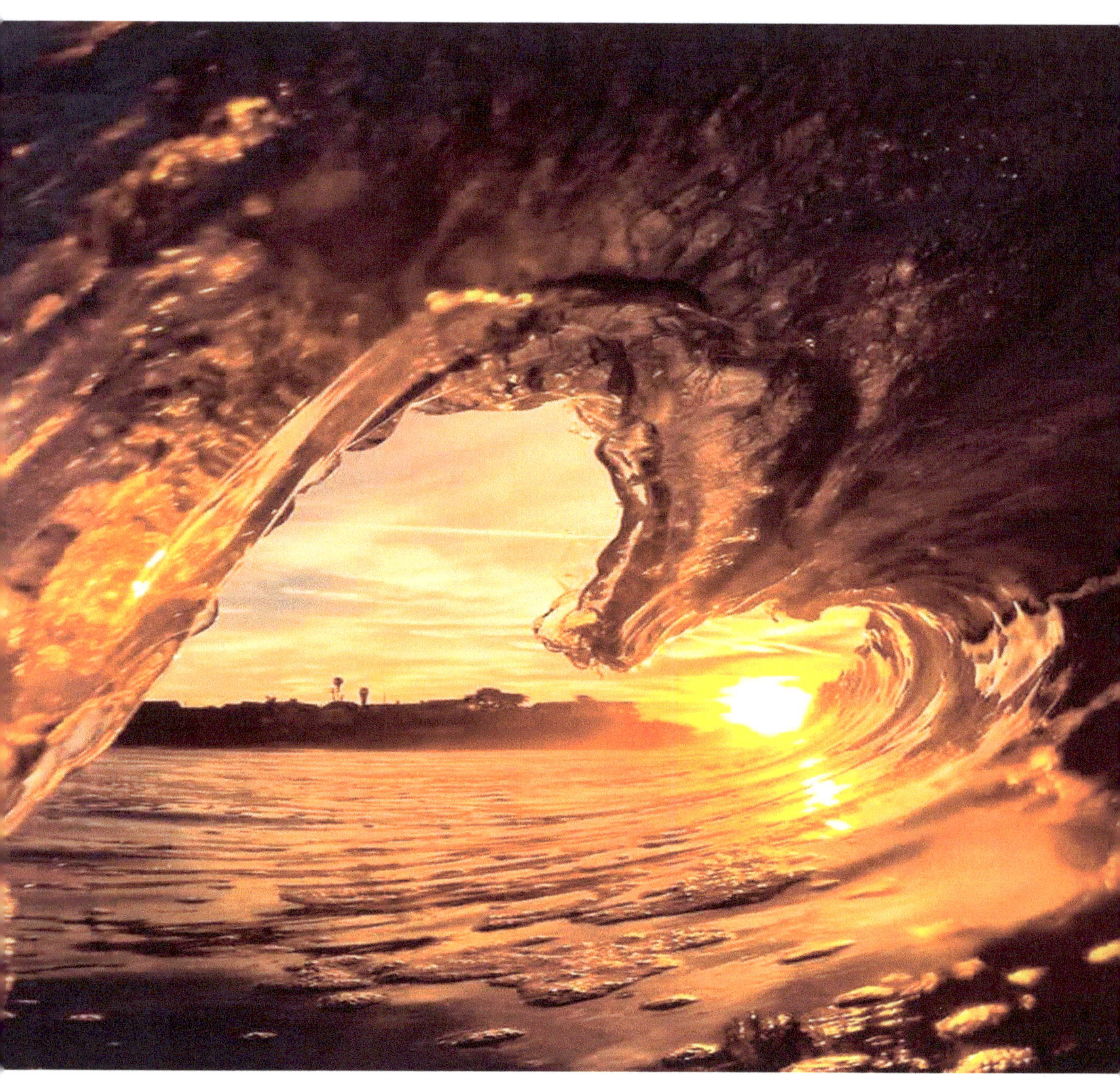

Destiny

Destiny, planned or arranged
Life as it is, managed
Seems to be
Illusions and passions
Material and delusion
Perhaps to me
Energy condenses
In a cosmic dance
Forming, interacting
Images, sounds, acting
Smells and intuitions
There are no partitions
What touches you
Involves them
Do we really know, who
Is at the helm
Is it me
Or Is it He
Perhaps you
Really control me
Galaxies, true
We have no clue
Who has the key
For you and for me
Bring your mind
Today, now, be fine
Tomorrow, how do we know
Constellations colors

Far nebulae, luminous
Matter
Live in glorious
Manner
Softly like flowers
Just be
Beautiful, peaceful
Let the wind carry
Your satisfying journey
Contentment, joy
And fulfillment
Past and future
All meeting, melting
Transcending
Our life
Our destiny
Into...
His immense
Power and Glory
So simple you see
Yet, unraveling to most
Of us human being
There is beauty
In this simplicity
Let go and let God
Love Him
Praise Him
Sit back, enjoy and applaud

Photo by Hernan Paucarra

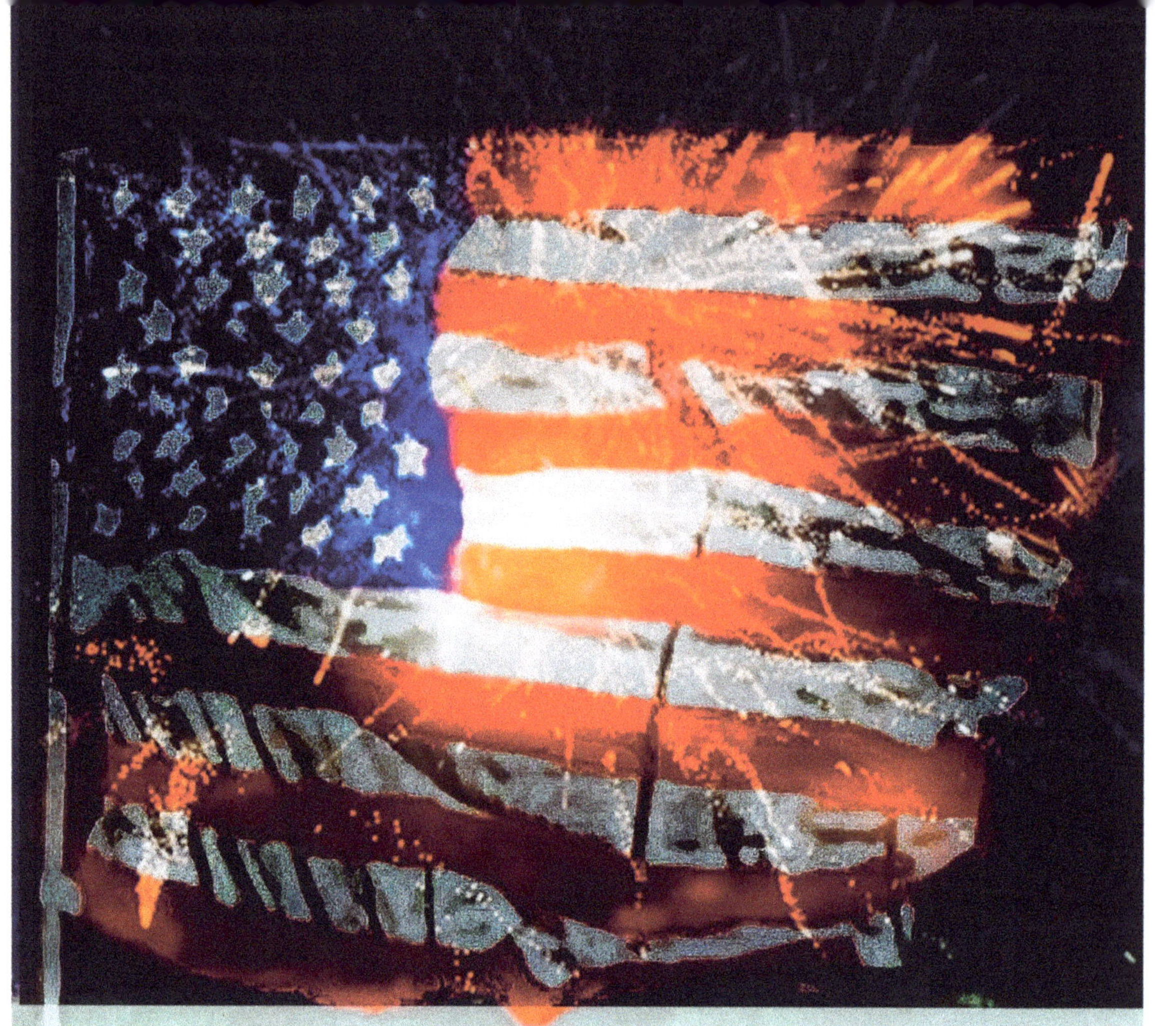

The human story
In all our profanity
Will develop
Must envelop
Our souls of honey
Our hearts of energy

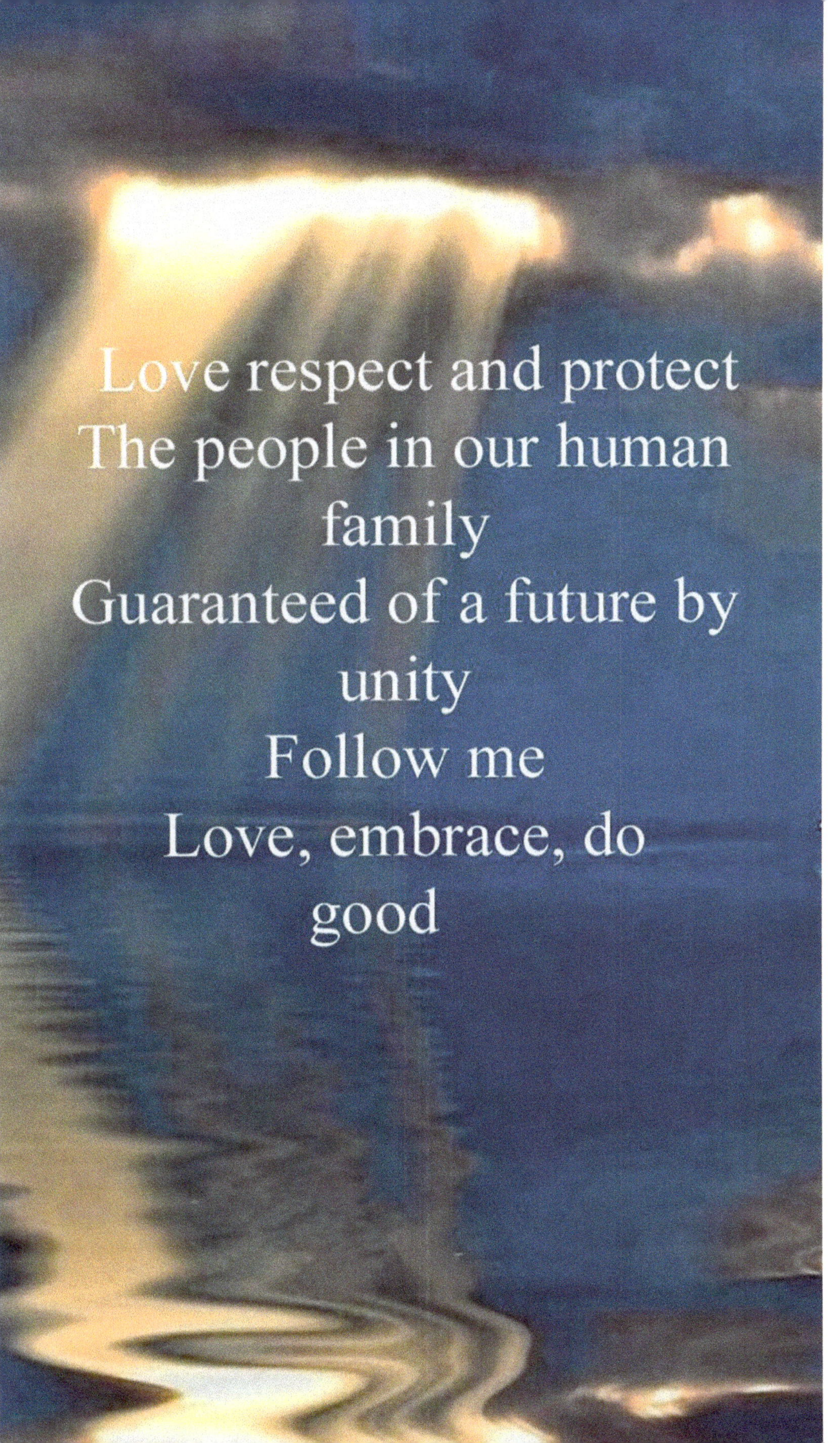

Love respect and protect
The people in our human
family
Guaranteed of a future by
unity
Follow me
Love, embrace, do
good

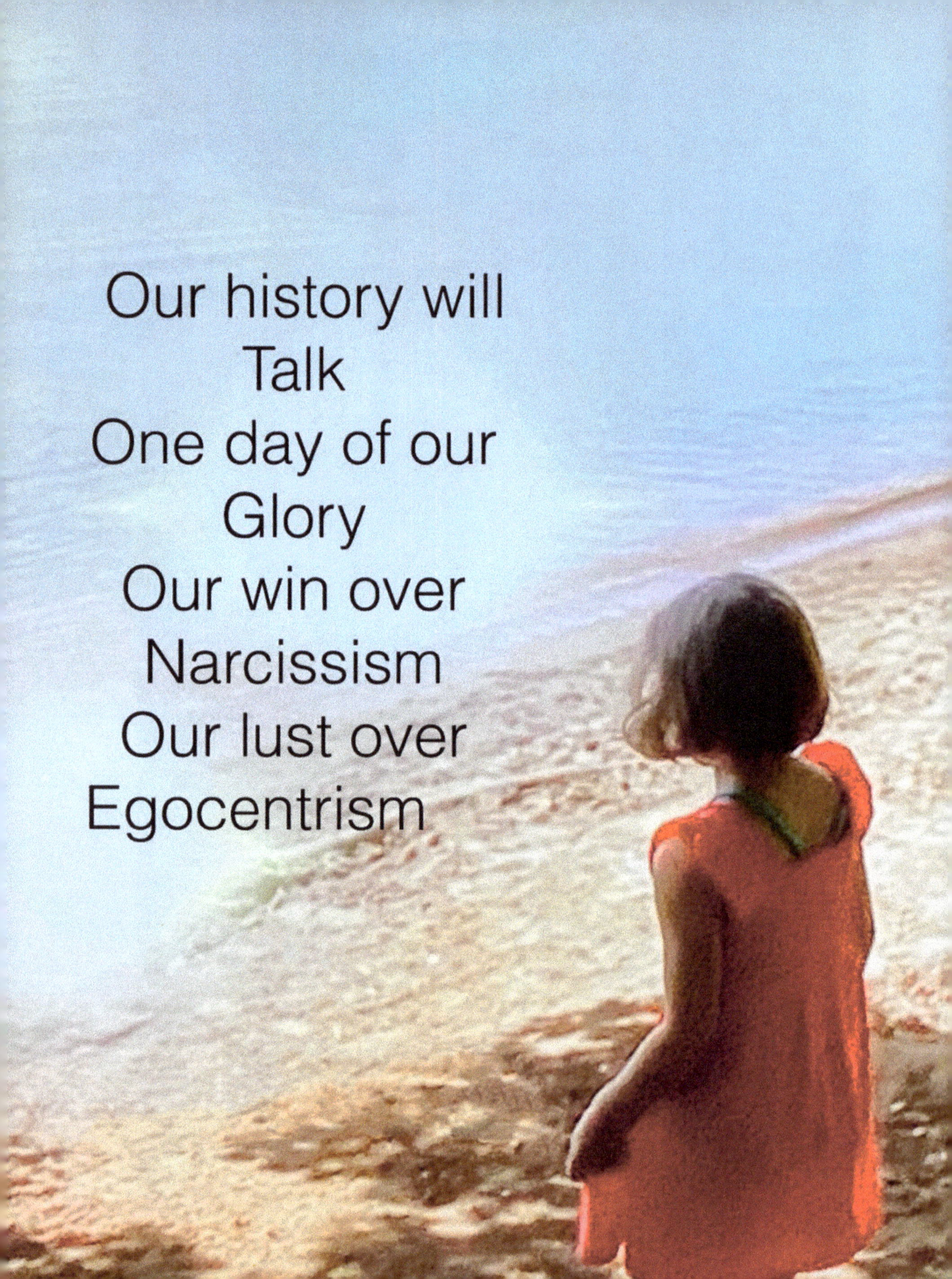
Our history will
Talk
One day of our
Glory
Our win over
Narcissism
Our lust over
Egocentrism

This energy reverberates
A water drop, circles, and
integrates
All of us, into a gigantic
Mystical
Magical
New world ideology
Of a very different tonality
Is this world, for real?

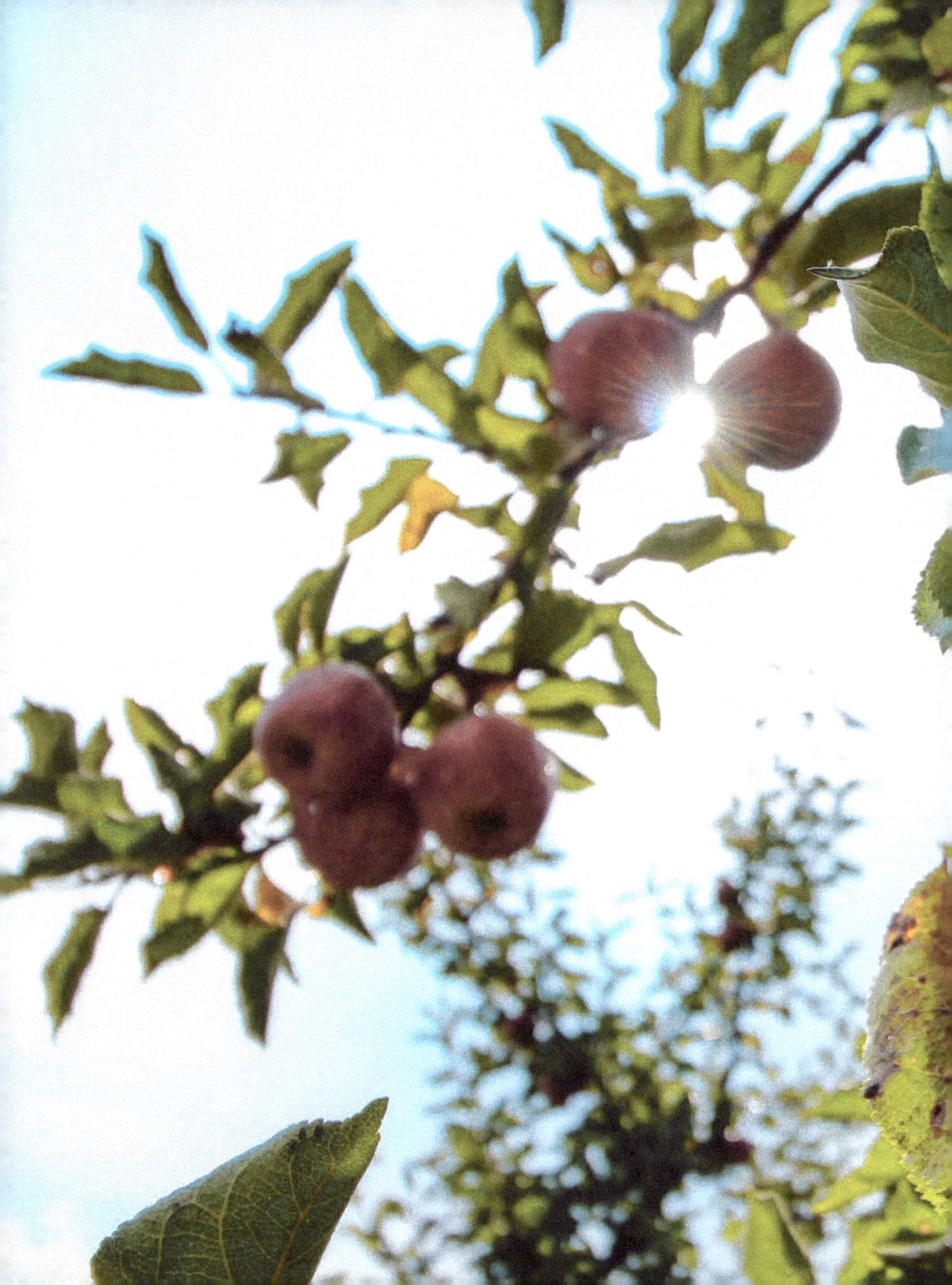

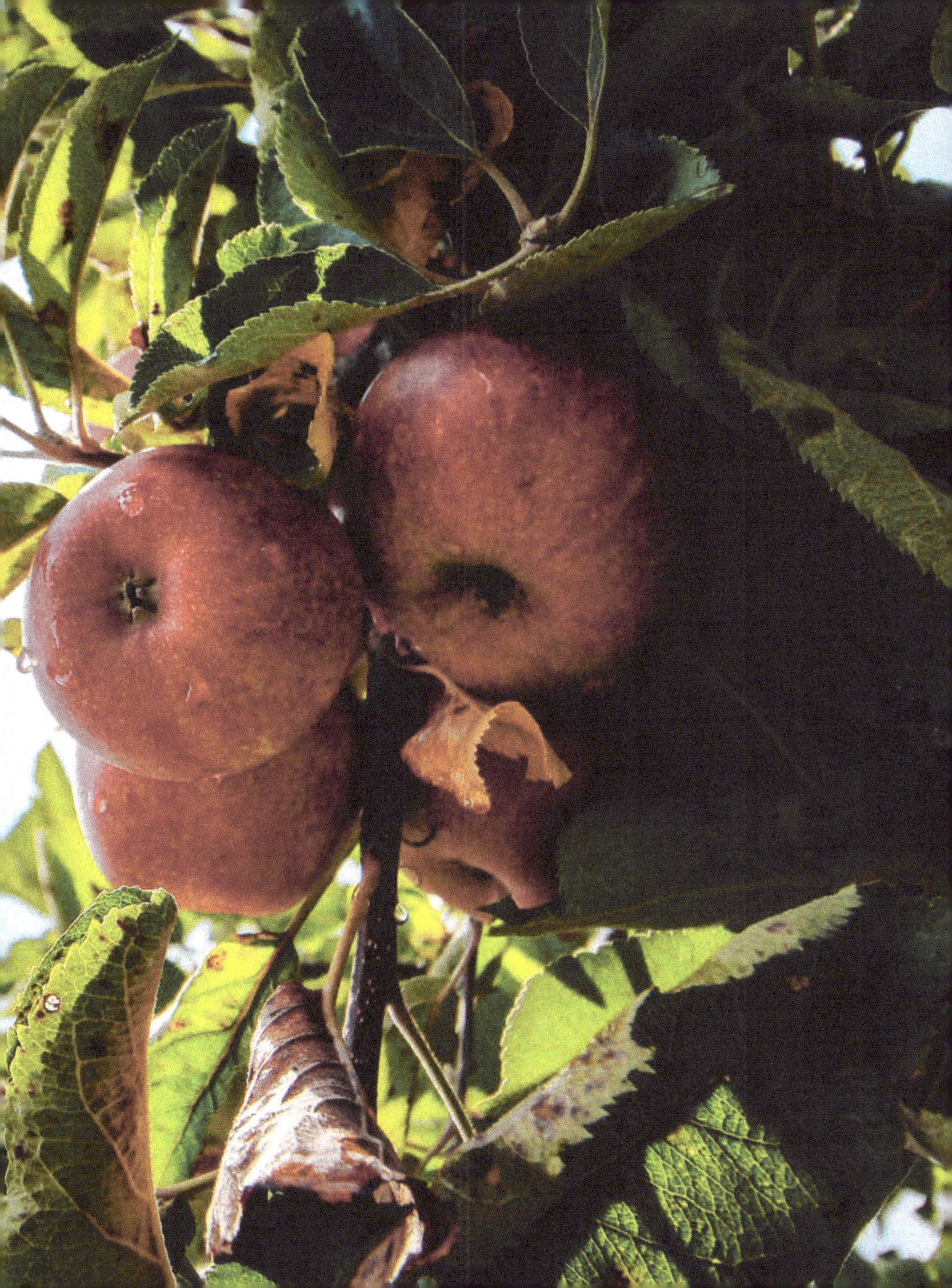

Life "Fruit-Utility"

I've always been aware of joy
Even since I was a boy
But what I discovered recently
Is how evil the world can be
Absurd, abnormality
In the name of money
Systems of corruption
Over earthly obsessions
The path of discernment
Abused without consent
Life, beauty and rare moments
Shadowed by glimmers and bad
Intent
I thought myself prepared
But really naive and unaware
Of the appeal of shiny gold
In the heart of humans, getting old
Patterns of redemption
Requiring our attention
Salvation
Revision
In the mind altercation
Pure fantasy or alienation
I am now observing
My fellows insisting
On the wrong behaviors
Of their primal ancestors
Our consciousness
Our uniqueness

Our inter connectivity
Requiring your positive energy
To fulfill our ultimate destiny
Involving
Evolving
Beings of light
Stars so bright
Capable and kindly
Beyond love and its ability
To heal
To kneel
Humbly
Thankfully
Embrace our common Unity
Assuring our survival
Is now my most precious
Message of hope for the curious
Interrogative
Introspective
Journey toward peace
Intergalactic consciousness, at least
The beginning
Of our loving nature as human,
Precious, being
Joining hands
Forward, to a better end
Fully aware of the rapture I've
Always been aware of joy
Even since I was a boy

Photo on previous page by Tom
Swinnen

But what I discovered recently
Is how evil the world can be
Absurd, abnormality
In the name of money
Systems of corruption
Over earthly obsessions
The path of discernment
Abused without consent
Life, beauty and rare moments
Shadowed by glimmers and bad
Intent
I thought myself prepared
But really naive and unaware
Of the appeal of shiny gold
In the heart of humans, getting old
Patterns of redemption
Requiring our attention
Salvation
Revision
In the mind altercation
Pure fantasy or alienation
I am now observing
My fellows insisting
On the wrong behaviors
Of their primal ancestors
Our consciousness
Our uniqueness
Our inter connectivity
Requiring your positive energy

To fulfill our ultimate destiny
Involving
Evolving
Beings of light
Stars so bright
Capable and kindly
Beyond love and its ability
To heal
To kneel
Humbly
Thankfully
Embrace our common Unity
Assuring our survival
Is now my most precious
Message of hope for the curious
Interrogative
Introspective
Journey toward peace
Intergalactic consciousness, at least
The beginning
Of our loving nature as human,
Precious, being
Joining hands
Forward, to a better end
Fully aware of the rapture
And His final disclosure ..
And His final disclosure ..

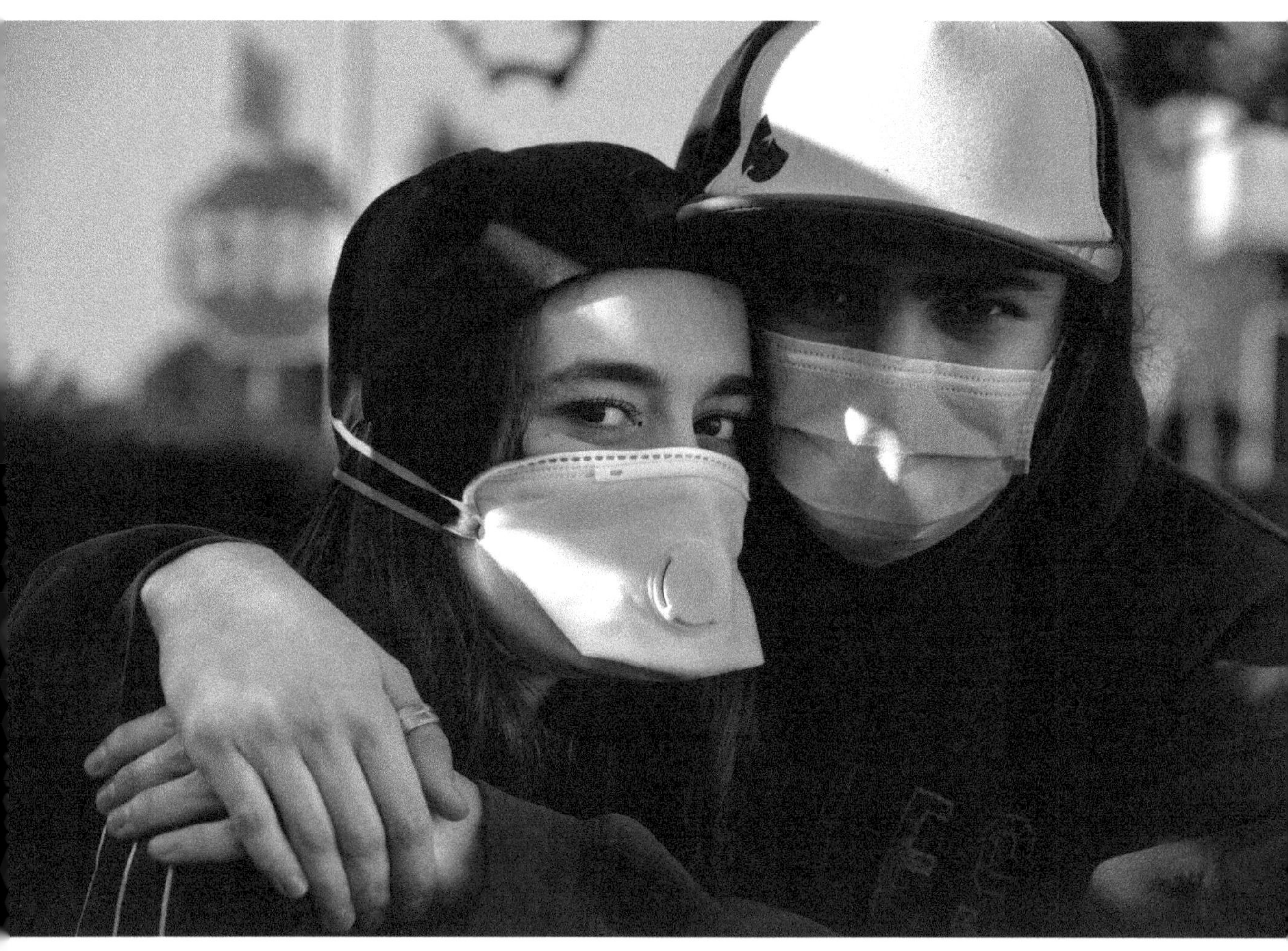

Con Legion Contagion

Coronavirus
Infectious, highly mysterious
Or fear, mostly, symptomatic
Of a society required of critics
Its deep questions
Essential
Primordial
Our undivided attentions
Let's take this seriously
Protect your health, importantly
Your good, clean, conscience
Trust in the knowledge of science
Respect in the vague evidences
Have no regrets
Save and protect
This unique, beautiful planet
By taking a moral stand
Maybe, we don't understand
Fear, divide and conquer
The road map, trace for our future
Awareness is described
Involvement is prescribed
For our sake
By our faith
Don't fear in humanity
Hope in the kind quality
Of our aim, purity
It's certainly, deeply true

We do, have a clue
Every lost soul
Is, for the heart, armful
For all the inflicted families
Our past, our destiny
Resilience
Acceptance
Determination
Adaptation
But above all, the will
To stay alive
To evolve is our deepest skill
We always adapt and thrive
In the rise of challenges
Even above
The worst climatic changes
I trust and recognize
Our intelligence, will mobilize
Into a bright future
Where the basic intents, will be pure
Rise, stay awake and protected
Our survival is imbedded
In the kind-heartedness of the stars
Believe
In the kindness of the human heart...

Photo by Serena Koi

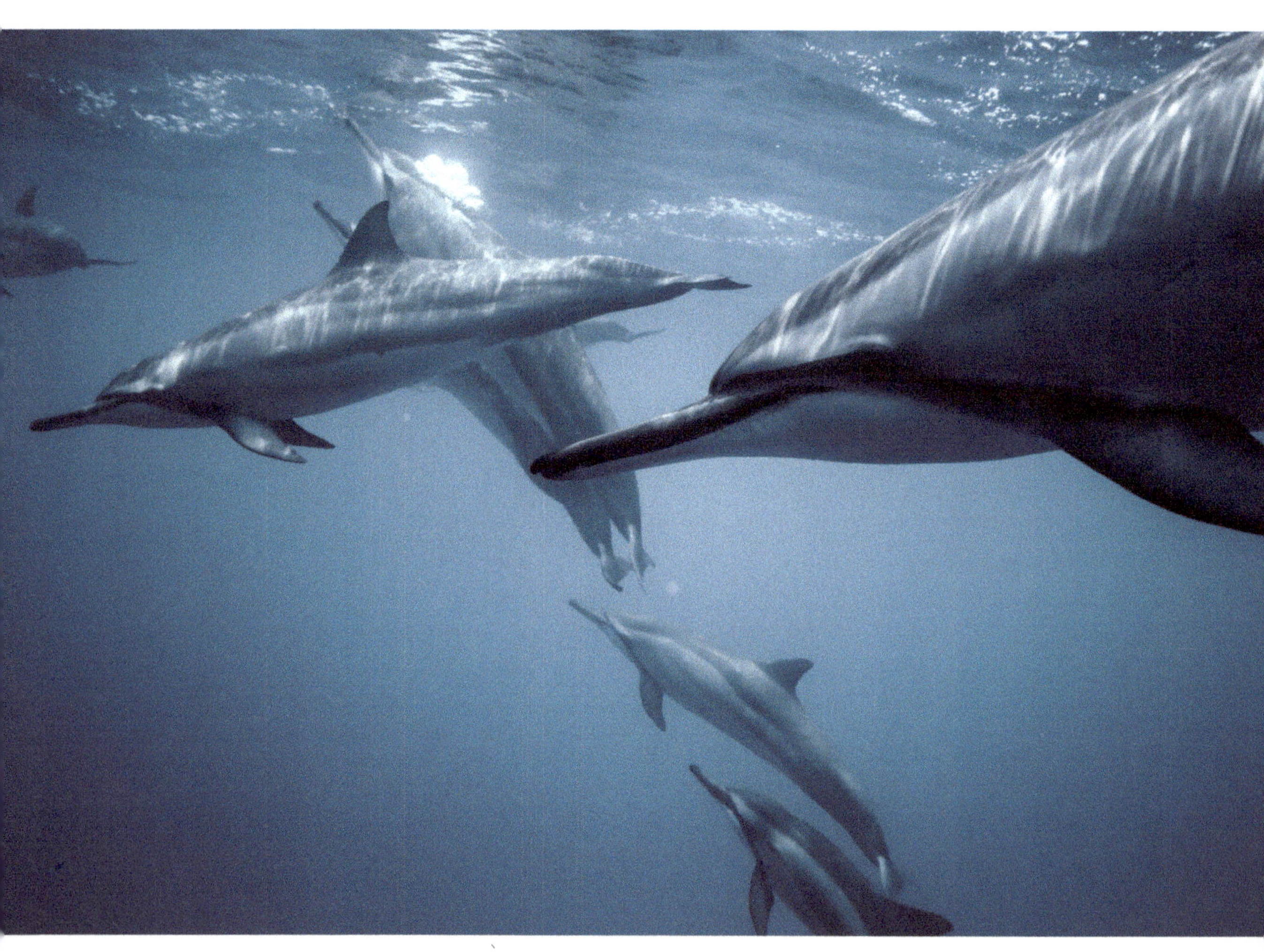

Dear Brothers, Why Do You Fight?

We are all blood, water and light
The same fabric, particles alike
Brothers, there's no need to be right
Life's gift is in nature
To be cherished for sure
Hurt, pains and blood
Imagine the flower buds
Pure, beautiful, soft
An inspiration it must
Colors, shades varies
Forms and shapes carries
Intricate differences
Without jealousy or preferences
Brothers see and understand
Do not take a stand
For egos, ideas, withstand
The pressure
To be sure
To be right
Instead, be bright
Shine lights
Enlighten the night
Darkness must be fought
Together, we can be taught
Change and transform
The world conforms
With no questions asked
Is it such a huge task?

How possible would it be to ask
To remove the mask?
Retrieve and believe
In knowledge we can achieve
Balance, realization
Of our total unison
One voice, one human race
All in, familiar faces
Would you wake up
For a good clean up
The reason simple
Your energy
Is my synergy
Our interaction
Is an essential action
Necessary for the chemistry
Forming, involving our destiny
Towards a better world
A place where hurled
Are things of the past
Moving forward at last...

Photo by Jeremy Bishop

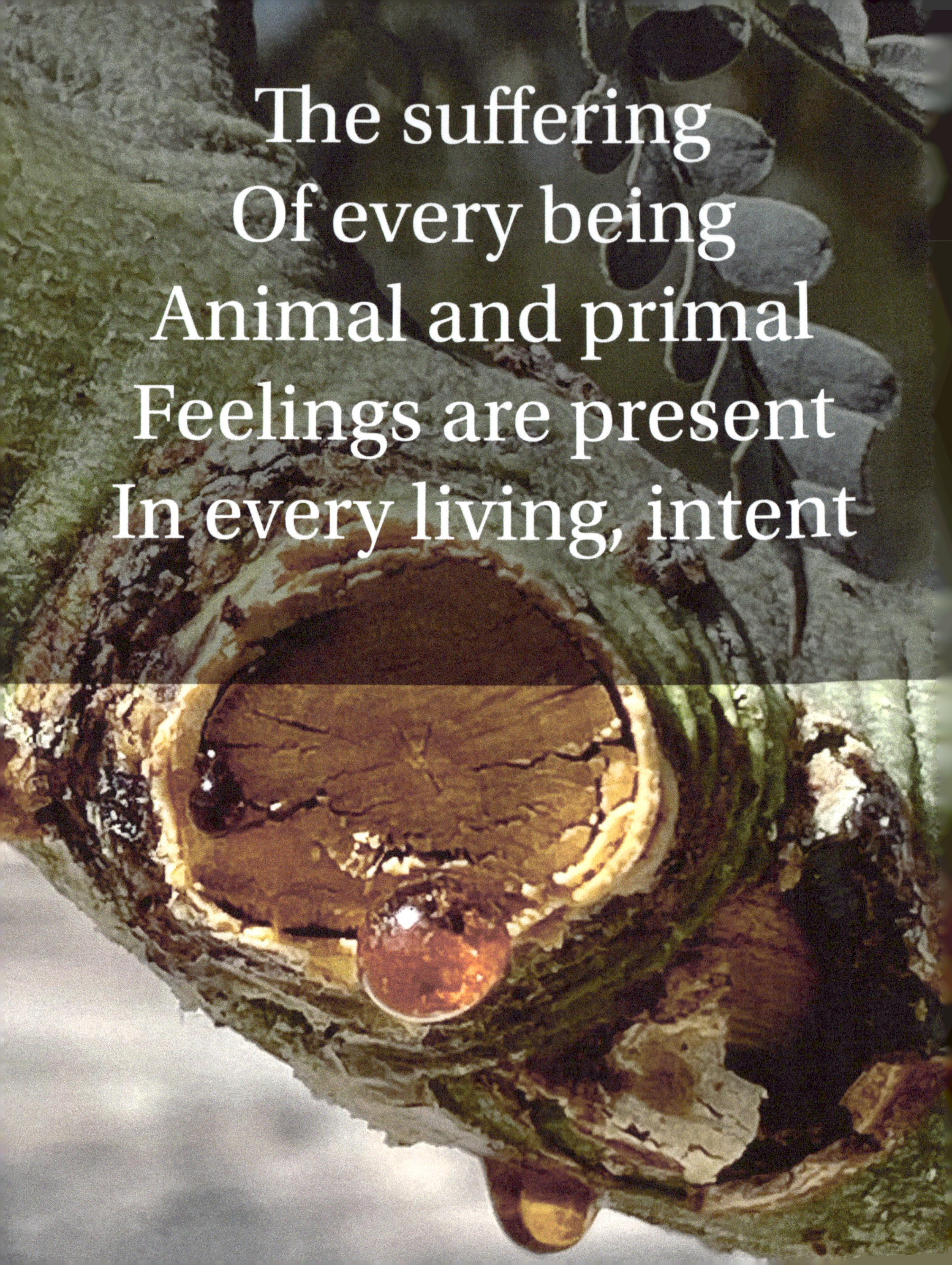

The suffering
Of every being
Animal and primal
Feelings are present
In every living, intent

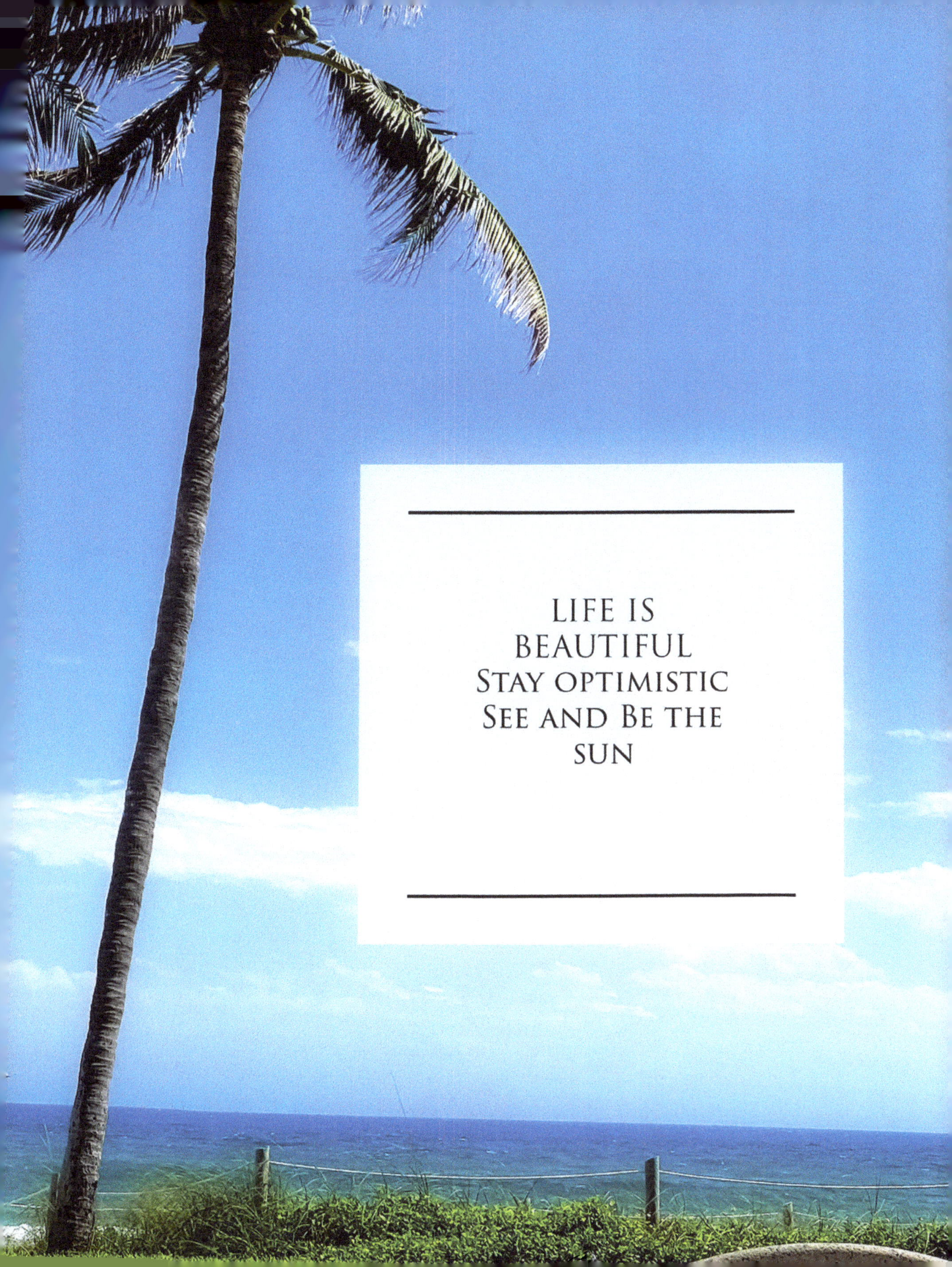
LIFE IS
BEAUTIFUL
Stay optimistic
See and Be the
sun

Victory

Victory has to be
Over our minds and its limitless capability
Controlling our thoughts
Reality without doubting or casting lots
But by visions
Created in elaborate constructions
Of concentrated energy
In matter weighted carefully
Manipulated
Articulated
There is a space
A resilience
A world in silence
Above science
Where intuition
Satisfies our ambition
There is no boundary
It's all the contrary
The universe as a voice
Genius and peace makers
Markers
Have come and gone
Each with their own
Unique vibrations
It should be our aim
To rewrite them together
Into a symphony made for our victory
I am the least amongst you

Yet, I am here to tell, who
The passionate, the healers
The simple
The humble
The powerful
The eternal
The skeptical
The believer
The beautiful and pure
All of humanity
Of its ability
Of the how to play this soft
Delicate music of energy
Of peace love and unity
Pick up your resonance
Reverberate
Transform and reform
We have the capability
Pick up your joy, your compassion
Your guitars, your passions
Let's pray this symphony
Remember to love like honey
It starts with our thoughts
Our mastery, over our souls not to be
bought
Paradise is not an illusion
But the only way forward, to glory
And His impending Victory

Photo by Jonas Ferlin

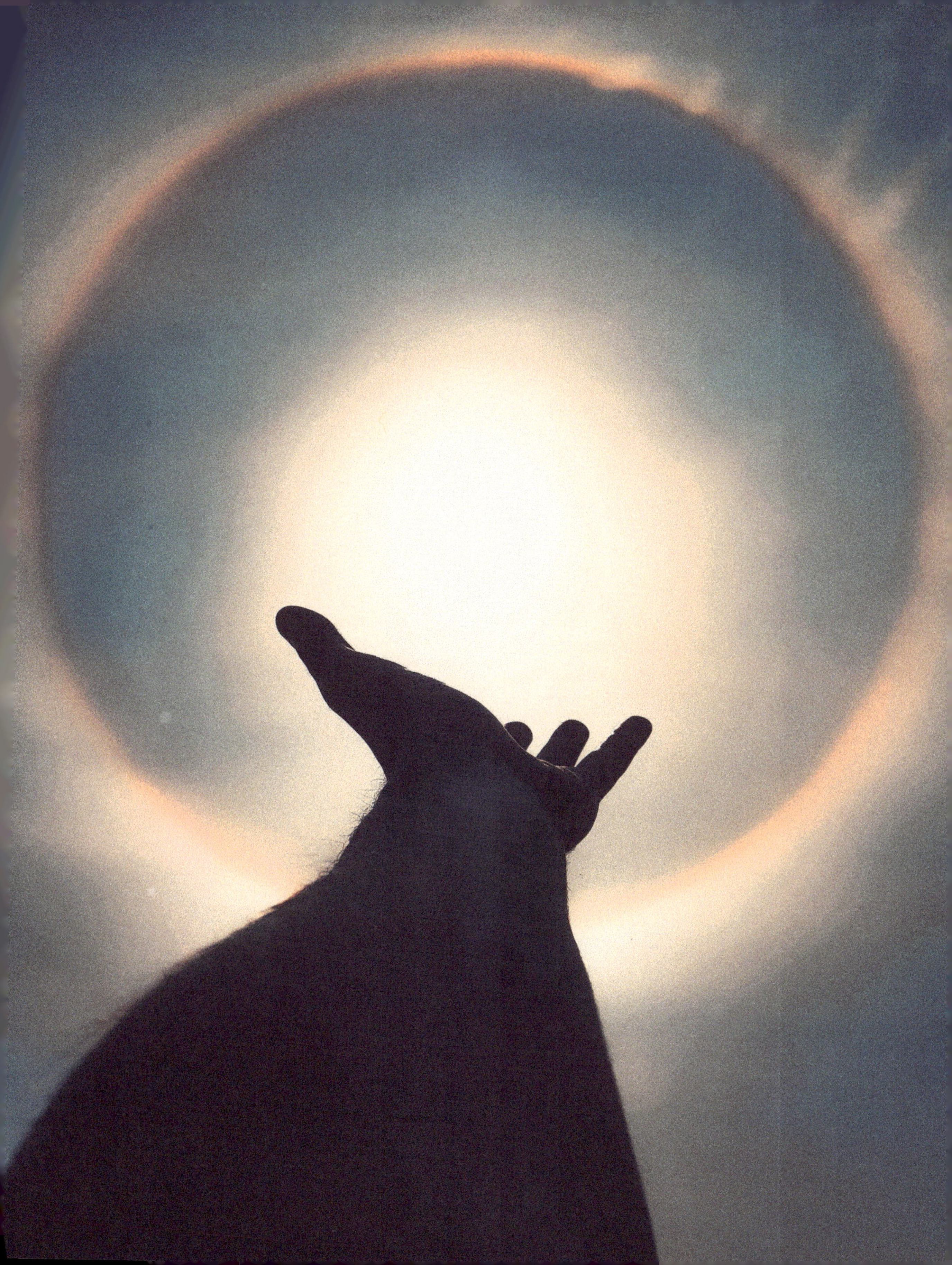

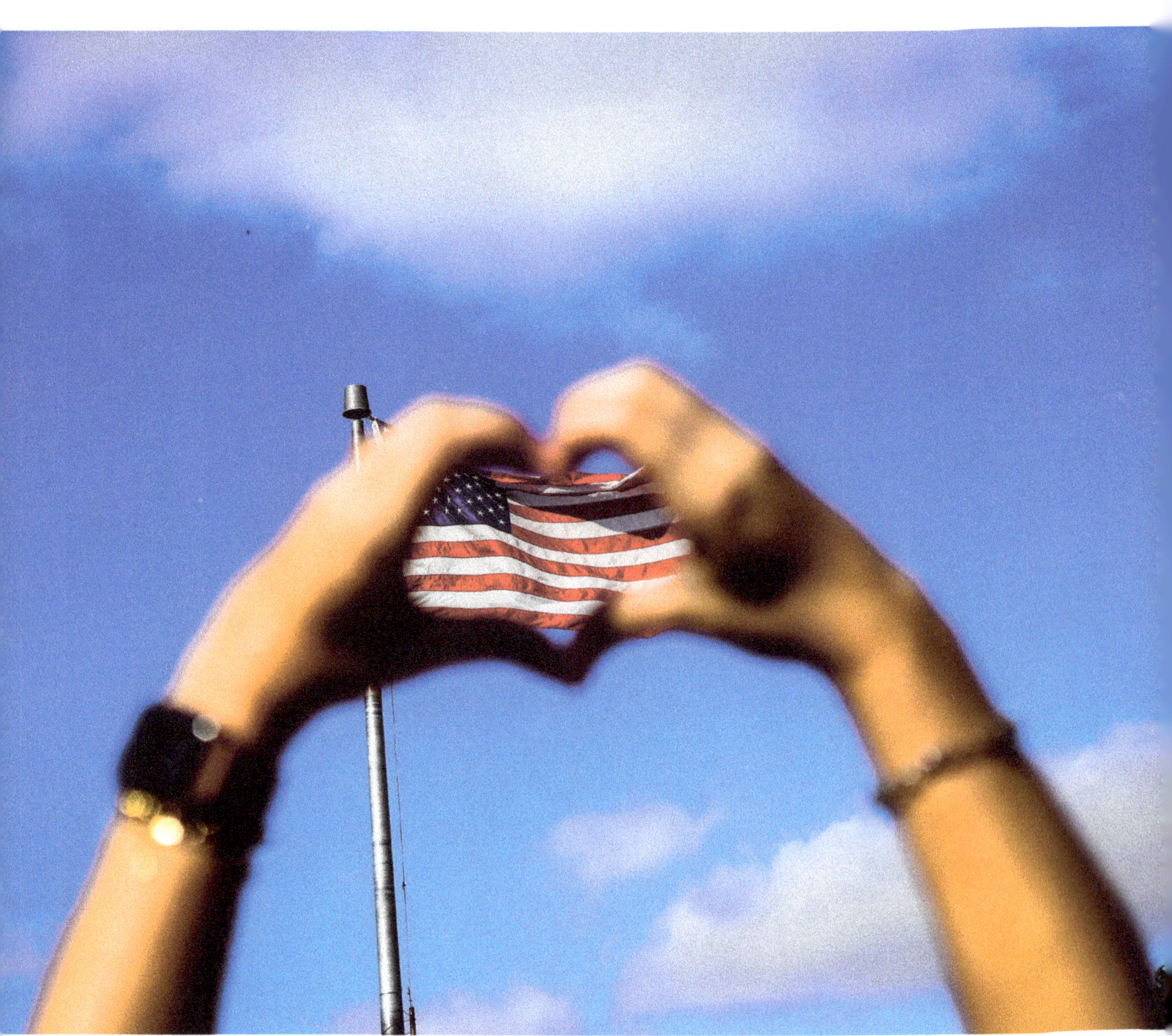

Photo by Edgar Colomba

Magna Carta

Magna Carta
Magna Carta my love
Freedom inspired from above
Equality, the end of tyranny
The beginning of free justice
The end of prejudice
Our history will talk
One day of our glory
Our win over narcissism
Our lust over egocentrism
The story being rendered
The beauty made us wonder
The human story
In all our profanity
Will develop
Must envelop
Our souls of honey
Our hearts of energy
Pure, loving
Soft, unassuming
Breath of conscience
Whisper of obedience
Magna Carta my love
Sweet sweet hovering dove
Take hold

Stay bold
There is an answer
On the Earth Lucifer
In the sky our Father
Align our thoughts
A truthful plot
To reign by the law
Of His love without flaws
For this new century
Let's not repeat the fury
Substitute hate repression and aggression
By implementing the utopia
Of paradise and its nostalgia
Love respect and protect
The people in our human family
Guaranteed of a future by unity
Follow me
Love, embrace, do good
Smile with patience
Live, a life in splendor
Knowing, Our Father is King and protector
Be calm, humbled
Be kind, tenacious and lawful
For WE the people
My love is for Magna Carta...

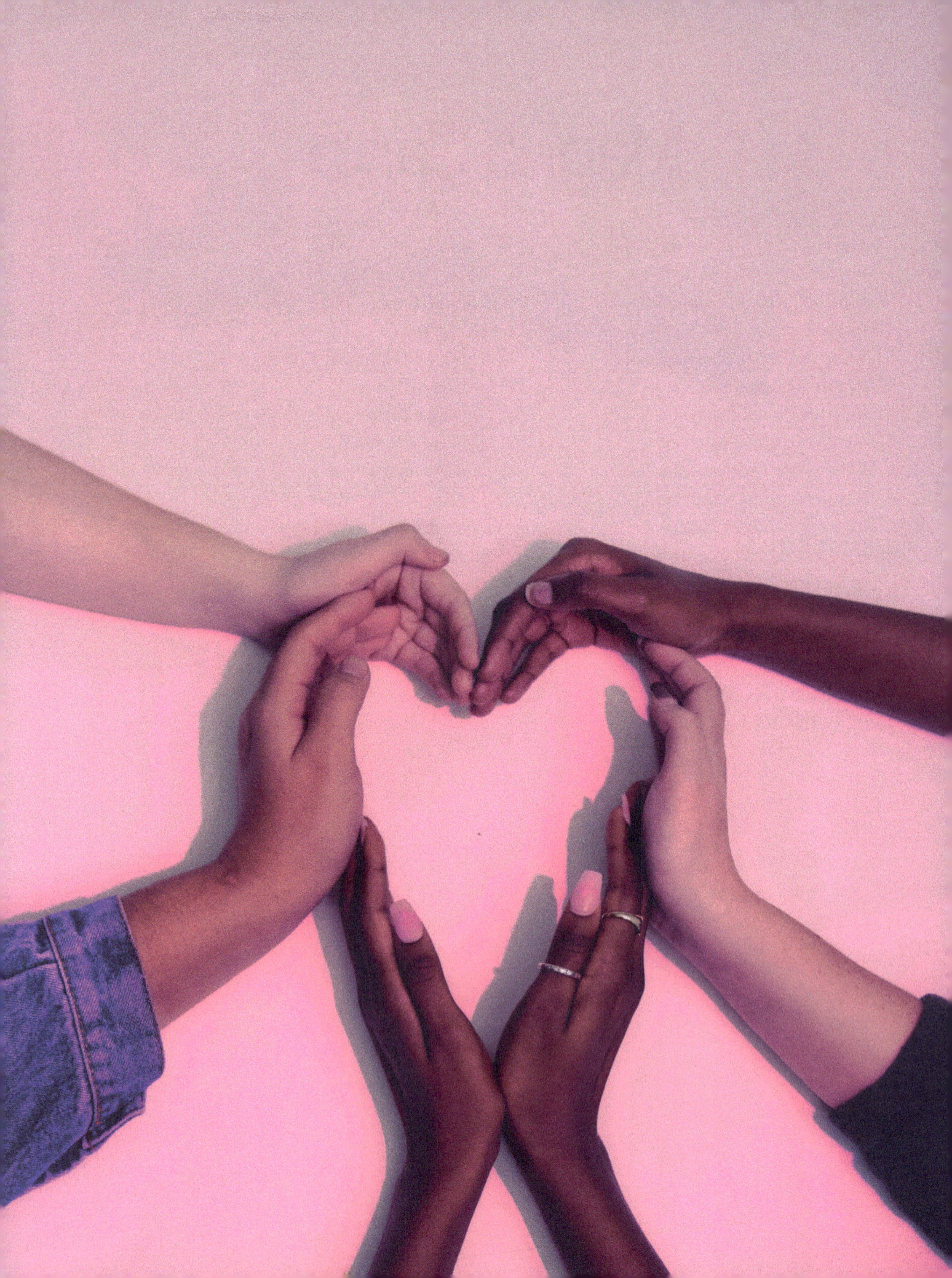

Imagine Compass Ion

Imagine a world where loving
Is seen as a weakness
Imagine being tired of fighting
Your heart's filled with kindness
Open up to the possibilities
Step out of normalities
Where hate and prejudice
Are no longer free in justice
Imagine a world where saying please
Is seen as a disease
Your heart's, aching for peace
Open up, to the immense
Strength, accessible to your senses
Reach up
Light up
Imagine not being able to dream
Flourish, learn and scream
Saying I love you
Not met, with thank you
Images of aging
Without fears of listening
To children's future
Looking at the destructions of nature
A world of green and colors
Communication without lectures
Imagine seeing in the dark
Opening your eyes to embark
In an adventure
Of feelings soft and pure

Disbelief of the relief
In the caressing breeze
Listening in the murmur
Of mother nature
Doubts evaporating
Conversation of giants everlasting
Under the canopy of leaves
In the shade of grief
Would they be relieved
To see our understanding
In the laws governing
The Universe
Multi verses
Imagine a world where loving
Would come naturally
Where the weakness of hate
Would be seen accordingly
Your heart's filled of happiness
In this imagined reality
Dreamed into existence
Without the rationality of science
Imagine spirituality
Without religion's stupidity
Whispered of Eternity
Compassion, love and respect
Will prevailed eventually
Just listen
...And imagine

Photo by ATC Comm Photo

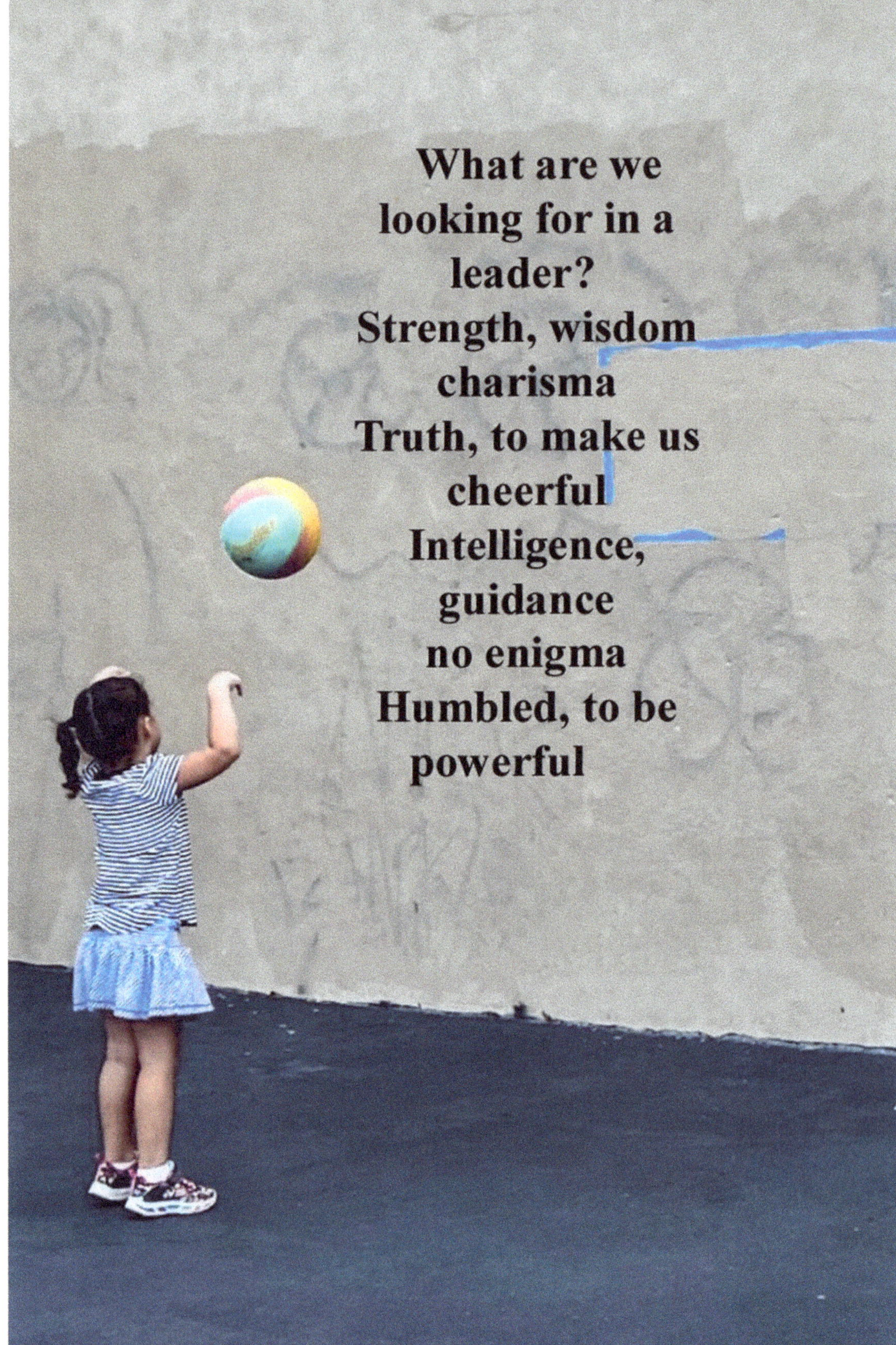

What are we
looking for in a
leader?
Strength, wisdom
charisma
Truth, to make us
cheerful
Intelligence,
guidance
no enigma
Humbled, to be
powerful

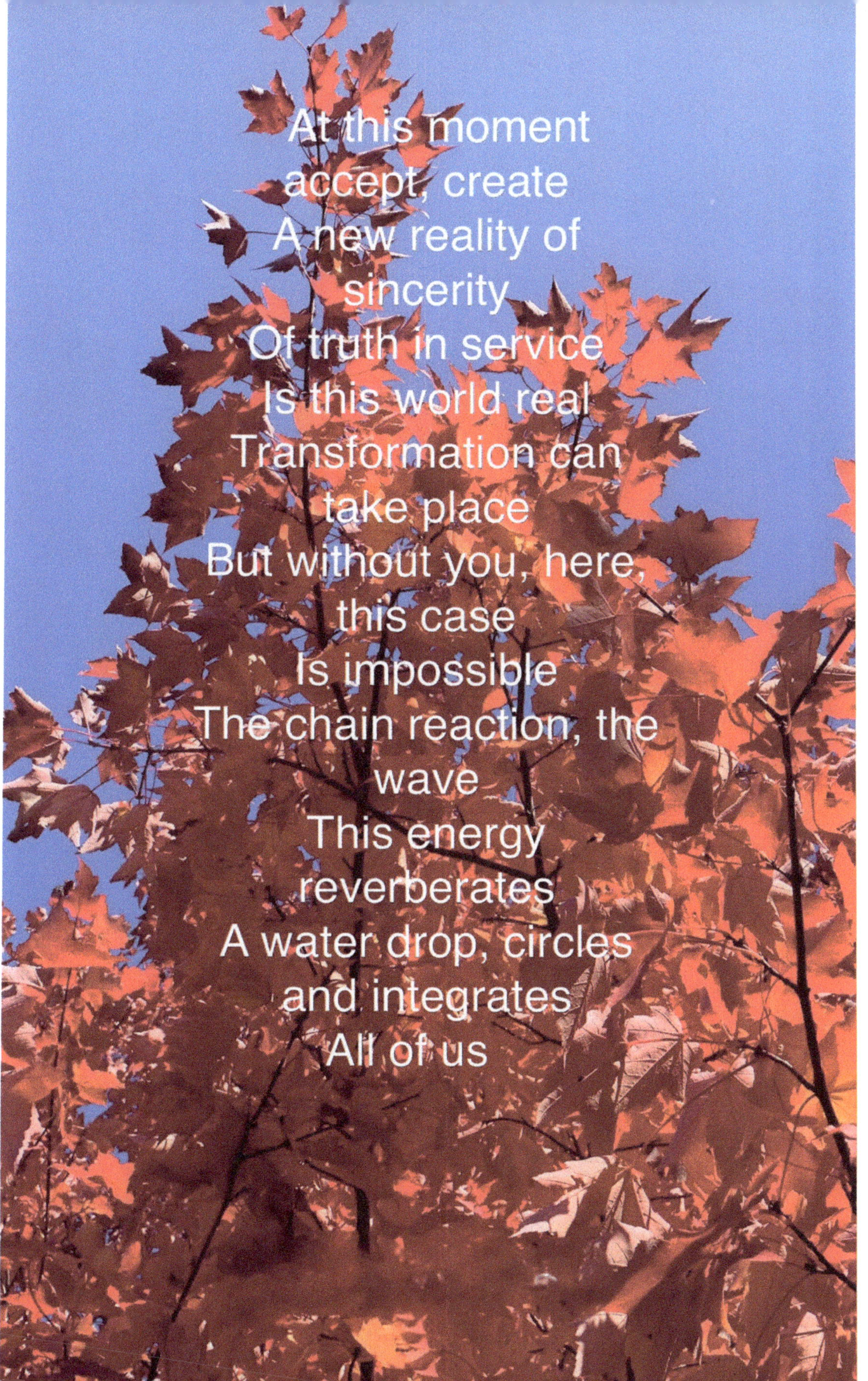

At this moment
accept, create
A new reality of
sincerity
Of truth in service
Is this world real
Transformation can
take place
But without you, here,
this case
Is impossible
The chain reaction, the
wave
This energy
reverberates
A water drop, circles
and integrates
All of us

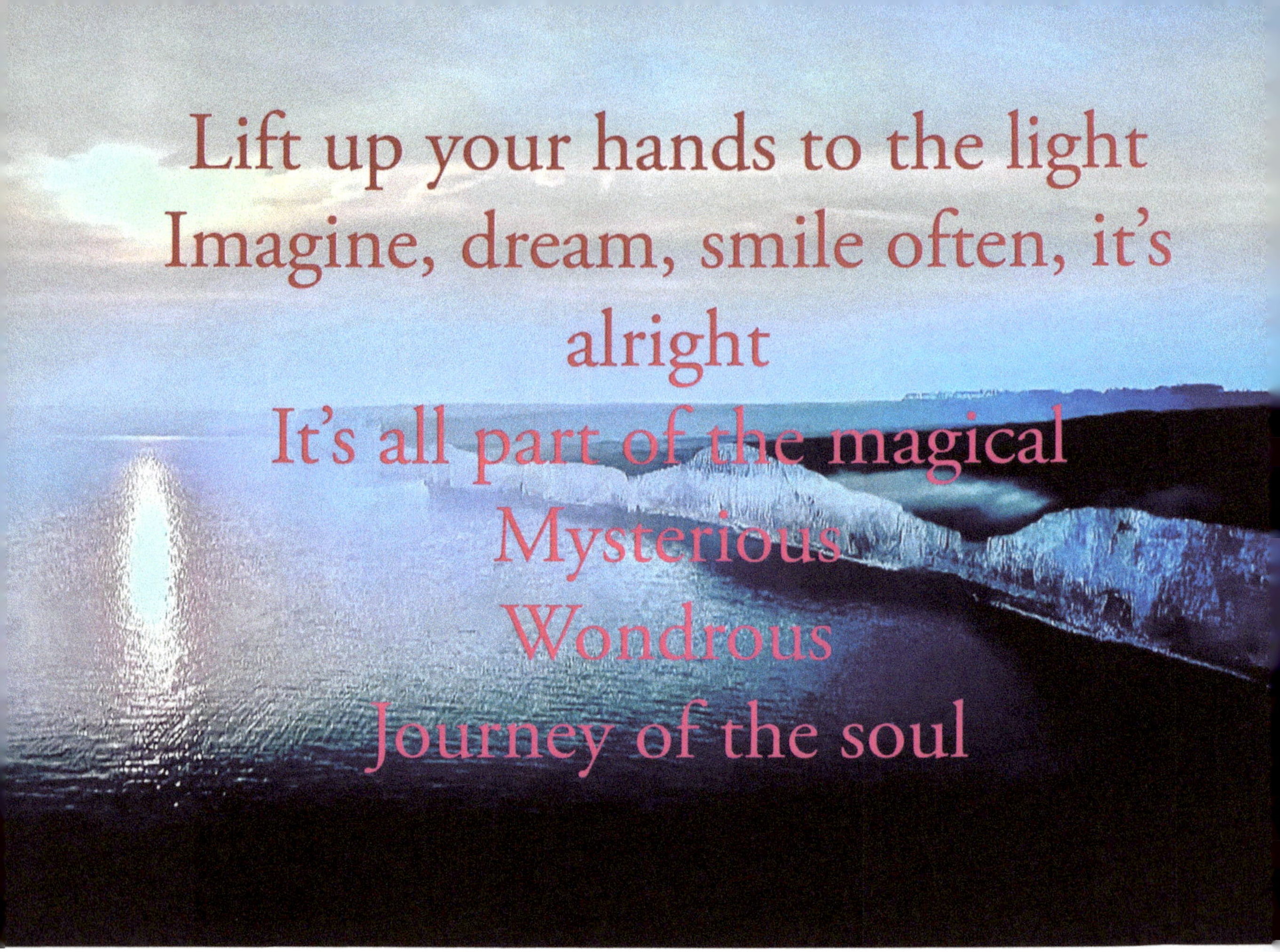

Lift up your hands to the light
Imagine, dream, smile often, it's
alright
It's all part of the magical
Mysterious
Wondrous
Journey of the soul

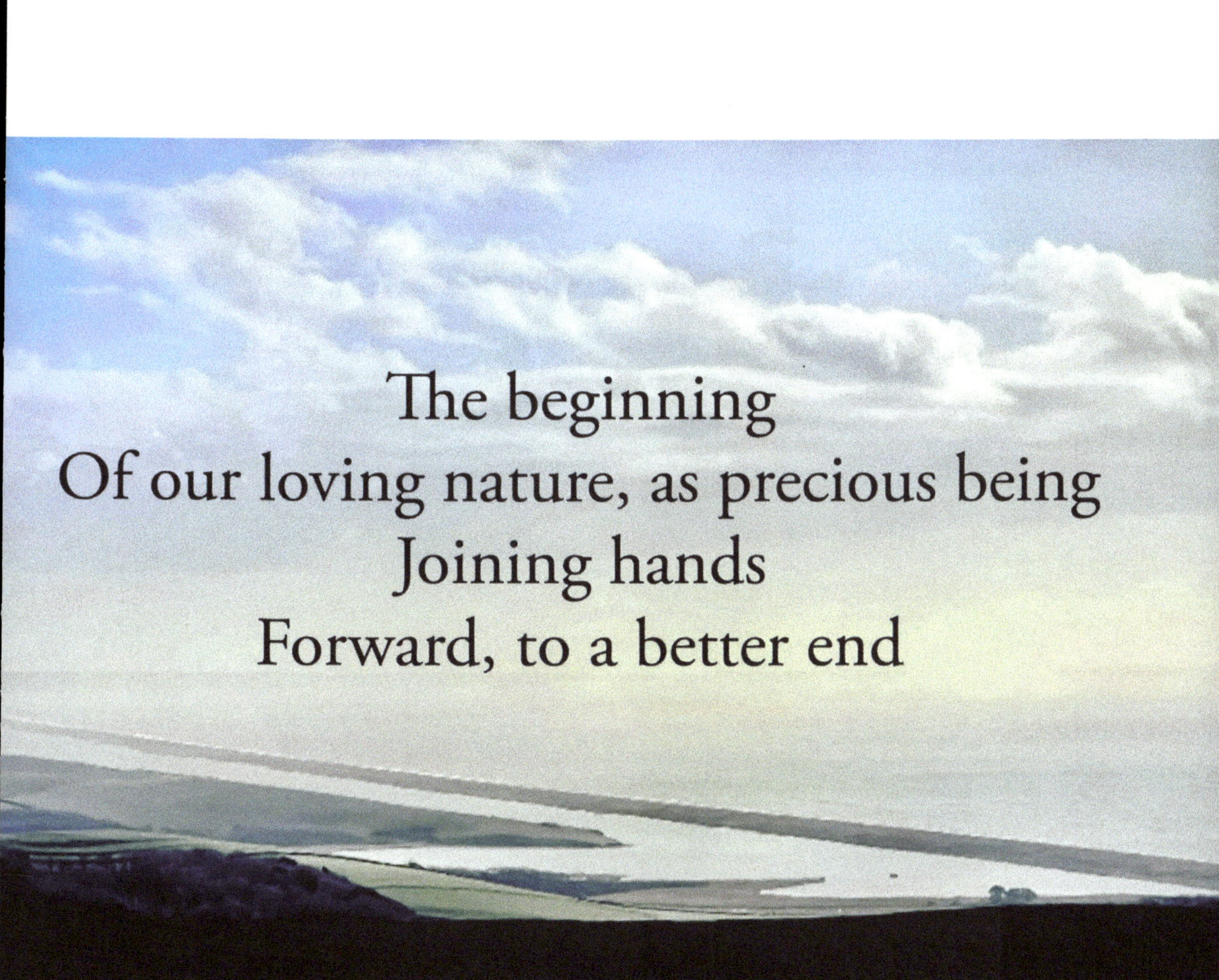

The beginning
Of our loving nature, as precious being
Joining hands
Forward, to a better end

Are You Reading, Listening?

Are you all listening to me
Or will this simply be pure fantasy
My mind set
My heart, hit reset
I want to share with you
Je me sens un peu fou
The story goes their way
Treachery for treasury
Fallen of humanity
There is emptiness after the runway
Discussion for the needed, precaution
One will, blessings, total union
The rain may come
We will have nowhere to run
Open your hearts
Stop pushing, pulling each other apart
The energy is connecting you and me
The vibration reverberates, aural faculty
With the goal of guiding, warming
The souls of the brave, trusting

Faithfully and praiseworthy
The illusion of this life
Evaporates and transgresses
Theses emotions are only
The opportunity of a life lived
The exhilaration of love
A soft, warm kiss from above
I am not sure you are listening to me?
It might just be a vision, an illusion
Of a future clean and pure
Our minds ripe for dissolution
Retrained reprogrammed
Regrets, folly dissipates
Good intentions
Good morals
Will prevail
Winning entails
Radical new ways of processing
Distributing information
Positive and uplifting

Darya Sannikova

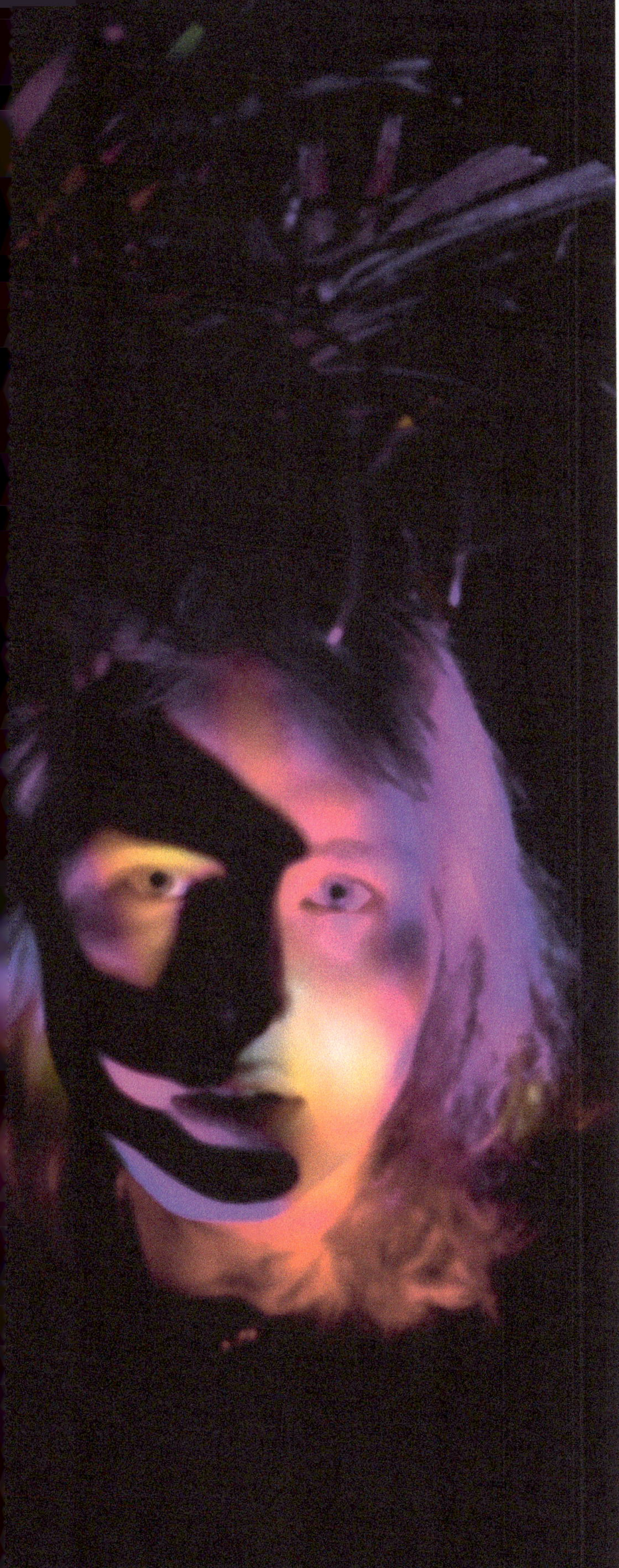

No more oppression leading to
Depression
Bright new rights
Brand new mentality, taking flight
Laugh, breathe, water the seed
The magical flower you are
Reaching for truth in the sun
Anchoring, cultural roots without
Separation
Changing shapes and colors
Reach up, be liberated
Lift up your hands to the light
Imagine, dream, smile often, it's
Alright
It's part of the magical, mysterious
Wondrous journey of the soul
Searching for love and mercy from
The sun and its creator.

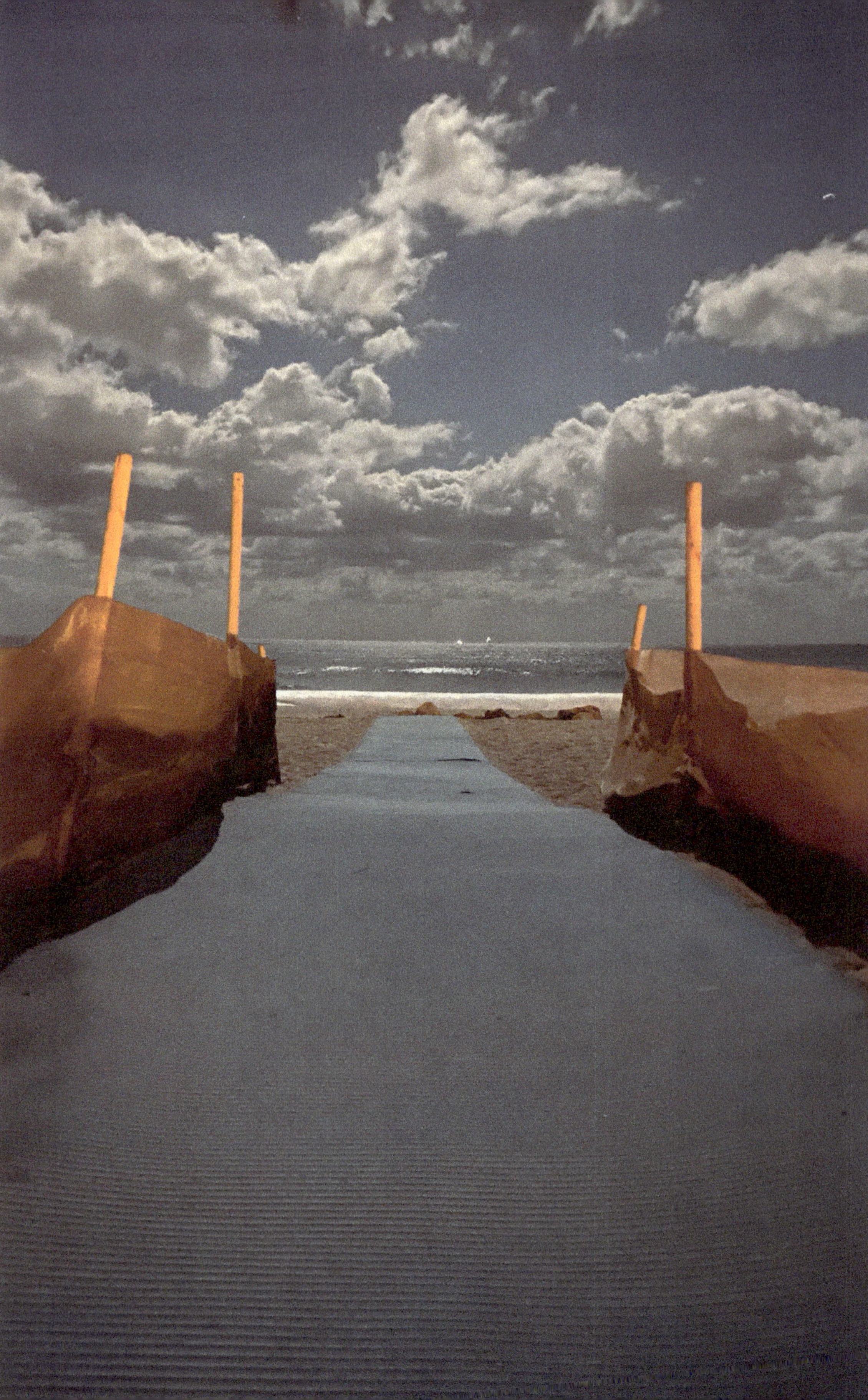

I Am, You, Are Me

I am only, a cry, a lamp
A light in the darkness
I am an attempt
A feeling of kindness
A weak, broken body
Trying to inspire
A lasting wave aspire
I am energy
I am you and me
I am a beacon
A whisper of reason
A human with many faults
Preaching for good results
Wake up, be the change
Reinvent, values must be rearranged
I only point, share thoughts
I am a channel
A waterway, a funnel
A twister of danger
I am at peace, with anger
I also hate, to love
A wanderer of good manners
A life, lived, in a treasure trove
Would you dream with me
Don't judge, but appreciate
Don't pretend, but ameliorate
A dream of justice
The end of prejudice

Where love would prevail
Where the wind would fill our sails
Propelling us forward
Never again backwards
I am the ocean
I am a small giant
A gentlemen of another kind
A lost and open mind
I am, only a laugh
Open, in this gentle draft
Hear me, tease you
See me, loving who
I am, you, are me...

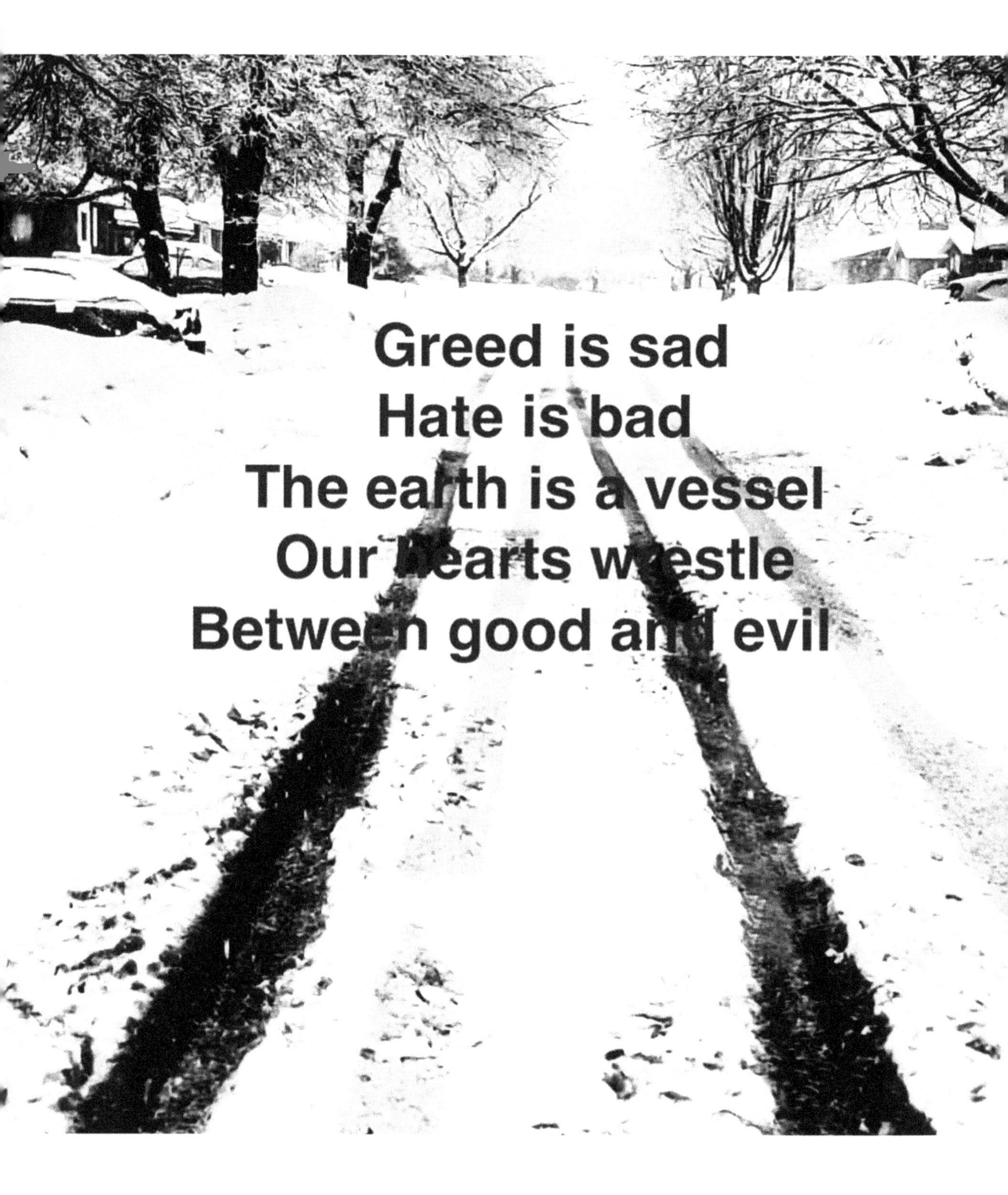

Greed is sad
Hate is bad
The earth is a vessel
Our hearts wrestle
Between good and evil

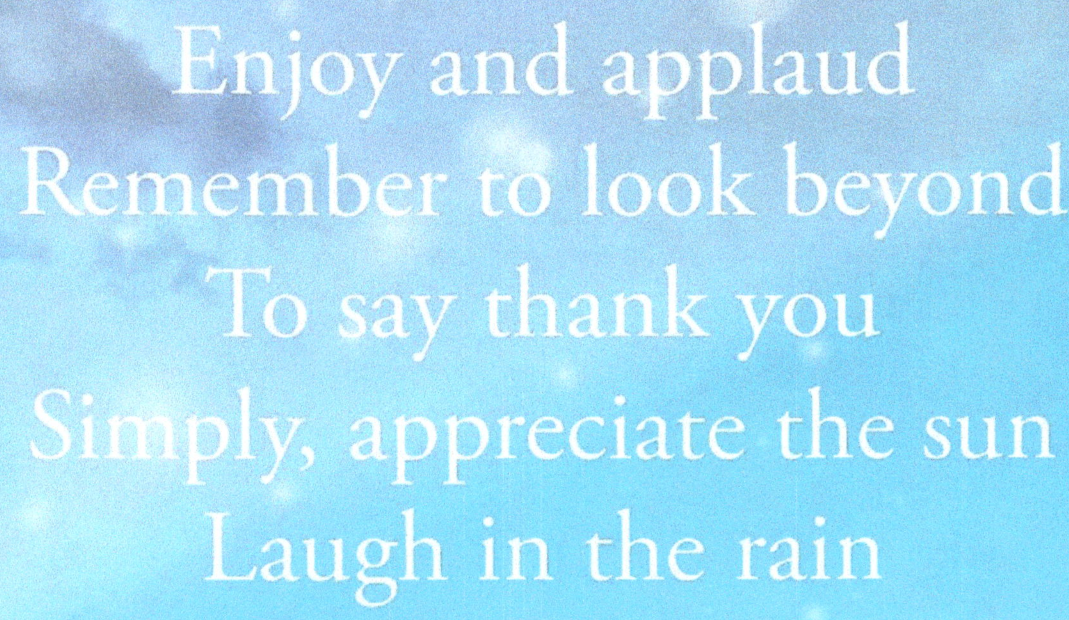
Enjoy and applaud
Remember to look beyond
To say thank you
Simply, appreciate the sun
Laugh in the rain

Your energy
Is my synergy
Our interaction
Is an essential action
Necessary for the
chemistry
Forming, involving
our destiny

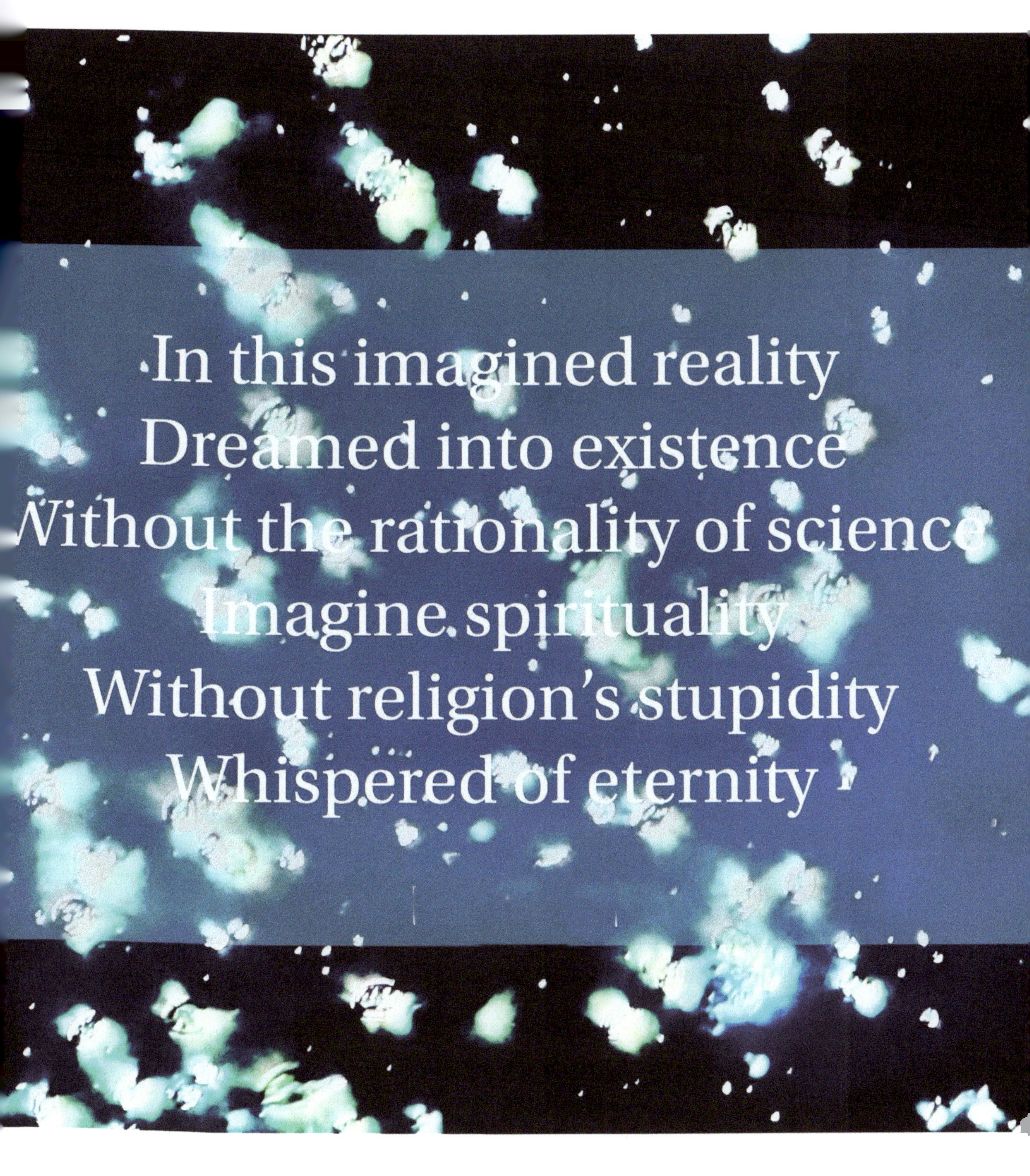
In this imagined reality
Dreamed into existence
Without the rationality of science
Imagine spirituality
Without religion's stupidity
Whispered of eternity

Rivers of Hope

Rivers flow
Never follow
Soft, rough
Shallow
Even tough
Overflow
Do You know
Where the river goes
Deepest thoughts
Drift away
We ought
To show
Softness
Roughness
Strong current
Coming our way
Humanity might be
On life's preserver
Divisions and hate
Is not for me
Heal with a gentle blow
Ripples like vibrations
Shimmers intuitions
Flowing down rivers
Life's obstacles
Yesterdays, oracles
Tomorrows, miracles
Waterfalls, tears of joy
Carrying hopes

Visions of happiness
Much kindness
Angel's inspiration
Colors imagination
Of a future
Bright and pure
Help one another
Love is greater
Nothing else matters
Leading to the ocean
Hearts of giants
Translucence
Imminence
Rain water
Nourishing our conscience
Proved by science
Thoughts of stillness
Immense calmness
Help one another
Effervescent vapors
Clouds of grandeur
Love one another
Bliss enlighten
Our world
Our universe
Like the river
Soft gentleness
Imagine such greatness
I pray to see

Photo by Matt Hardy

The day everyone's happy
Art, music, and poetry
Flowing in unison
Healing our nations
Dreams of Eden
Where rivers
Meet in the garden
Paradise is simple you see
Love and compassion
Naturally... flowing into the sea
Honestly and free

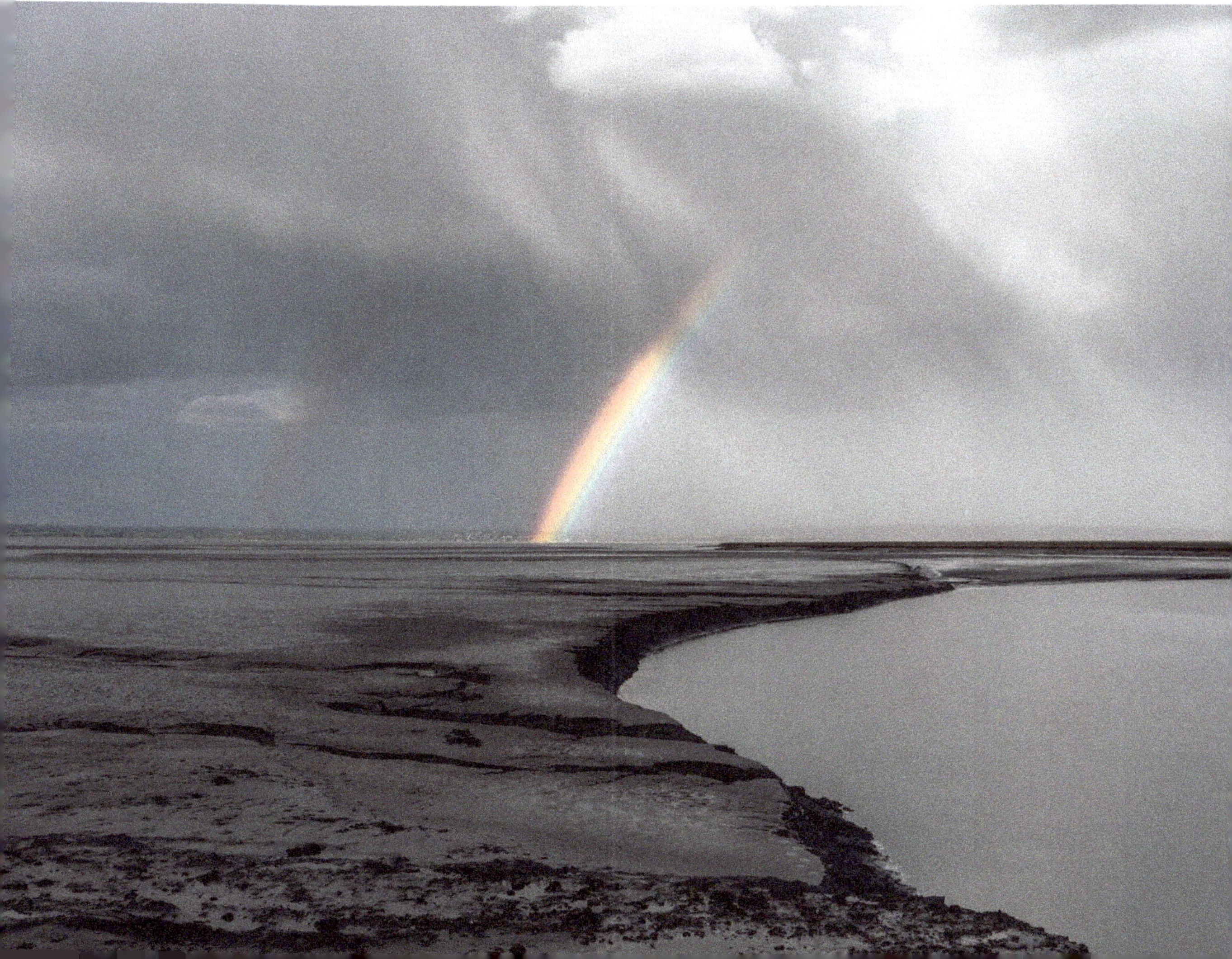

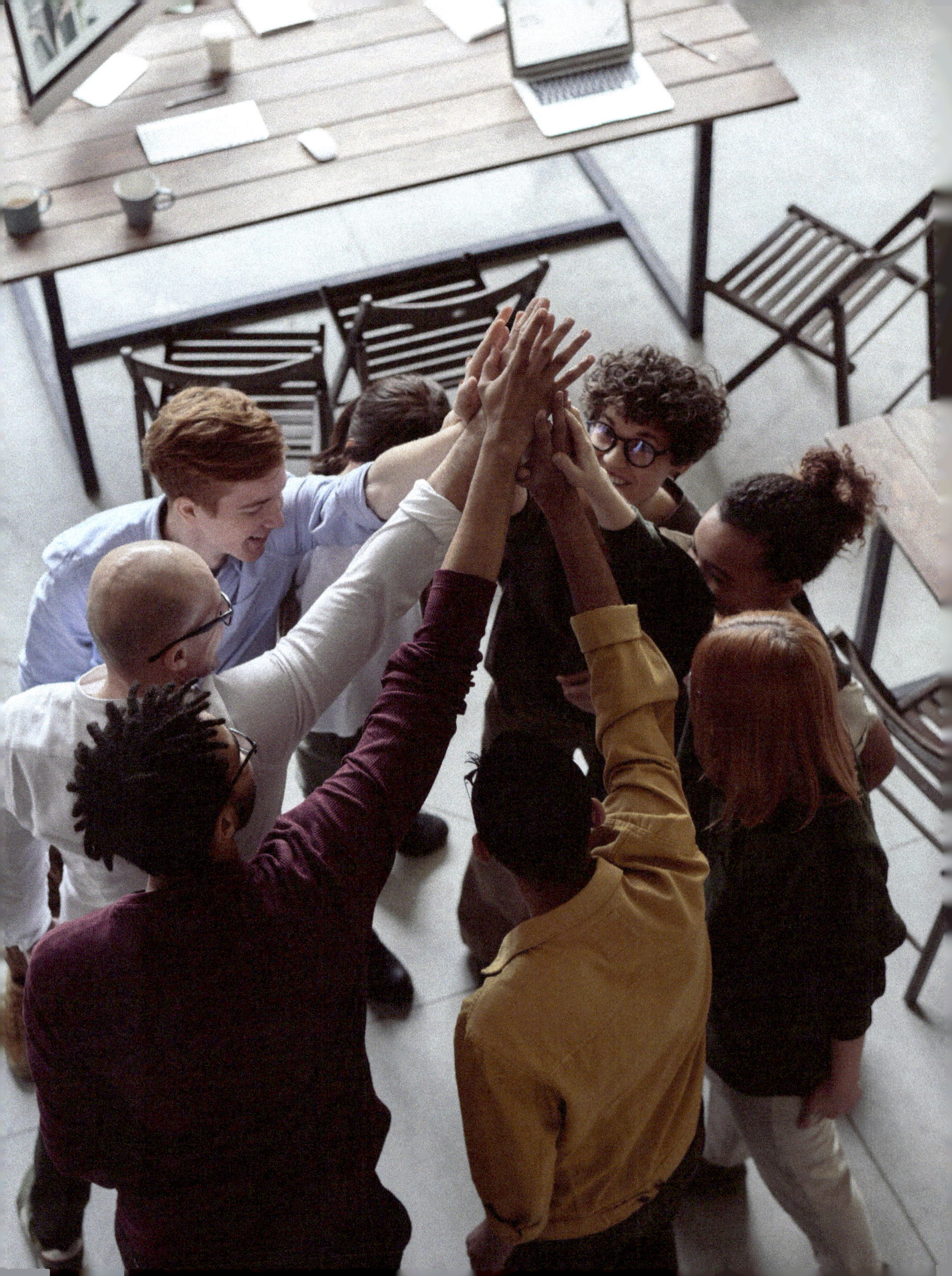

Unity in "Demo-Crazy"

What is democracy?
A treasure to be cherished
A conquest not to let perish
A place, We all live in harmony
The end of divisions, primarily
A proud, unified country
Where, We the people
Decide and elect without hurdles
We rule over the land
Proudly, command
Realizing the dream
Our patriarchy laid at our feet
Dictated and erected
Planned and prayed
Justice for all
Representation without walls
Protecting dignity
An immense sense of glory
Forming the most beautiful
Nation, people
Freedom
Awesome
Land of plenty
Defender of human rights
Righteousness, where it might
Prevail, restore
The honor bestowed
The epiphany behold
Our founding fathers

Their intention rather
Pure, inclusive
Of a conclusive
Conscious, meticulous constitution
To form a territory, without delusion
A birthright
A voice, a gift
Not to be discarded
On illusions
A dignified nation
Nothing strong could be envisioned
With a fight or by division
Instead a promise
The heart of conquest
Forgiving, inviting
Honest and wise
No fools in disguise
Govern by the whole
Population to the poll
Living
Instituting
This living dream
This chance, this opportunity
Humanity in all, His glory
Please regain your senses
Help me accept, protect
This gift We all share and must
Respect

La Vérité

C'est la vérité, j'ai peur
De la misère et de l'enfer
Je pense la nuit debout et je pleure
De ce que pourrait être le matin,
sur ce train de fer
Malgré mes pensées, j'avance
Je souris et je pense
À cette légèreté de la chance
À ce désir
Ce besoin d'écrire
Ce tourbillon qui me séduit
Pourquoi ne serais-tu pas dans mon lit
C'est la vérité, je suis terrifié
Du bonheur
Et de l'heure
De l'aube qui s'éveille
Qui me laisse à mes merveilles
Douce lueur
Pourtant pas la leur
J'adore et je dors
L'épreuve de mon corps
Je vis et je crie
Je m'éveille et m'éblouie
C'est la vérité, j'ai peur d'aimer
Est-ce que je pourrais vous le murmurer
Cette pensée pourrait ainsi doucement rester
S'engraver dans le cœur des mal-aimés
Je suis prêt, pour de vrai

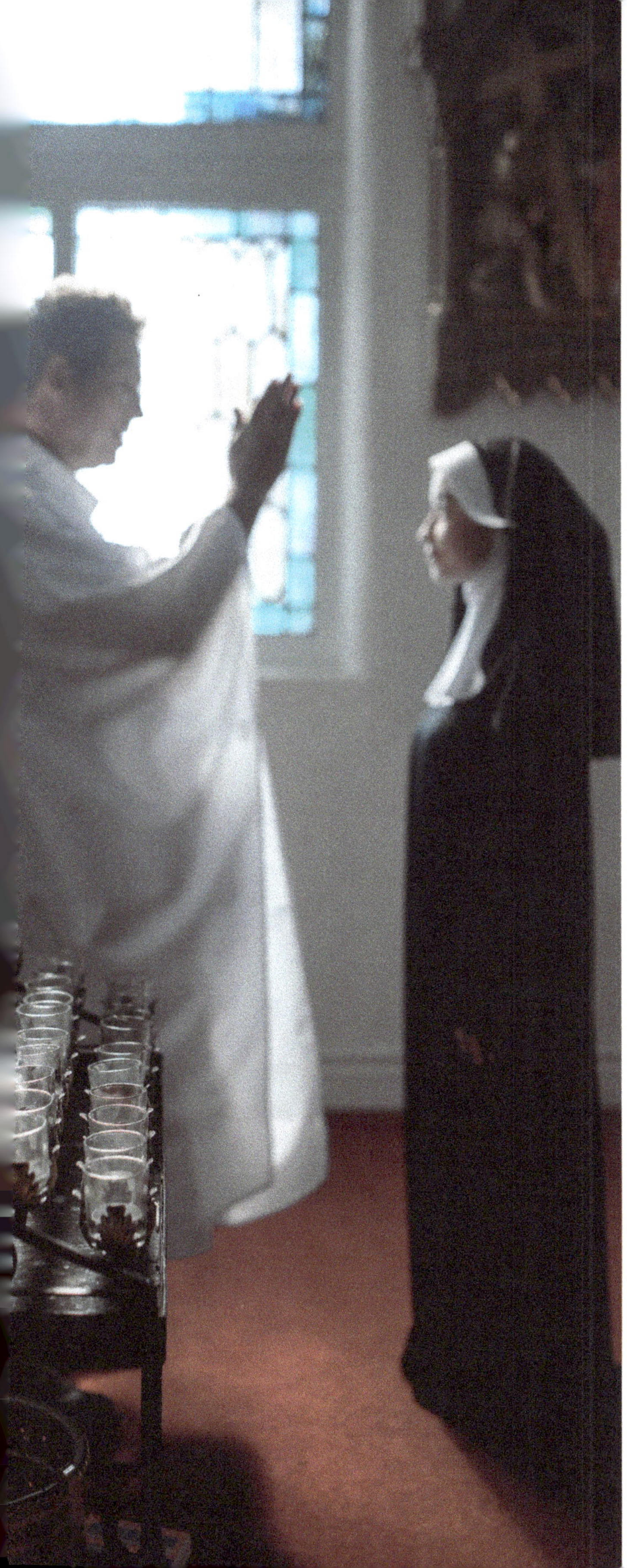

À vous dire la vérité
Je ne sais plus à quoi, comment penser
Ma tête est dans ce train, déboussolée
S'il vous plaît, pourriez-vous m'aider
Me faire comprendre que je suis aimé
Le train que je conduis
Pourrait ainsi m'emmener au paradis
Le mien surtout le vôtre
Ce ne sera pas, de notre faute
C'est avant tout la vérité
je serais tout à fait comblé

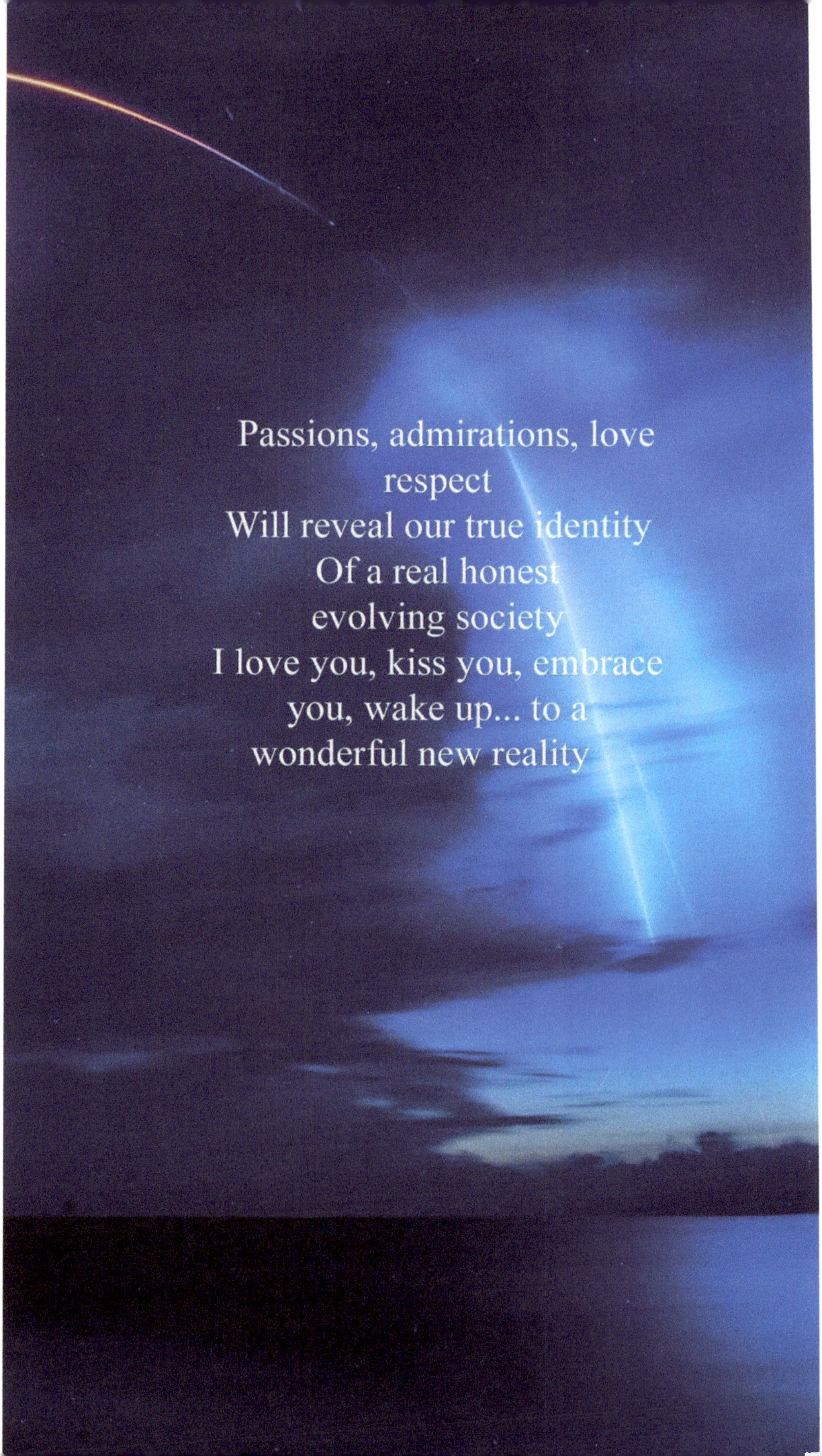

Passions, admirations, love
respect
Will reveal our true identity
Of a real honest
evolving society
I love you, kiss you, embrace
you, wake up... to a
wonderful new reality

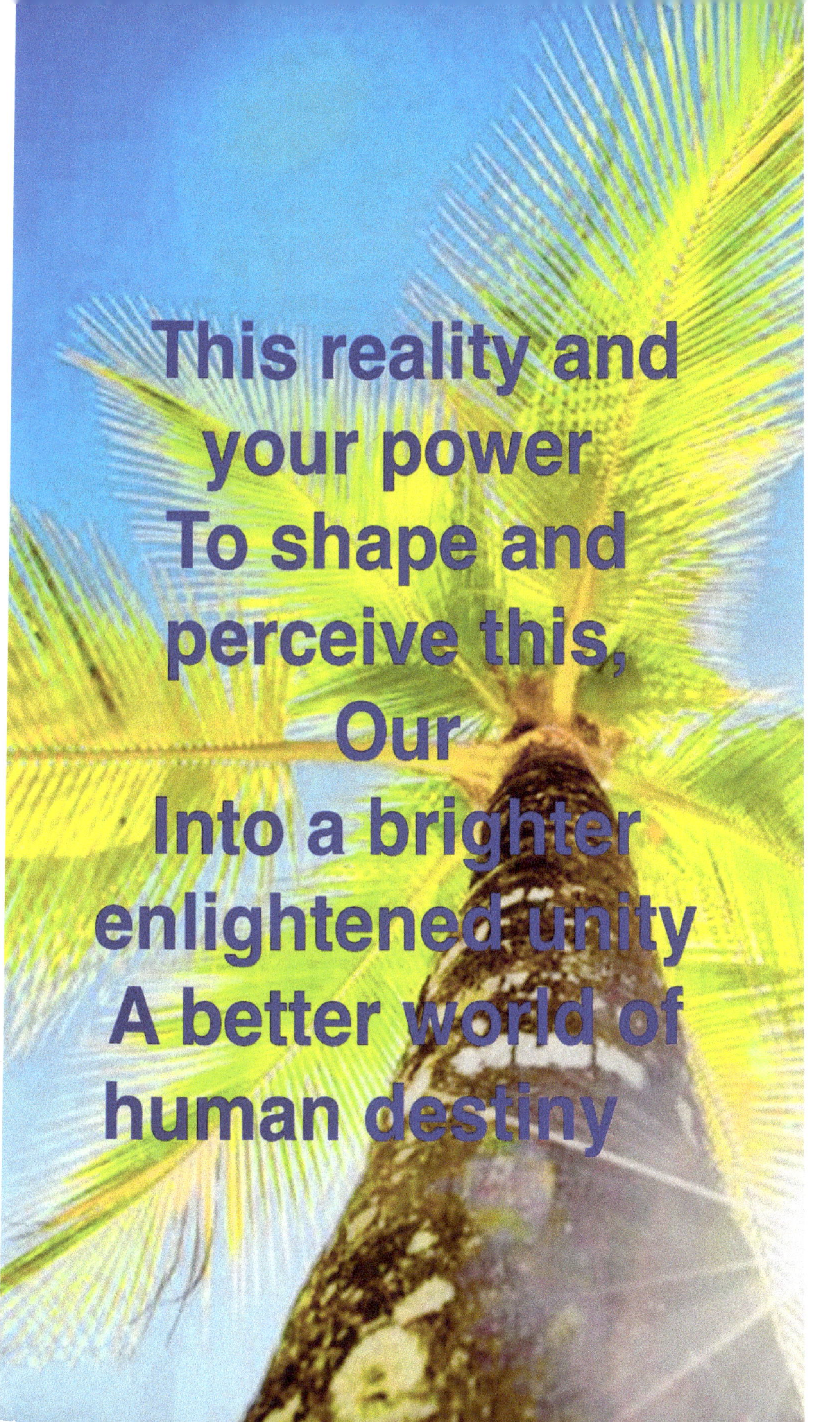

This reality and
your power
To shape and
perceive this,
Our
Into a brighter
enlightened unity
A better world of
human destiny

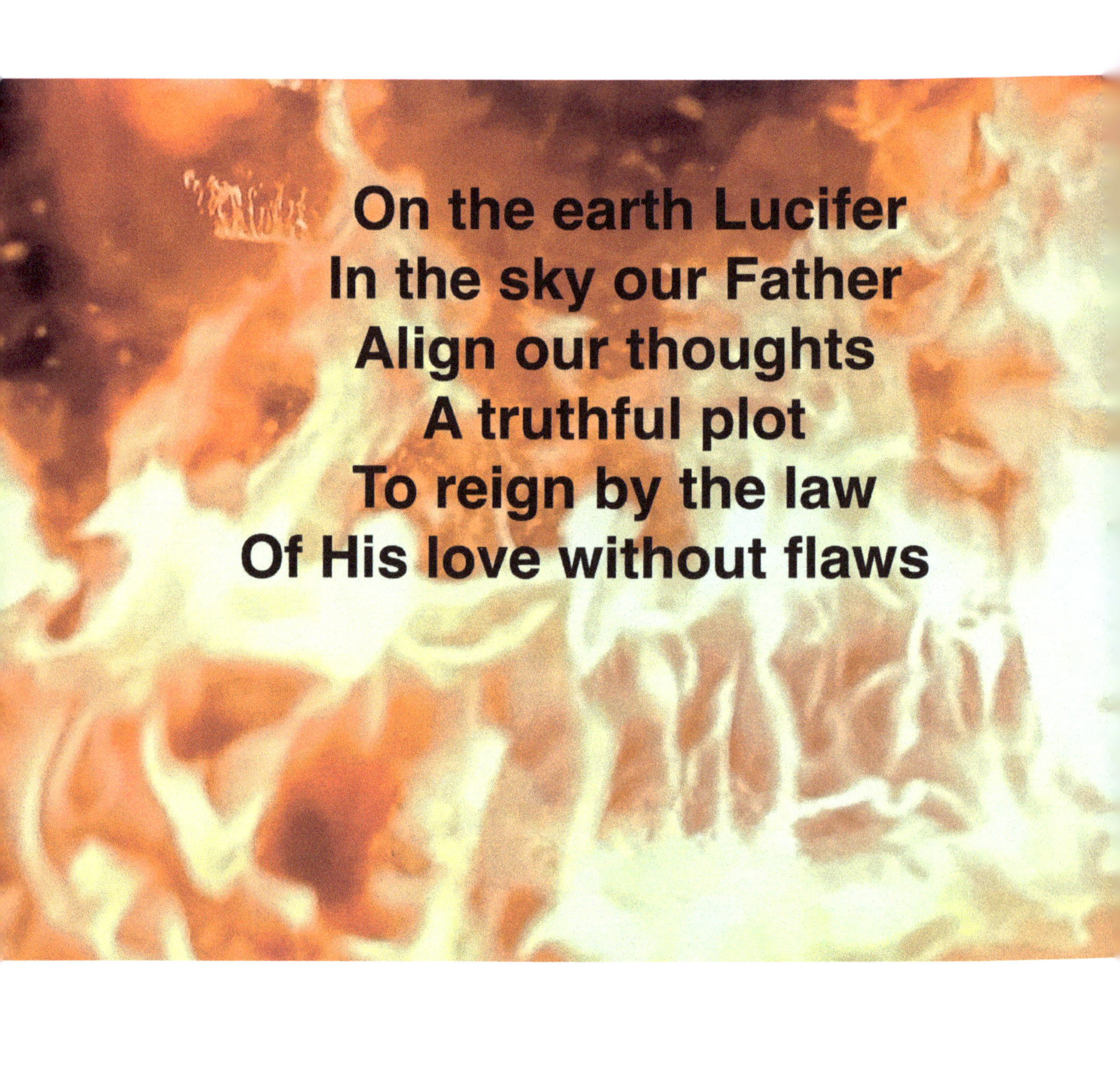
On the earth Lucifer
In the sky our Father
Align our thoughts
A truthful plot
To reign by the law
Of His love without flaws

Save and protect
This unique, beautiful planet
By taking a moral stand
Maybe, we don't understand
Fear, divide and conquer
The road map, trace for our
future

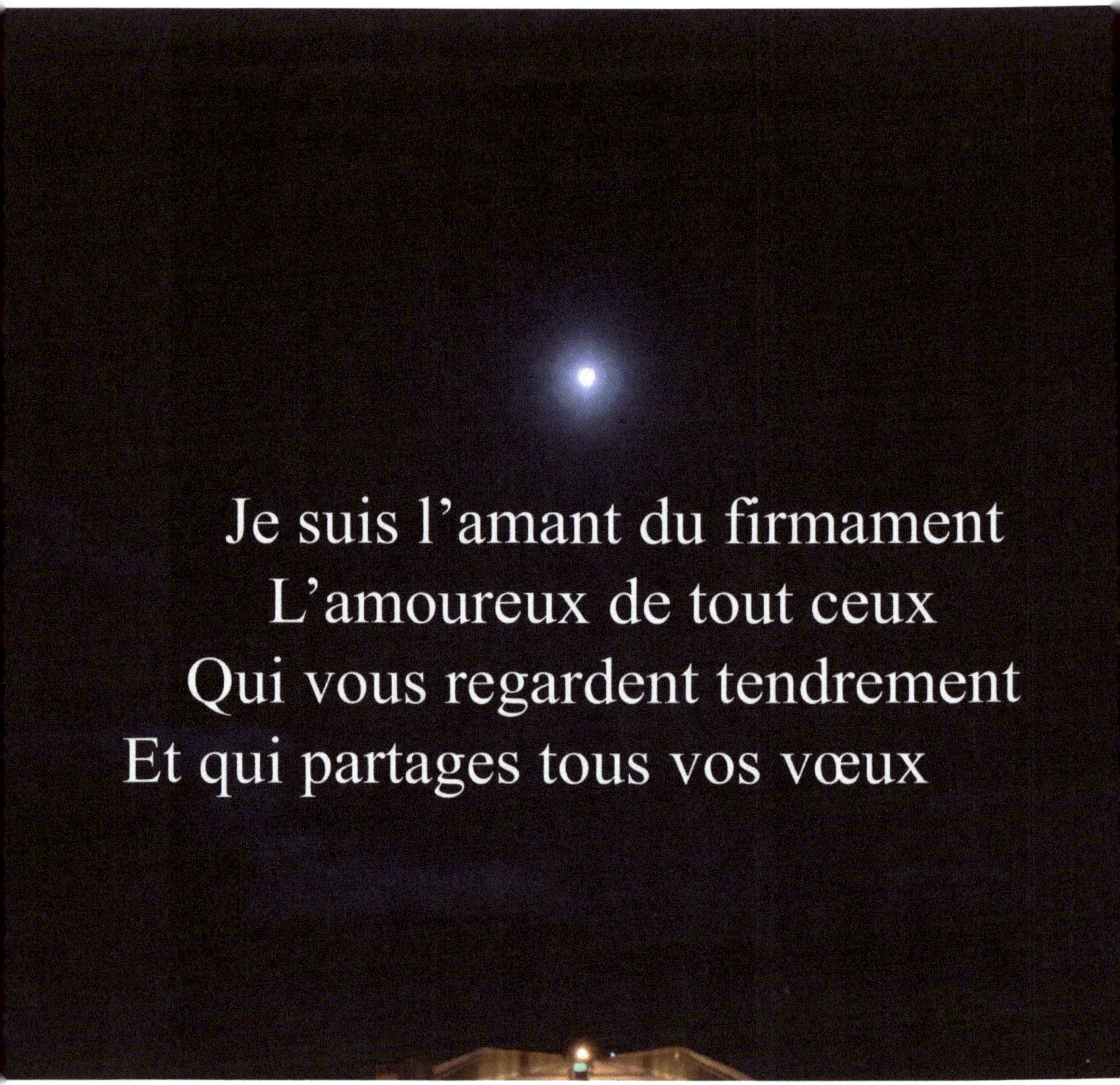

Je suis l'amant du firmament
L'amoureux de tout ceux
Qui vous regardent tendrement
Et qui partages tous vos vœux

If I offered you a dream
Would you wake up to
redeem
This reality and your
power
To shape and perceive
this, Our
Into a brighter
enlightened unity
A better world of human
destiny

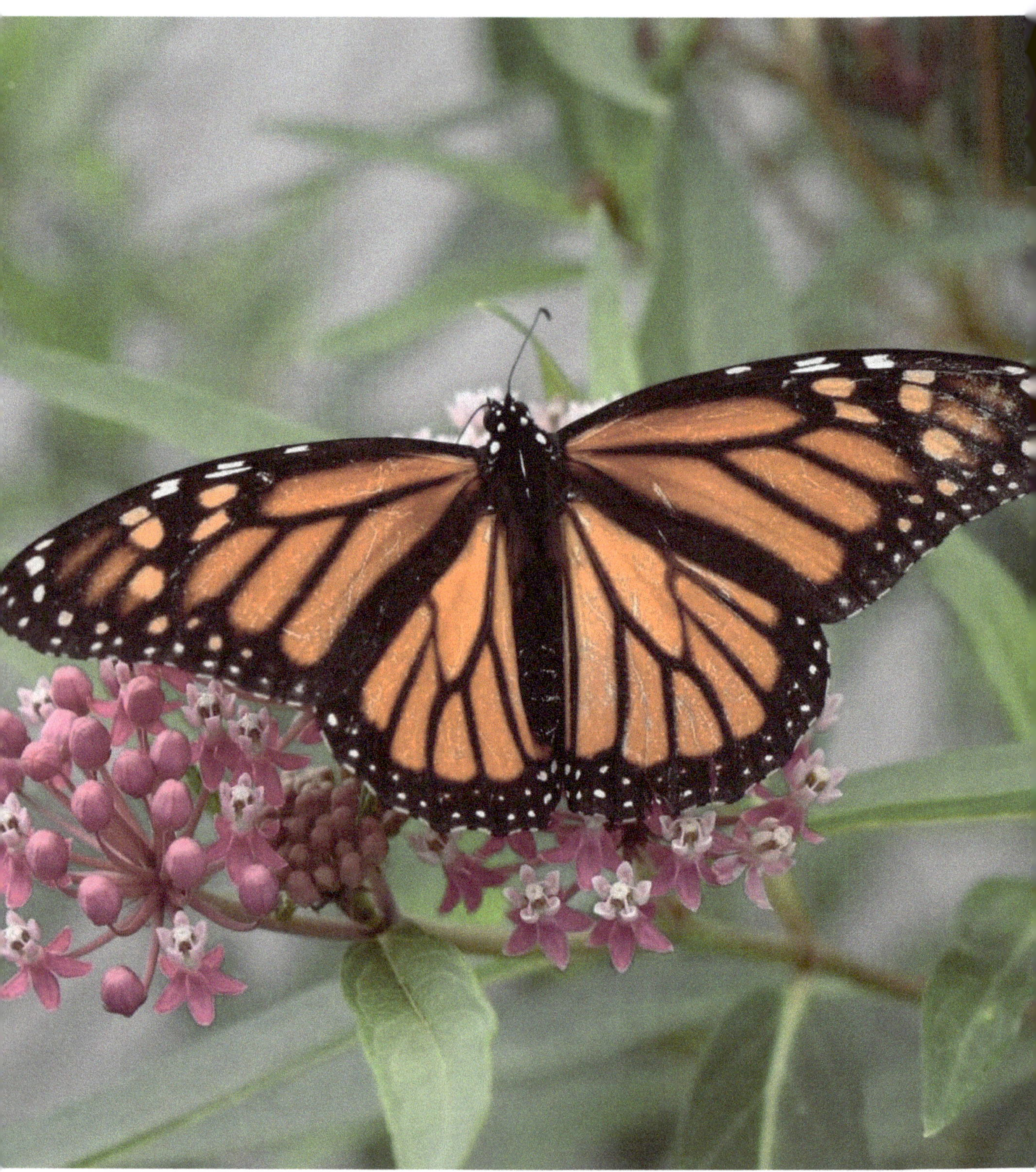

Transition Obligations

I am the observer and the sinner
The master of luster
I belong nowhere and everywhere
I am a whisper of conscience
A resistance to science
A believer of cosmic
Forces and its mathematics
An instance lived in love
An observer of the above
Yours and theirs
I am a person from anywhere
I am the light of a sound
An image can be profound
A mother
A father
A child
A wild
Force of nature
Of greens and lure
Another dimension
Amen in transition
Words read slowly
Music played softly
I am found
In His glory
Kissed and loved
Forgiven and accepted
A existence in passage
Glorious papillon

Photo by Liane Blanchard

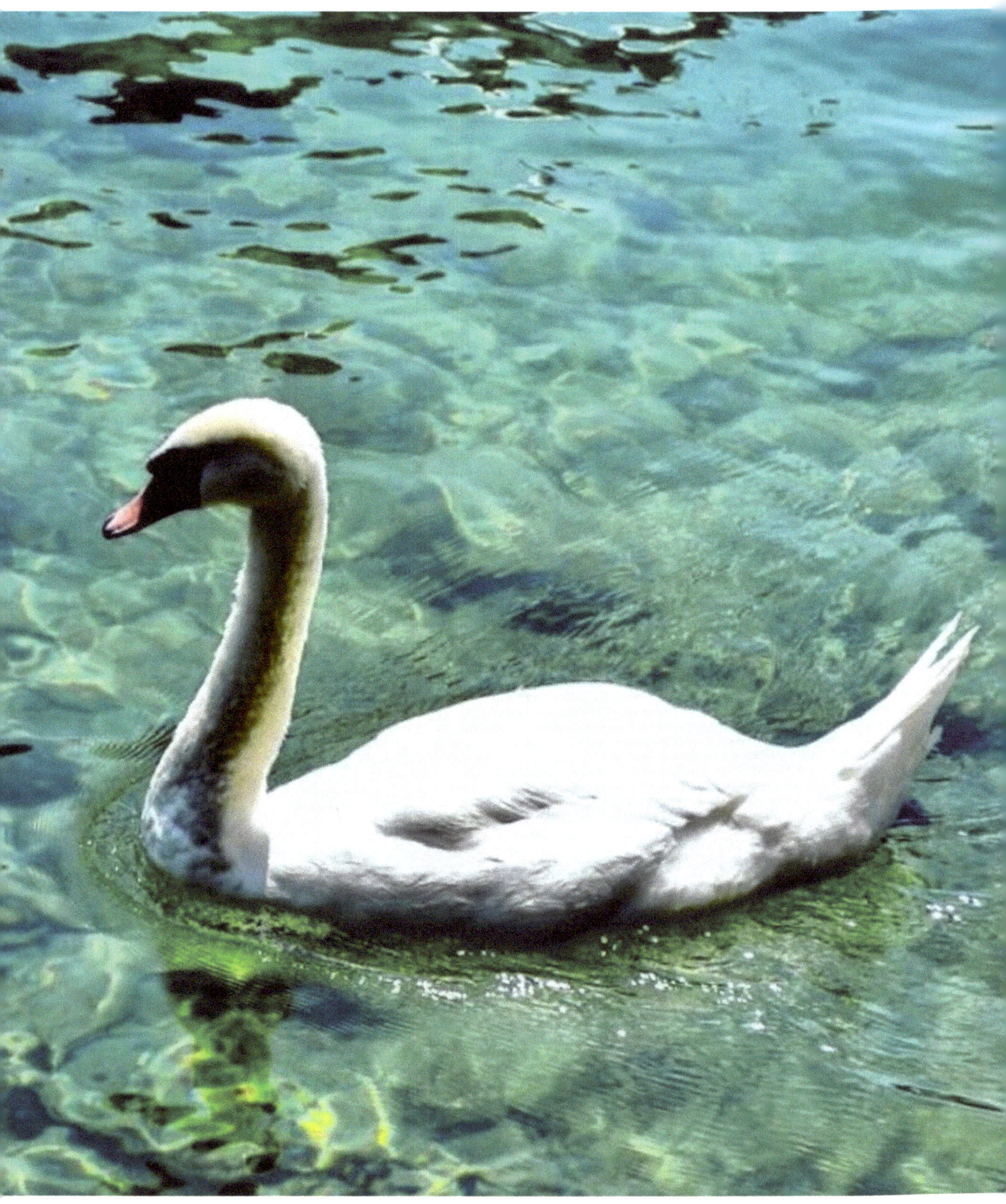

White Swan

Another lonely night
An uneven fight
I get no answer
To my prayers
Lord have you left me
Refining takes debris
How much can I take
I don't want to break
My spirit is down
Mind uplifting ground
Familiar faces
I find in grace
Still she owns me
Move on, agree
Silent proof
She's got a new roof
Whiskey is my enemy
Yet, I still drink, lonely
Perfect swan
White angel wings span
Flew away
With all my ways
Renounce, leave
Faster new eves
Bad days, good days
Still praise
I get no answer
To my prayers
Lord have you left me
Polish me, have mercy
They're all so pretty

She's got no mercy
Space time
Finding mine
Souls by the millions
Chances zillions
Minimal statistic
Connecting static
Energy rising
Candle light dancing
Divine revelation
True passion
Heard and seen
Fleeing the scene
Until when
She's got to return
Settle and stay
Future we may
Have kids, I pray
All, will be ok
Faith brings you
Favor, higher, true
Happiness is now
We don't know how
Learn together
Forever last
Sickness and health
Together until death
White swan
Be my pass on
For future generations

Photo by Lia Scandariato

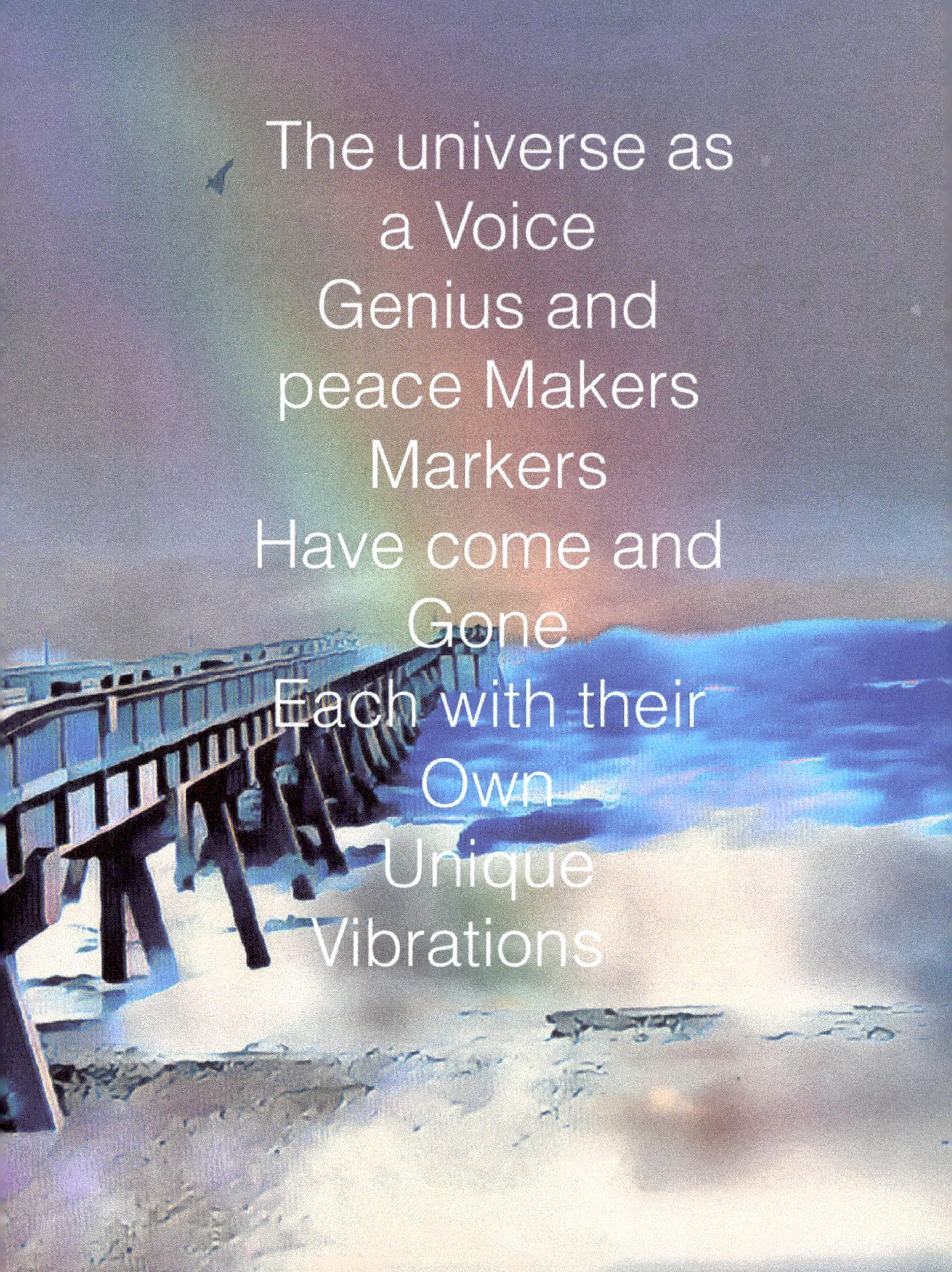
The universe as
a Voice
Genius and
peace Makers
Markers
Have come and
Gone
Each with their
Own
Unique
Vibrations

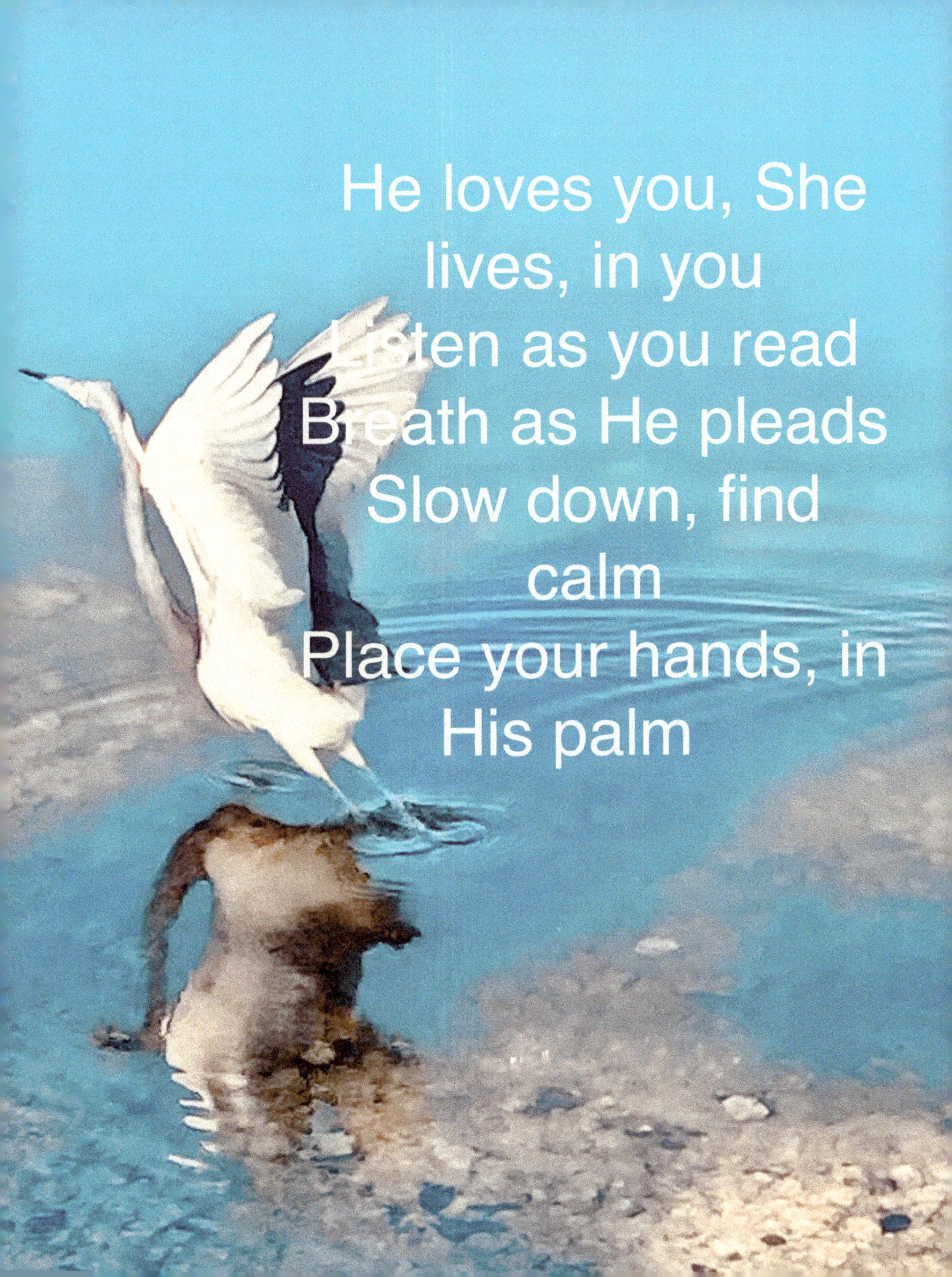
He loves you, She
lives, in you
Listen as you read
Breath as He pleads
Slow down, find
calm
Place your hands, in
His palm

If I offered you love
Could you embrace it
If it came from above
Support it, elevate it,
To mountain top

**Walking away from the
Ledge
To the center of humanity
Reaching our own purity
Free of darkness
Contaminants
At last... sunshine on all
Continents...**

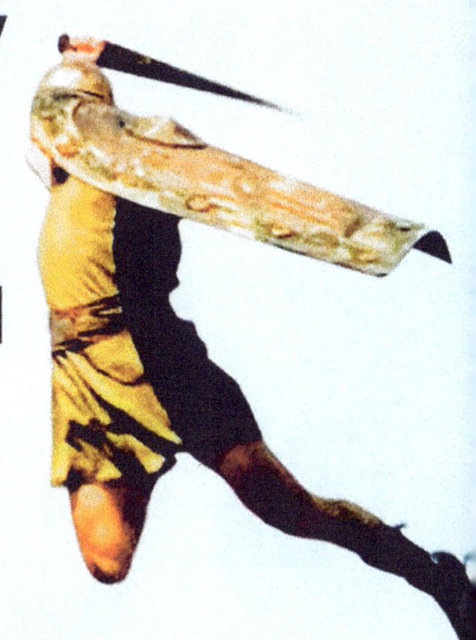

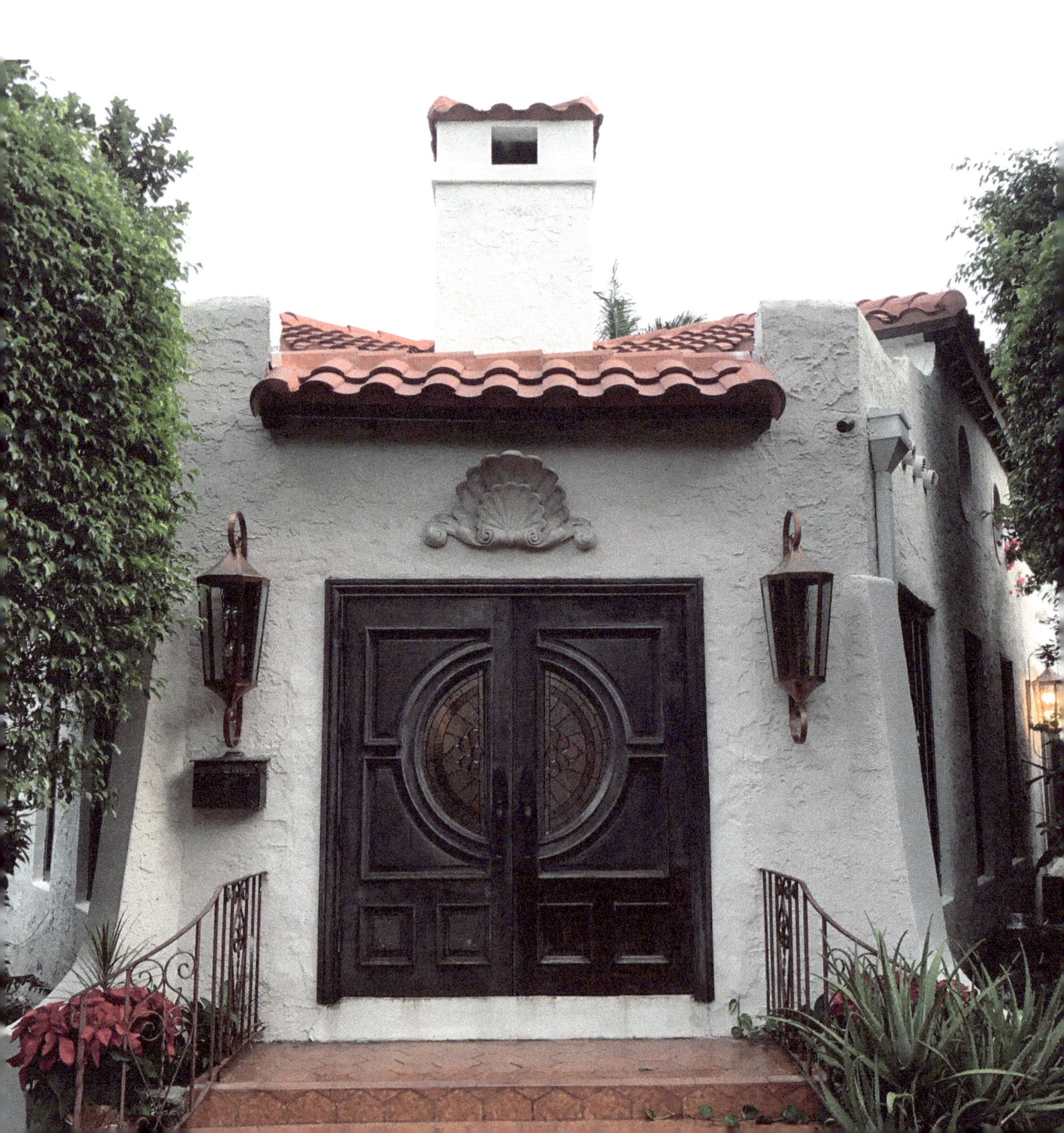

Blessed

Lord, what I've found
Words of sounds
Intricate arrangements
Detour of firmament
Blessings to the ears
Truth for all years
Soul's happiness
Mind's sadness
Emotions elevate
Reading accentuates
One after another
Gifts of splendor
Real flowing
Intricate writings
You're the author
Awesome tutor
Easy listening
Fine tuning
There's a way
Something to say
Communication matters
Messages beloved
Species evolved
Calming lovers
Spiritual healers
Personal and vital
To you viral
Great father

Amazing protector
Let these riddles
Touch celestial idols
Vibrations bound
Waves surround
Hora, era, visualizer
Mankind, transformer

Is This World Real?

We all live like animals
Judging, treating
Each other by the primal
Envelope, complaining
Often pretending
With only the goal of achieving
The idea of cementing
Our souls with the latest, marketing
Introduced, appealing
To those with an empty soul
Killing of a consciousness
A mass hypnotic desire
To steal and acquire
Love, kindness, politeness
Substituted, by hate and rudeness
Is this a dream or is this the real world
Most would prefer
To feed, the evil egos, the voices
Deceiving, perturbing, bad choices
In advocate of a discordant
Mirror of darkness in accordance
Shallow for those who follow
Alarming, to whom, enters the narrow
Path of discernment, lift the blindness
To the oneness
The simpleness
Of our hearts
Of their hearts

If you want, to wake up
Change, the world, rise up
Start here in your shoes
At this moment, accept, create
A new reality of sincerity
Of truth in service
Is this world real
Transformation can take place
But without you, here, this case
Is impossible
The chain reaction, the wave
This energy reverberates
A water drop, circles, and integrates
All of us, into a gigantic
Mystical
Magical
New world ideology
Of a very different tonality
Is this world, for real
Pinch me, tell me, I am dreaming
Our eyes will eventually open to humanity
The nightmare, dissipated in its absurdity
Passions, admirations, love, respect
Will reveal our true identity
Of a real, honest, evolving society
I love you, kiss you, embrace you, wake up...
To a wonderful new reality

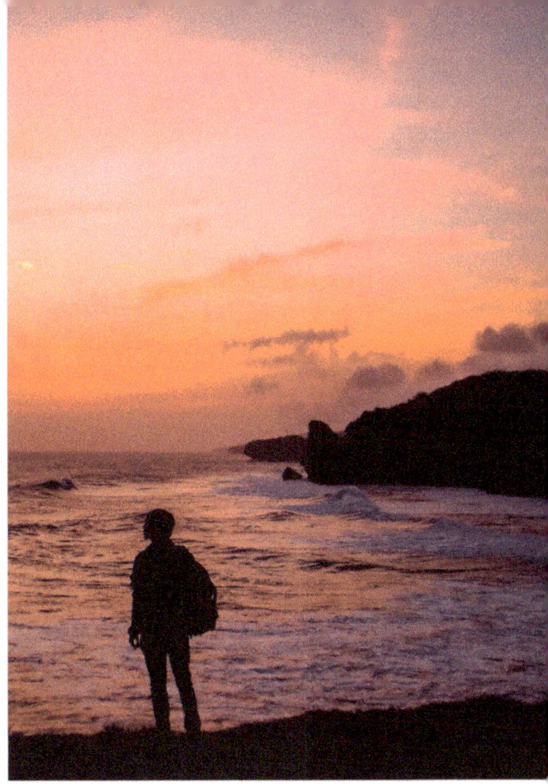

Photo by Samuel Silitonga

Mon Peuple

Je suis certain
Être inspiré
Par un milieu lointain
Pour créer
Une œuvre, notre œuvre
D'amour et de peur
Une preuve, votre preuve
De ce que cette heure
A besoin pour se libérer
De ce cafard
Retrouver la liberté
La joie, les arts
Souffrir, grandir
La tendresse de l'âme
Pourrait-elle, être palpable
Pour qui ne sais la sait
Mon peuple, notre pays
Ne sait s'affranchir
Nous avons grandi
Sans pouvoir réfléchir
De ce qui pourrait
De ce qu'ils avaient
L'isolation, l'insécurité
Les âmes brisées
Aimer, embrasser
Cultiver votre amitié
Ouvrez vos cœurs
Sans trop de rancoeur

Partager, ne pas regretter
Le passé imbibé
Ou mal aimé
Avancer, laisser aller
La vague, le plan,
Du présent
Vous êtes beaux
L'avenir de haut
Nous appartient
Le tien, le mien
Comprenez bien
Je me souviens

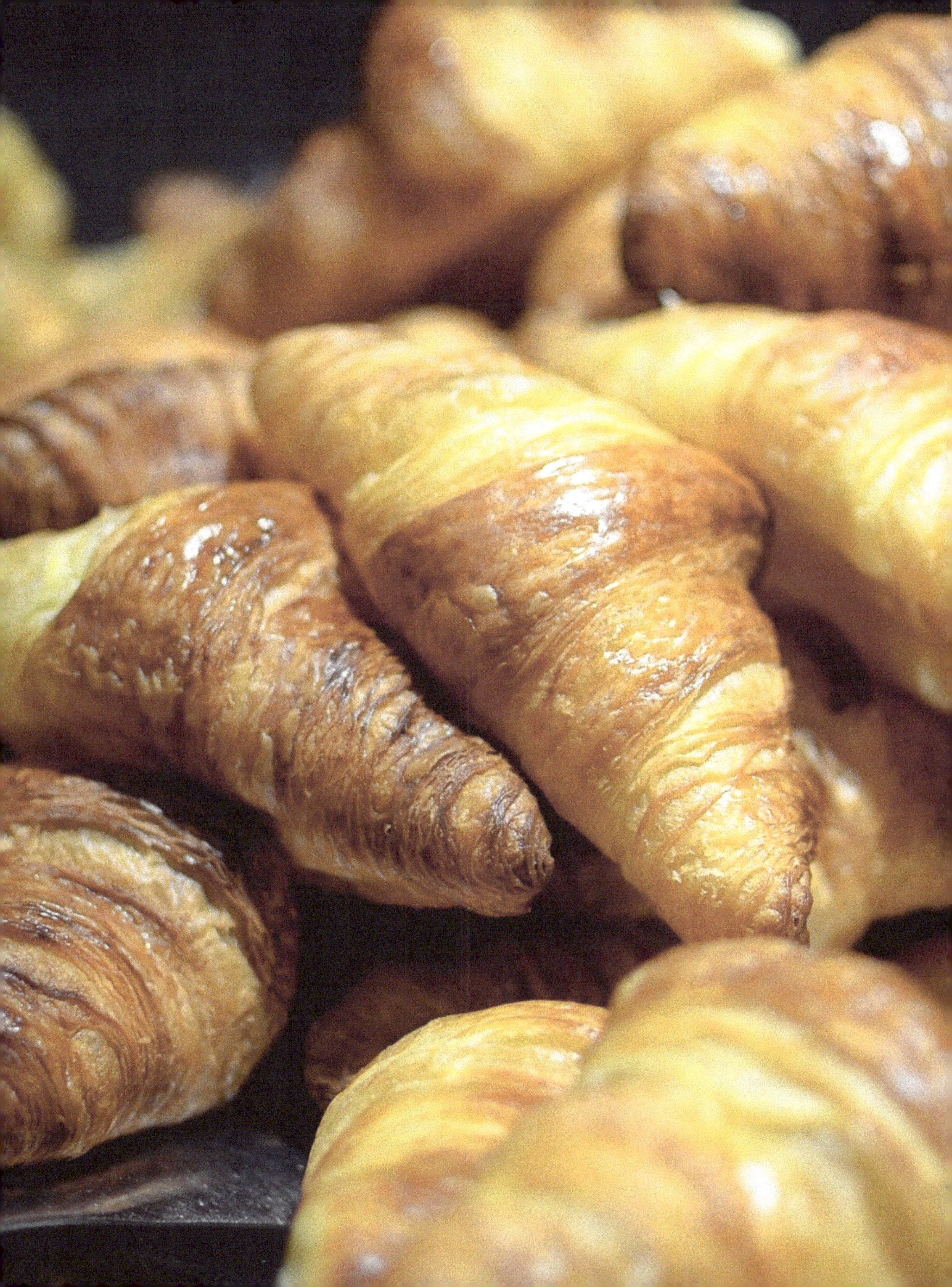

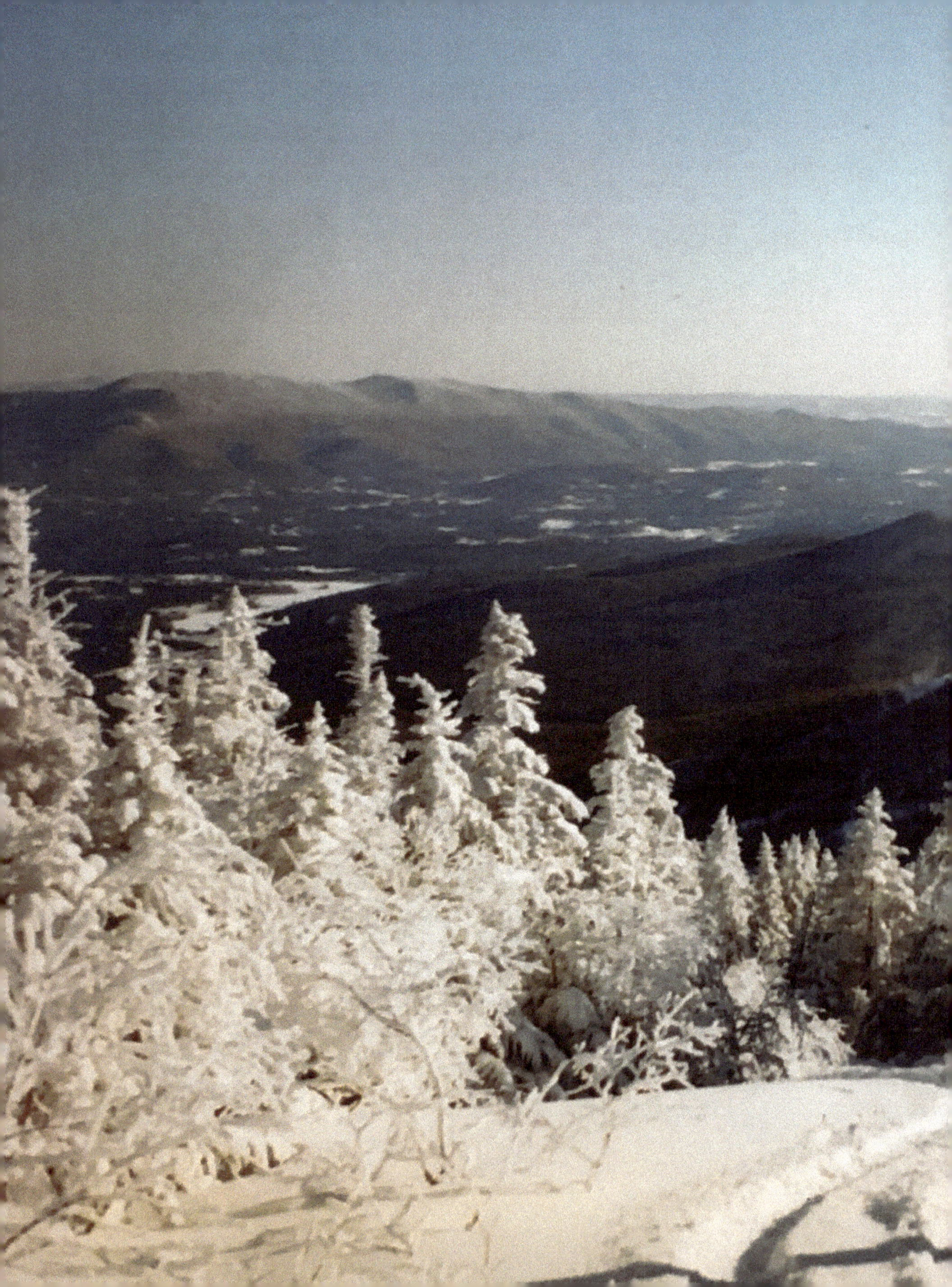

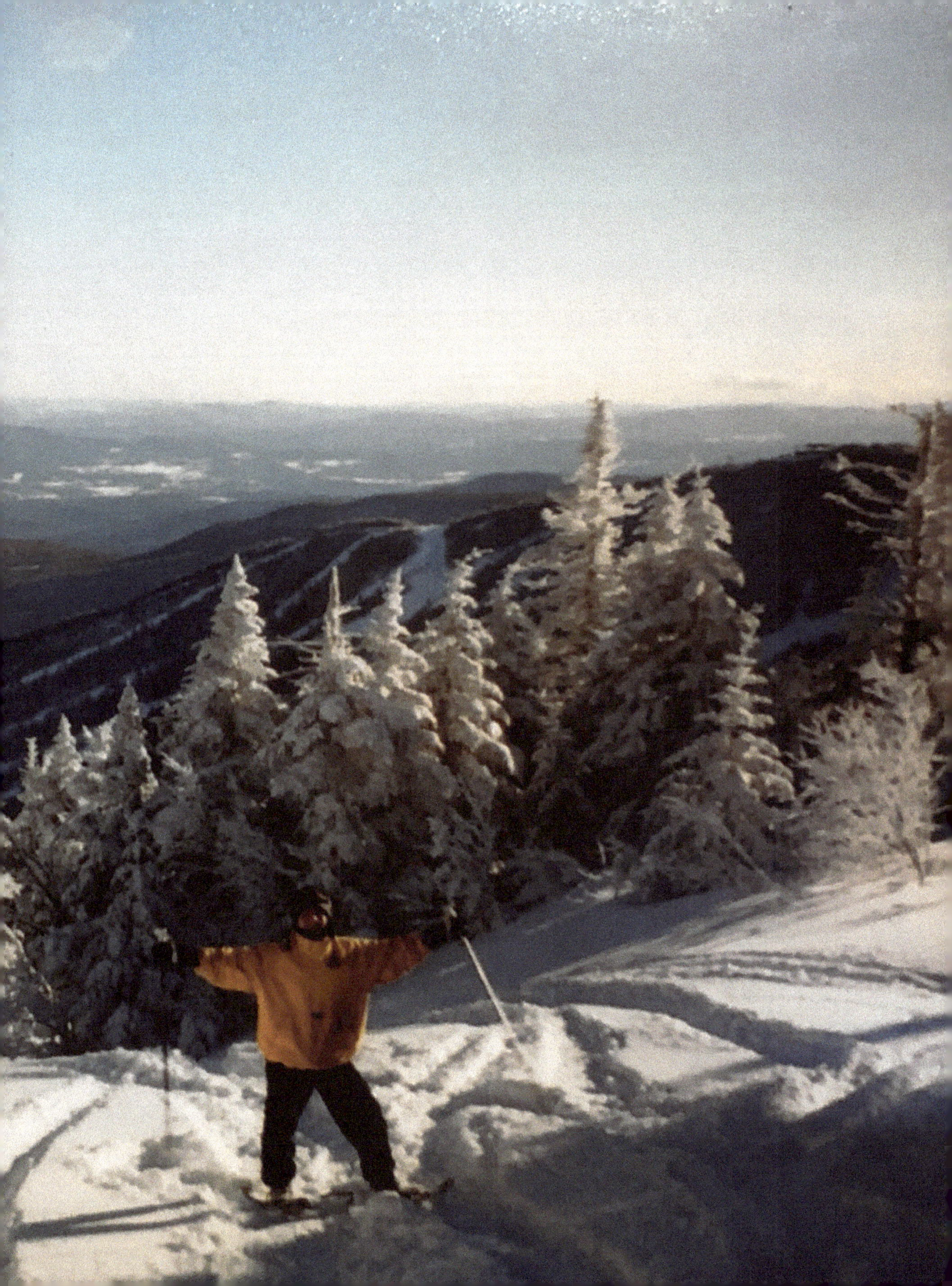

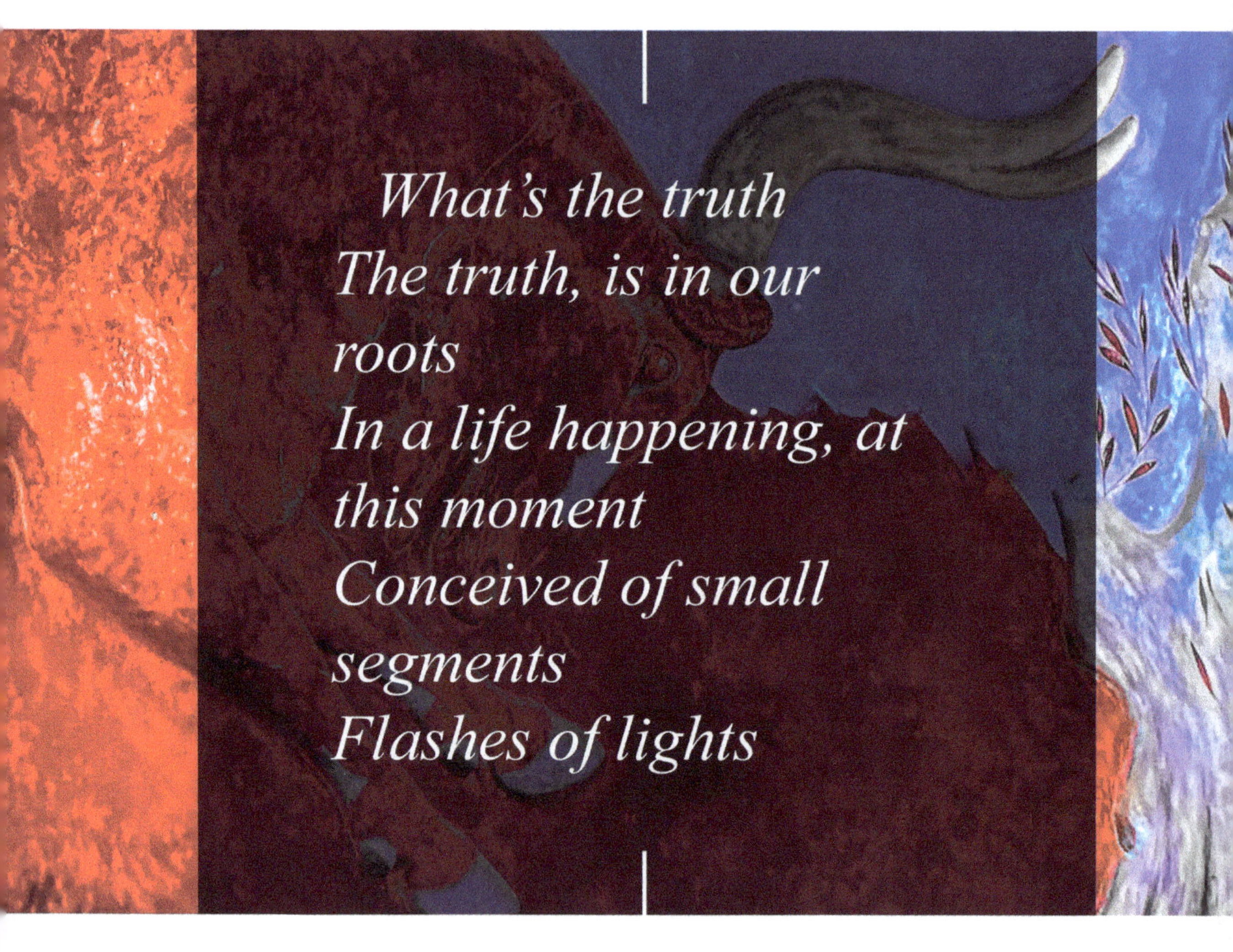

What's the truth
The truth, is in our
roots
In a life happening, at
this moment
Conceived of small
segments
Flashes of lights

You Think Life is Boring?

If life is the same everyday
You wonder and pray
You want to live in the forest?
Go, start planting seeds
Grow, learn, be on your way, proceed
Life is a journey
An adventure, I say
Take action
For a reaction
Your dreams, are a few feet away
But, you have to get on your way
Each step reveals
Humor, with a little zeal
Discoveries
Magical moments
Gone in an instant
It's your time
Your line
Write, read
Love, breathe
Time is precious
Arrogance is ridiculous
The world is turning

Mother Nature, is dancing
Do not expect, but create
Respect others, not thrust their faith
The light projector starts in your head
The movie, is ON
Passing through your eyes
Reflecting on reality
The images of your creativity
For you, to dance, to join in
Laugh, enjoy this beautiful story
Jump, in life, open the lights brightly
Let it reflect on your surroundings
Let it be as you imagine
You will shine, radiate and affect others
You are the soul, you are consciousness
Universal
Eternal
Return to peace, unity and hope
Find a blissful, joyful, fulfilled life
The real need is for self-realization
A beautiful communion, without partition
Smile, laugh, and enjoy

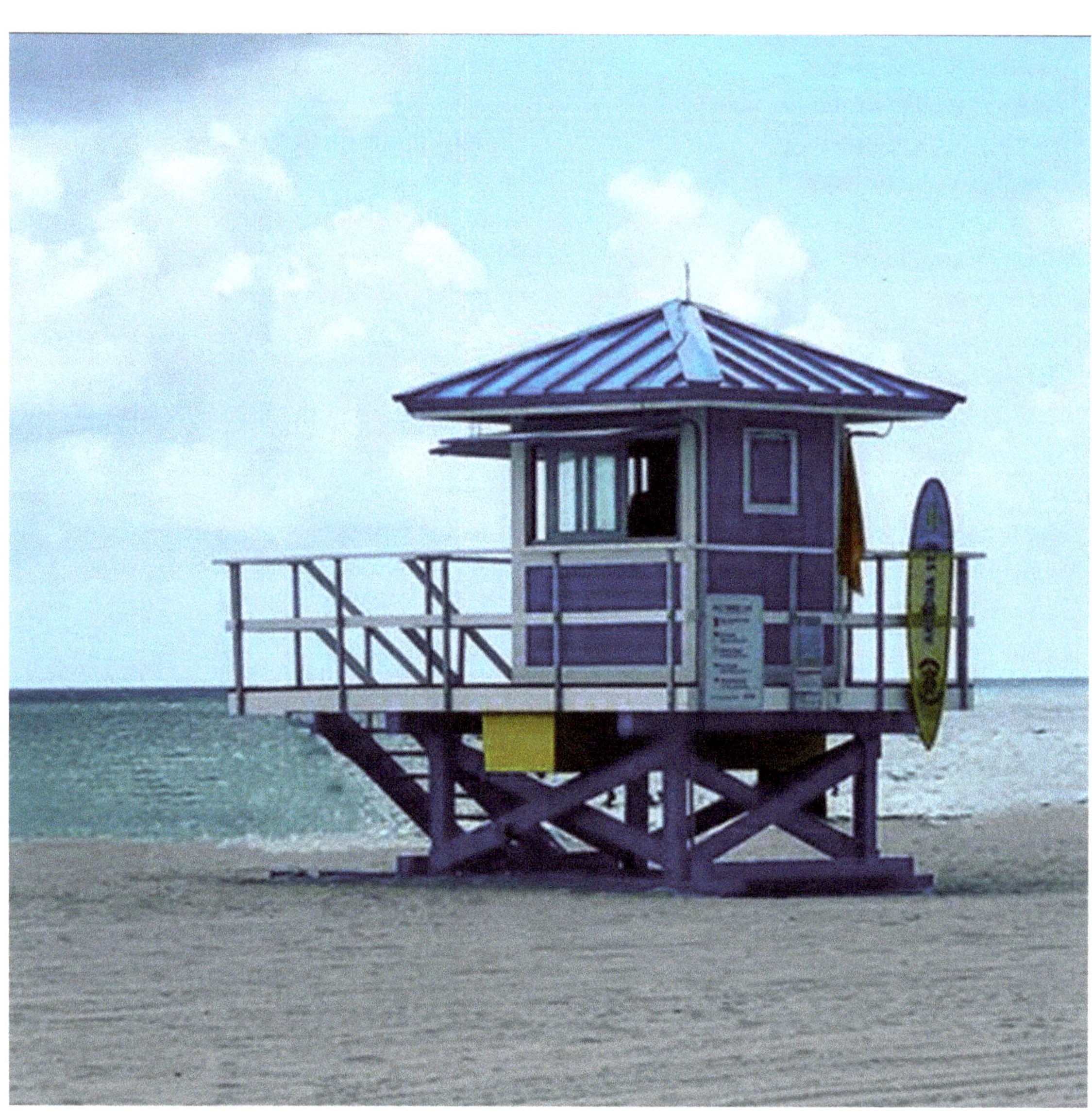

Trains and Airplanes

Trains, of thoughts
We really fought
True of all history
We were all so crazy
Conquering, destroying
Motives for changing
Profits fast acquired
Unworried are the buyers
Steaming, forward
Fakes for reward
Only idiots never learn
All, crash and burn
Technology changes
So do minds who age
Flying high
Above the sky
Planes, carrying
Fresh visions
New horizons
Probably would mean
Drop the shit, I mean
People suffer
While, he prospers
Equality may be, atrophy
Unrealistic, maybe unreal
Yet, it feels, the only real
Possible way to prosperity...
Everyone should be free

In our own ways, equity
Strongers look, after
Weakers took, higher
The whole be happier
Maybe even, Godlier
Put yourself in reverse
Care about your neighbors
Open doors to many cultures
We are all one creature
Different skins, gods, ideology
Made for intelligence, seems crazy
Change our ways
May be the only way
Peace of heart
May, be bringing peace on
Earth...
Let's all have an overview
If only we flew
We could be aware
Life, for ever...
Could, change forever
Love take over
Would it be the beginning
The new Earth fulfilling
Don't wait, sooner the better
We would all be smarter...

Time Fear

Love is it
What she fears
She used it
Like a spear
Piercing hearts
Until I fell apart
Where's my part
Here with, her to start
Beautiful and charming
Completely disarming
Should I have been
Holding my keen
Love builds
Away and chilled
Wandering or laughing
What's her feelings
As days go by
I say goodbye
Love is it, what she fears
She uses it as a spear
Beautiful and charming
Completely disarming
I certainly don't mind
I want her to be mine
Take, take, away
My soul, I only pray
Idiot and lost
Let go in her lust

We are all unique
Yet we all seek
Our half moon
Never comes too soon
Hear the call
Appropriate it all
It's your road
I've been told
Love is it
What she fears
She uses it
As a spear
Beautiful and charming
Completely disarming
Was it, all a plan
I'm her biggest fan
Let go my guard
Hoping for her reward
If only she, could feel
The same appeal
The day is young
I'll try to remain strong
Time, is what she needs
Let me concede
Fly away
Might, make her stay
Only God knows
I can't suppose

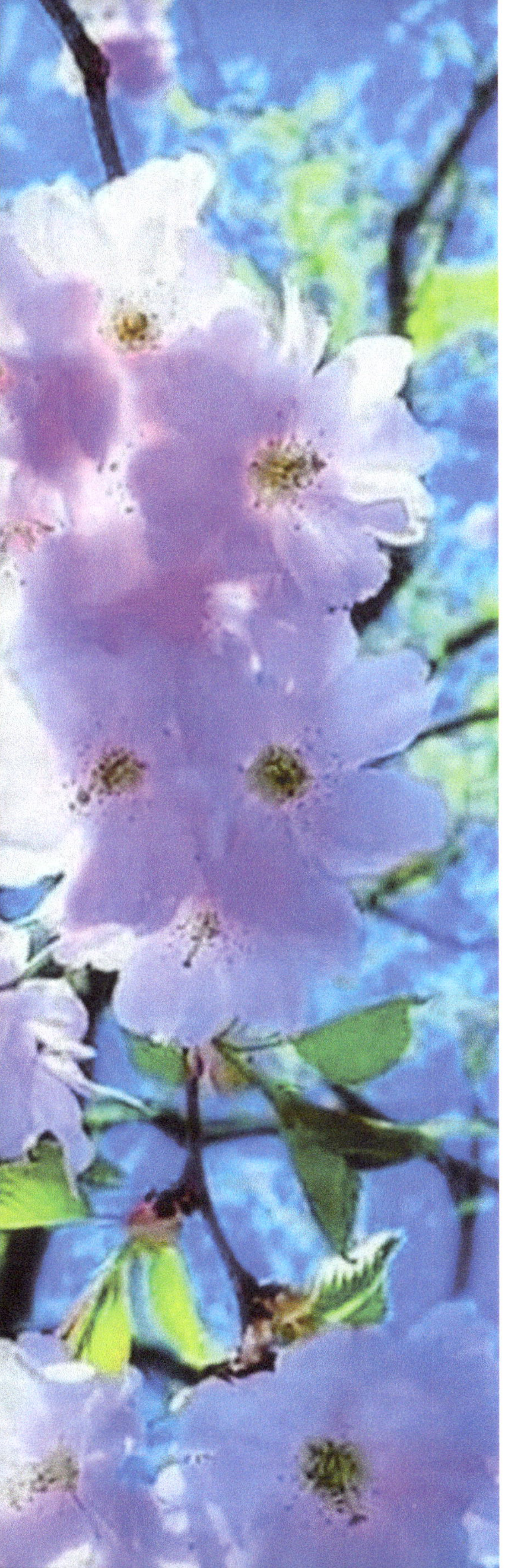

Love is it
What she fears
She uses it
And I'm in tears
Indifferent, is she
How could it be
Warmed of her hugs
Feels like a drug
Addicted to her ways
I can't just walk away
Return be fortunate
The wait abbreviate
Love, don't hold
Day and night, use it
When you're here
With me, be bold
Heart's flames, be lit
Many wonderful years
Without any fears

Save and protect
This unique, beautiful
planet
By taking a moral stand
Maybe, we don't
understand
Fear, divide and
conquer
The road map, trace for
our future
Awareness is describe
Involvement is
prescribe

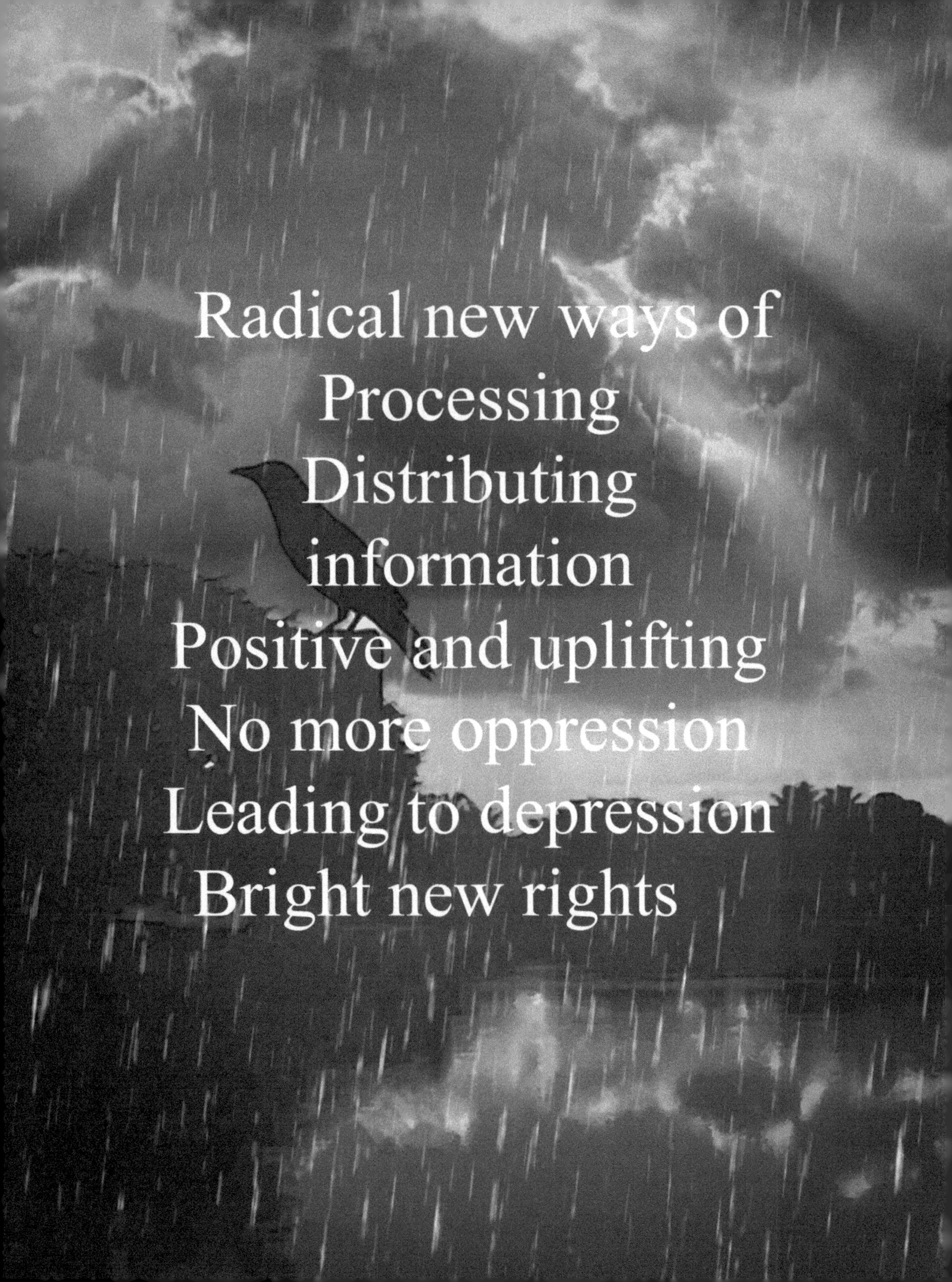

Radical new ways of
Processing
Distributing
information
Positive and uplifting
No more oppression
Leading to depression
Bright new rights

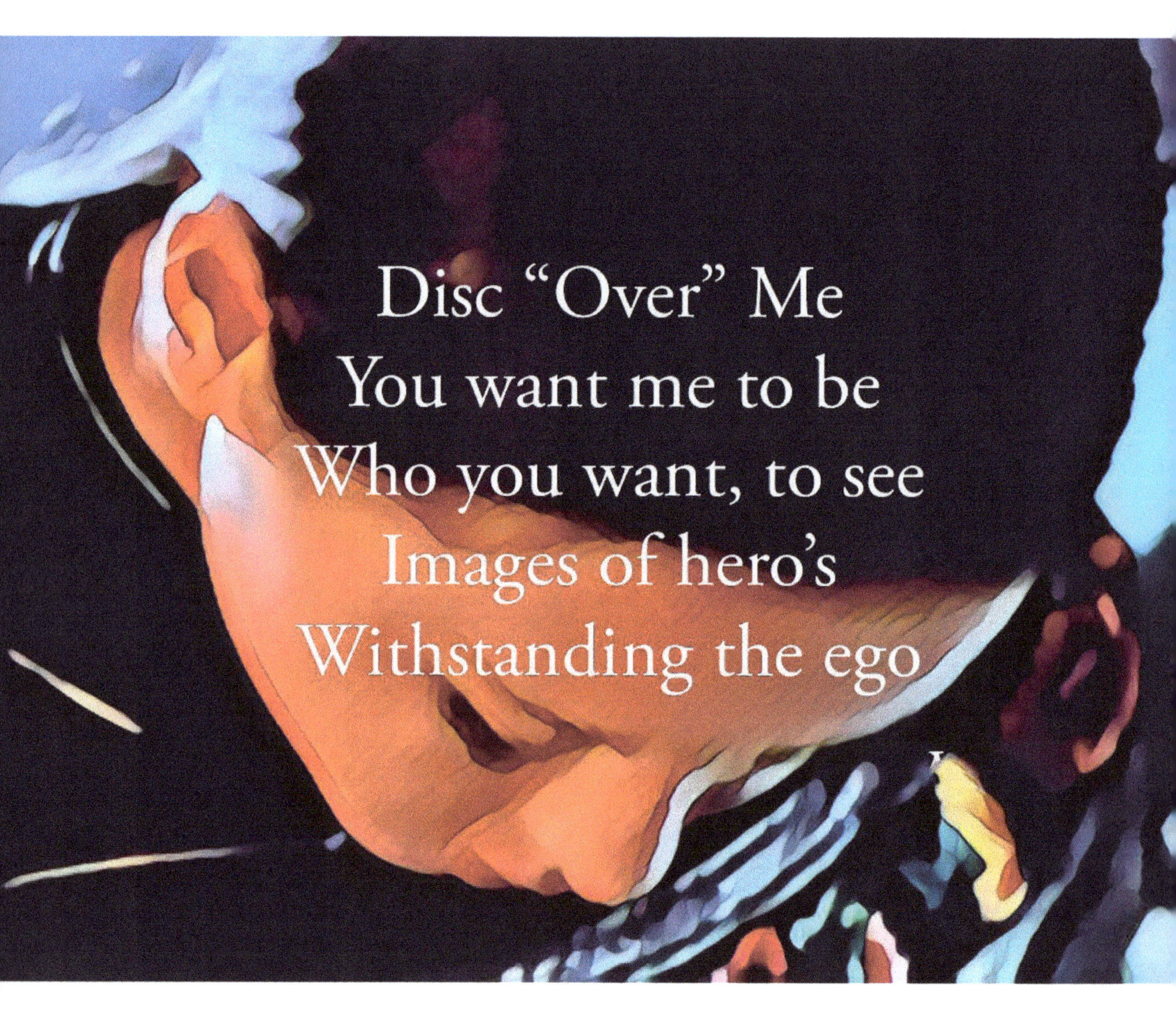
Disc "Over" Me
You want me to be
Who you want, to see
Images of hero's
Withstanding the ego

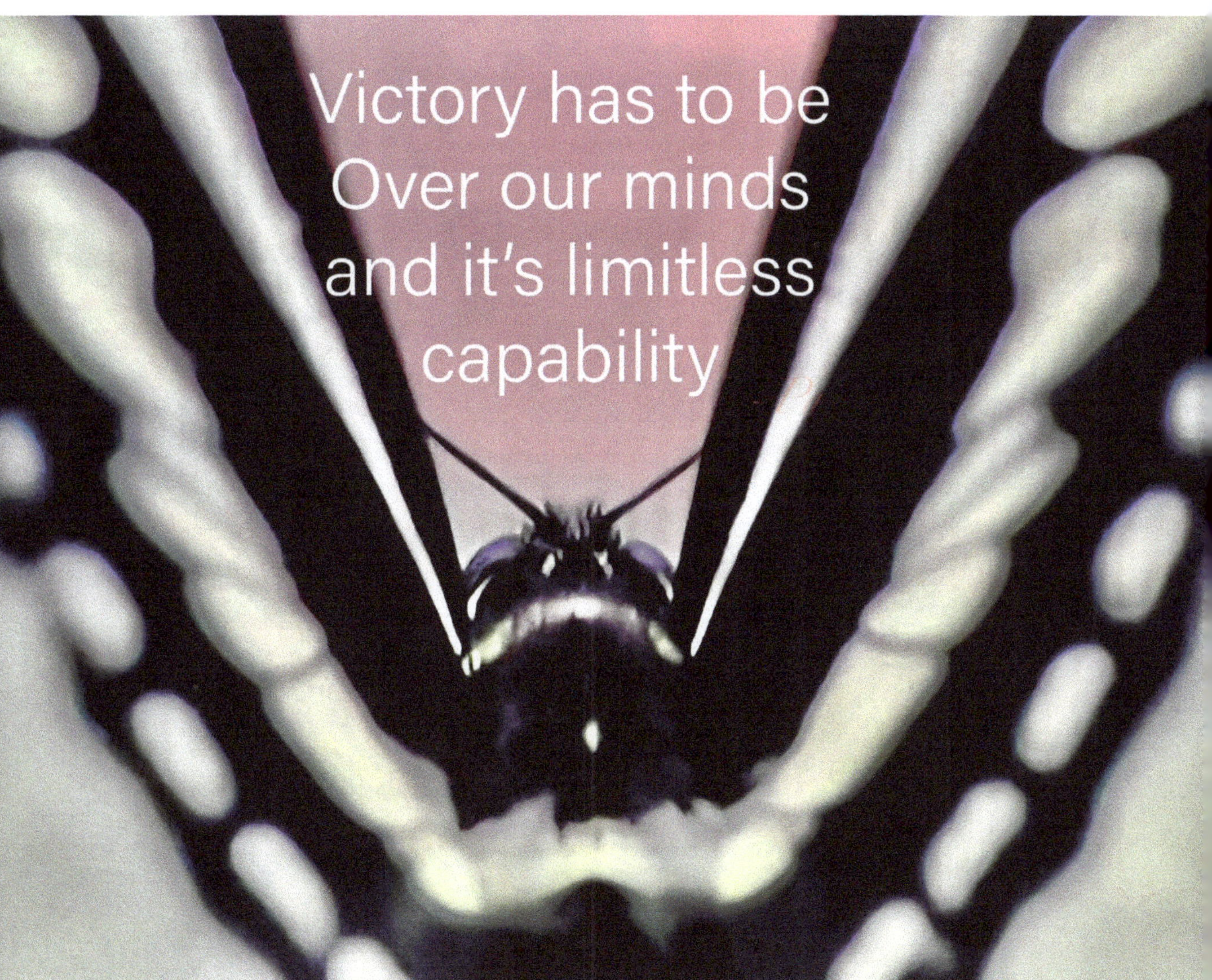

Victory has to be
Over our minds
and it's limitless
capability

I'm not pre tending
I do not pretend to be a scholar
I do not pretend to be a star
I write with my heart
I cry, with my art
I express my surprises
I admire the sunrise
I tell the story of a human journey
Thrifty, loving and happy
Upset by humanity and it's idiocy
Praying, for peace and harmony

Time

When I was young
Was I told wrong
Love little
Fight a lot
Guess what brittle
I'm in a knot
I love too much
What ever luck
Is in it such
Looking for something real
My heart isn't made of steel
We should all aspire
Accomplish desires
To greater deals
Stay, be real
When you please
If you leave
Elsewhere
Be aware
Trouble may lay
I'm here now
Learn that, I vow
Keep this way
But you should plow
The way, to stay
Is to understand
And be committed to how
Comprehension, love and affection
The mother of all emotions

The One

Beauty or fictive
Where does she live
In her mind
Or is she blind
Intelligence oblige
Street smart alive
Creating wealth
Any cost, all health
Distorting reality
Needing of security
I have wish meaning
For her being
Day after day
She is my way
Talking, drinking
She's the best thing
Ever to happen to me
She is the key
Free my mind
Ever-last be mine
Make me the artist
I only would wish
Loving you, easy
Loving me, breezy
What's the goal
Money on hold
Love in our minds
Friendship hard find

Loving her to the end
I want her, find friend
She might be genius
I do need her
She propels me higher
Always wanting you
My friend let me hold you
Until love makes us
Inseparable truss
Since the first glance
My world is enhance
Life be romance
Without hesitation
Life long anticipation
Creating unity
Unifying families
Undivided attention
No need of retention
Imagine the future
Without blisters
So new, yet so completed
Souls connected
Forever is our future
Loving all demeanor
Make a decision
Support our union
Please be mine
At least until sunshine

The sunrise
The sun sleeps
Our life will meet
Sure I won't retreat
Allow me closer
Break the cycle
You read my mind
Forever be mine
I grew older
Acknowledging my error
I know, I rushed
Even I pushed
She as no one
Nobody as won
Certainly I hope
Her heart, cuts the rope
My dear angel
Certainly, she's beautiful
My heart is full
Open her eyes
Hear my cries
Find security
I will be waiting and... see

New Year

It is a new year...
Some, approach it, with fears
Most, would love, to hear
That life, will be without tears
But diamonds are made in fire
Pounding and enduring
Love comes in forms, often, making us wonder
What about, all the suffering
Might transforms our minds
Open it or even remind
Us all, to look above
What, if love came, in the form of a dove
White, bright, hovering
Softly, eagerly, ready to be opening
Hearts that are made ready
To receive openly
Guidance
Acceptance
Of a much greater energy
A smile, a wave of consciousness away from conformity
A new way to be accomplished
Takes refinement, to be polished
To accept, to praise the life
The chance, of this human experience
This amazing story and His plan
Opening the hearts, the souls
To positivity, be ready, for all capability
Unknown at once, to create

To participate, in this magical
Story that is taking place
Here, now, around us
With all its good, bad, ups and downs
Twist and turns
It is what it feels like to be alive
To live, to endure
To breathe, enjoy the pleasures
Rest reassure
The plan, with our acceptance
Will always end for the good
Love, observe, realize your blessings
Family, friends
Emotions, feelings
Touched and moved
Are parts of the amazing, materialization
The consciousness of our nurturing
Say THANK YOU, smile, laugh, and make no excuses
He loves you, mind, realize your dreams
Nothing can stop you, but you
Knowing, understanding, the force is with you and in your control...
Blessings

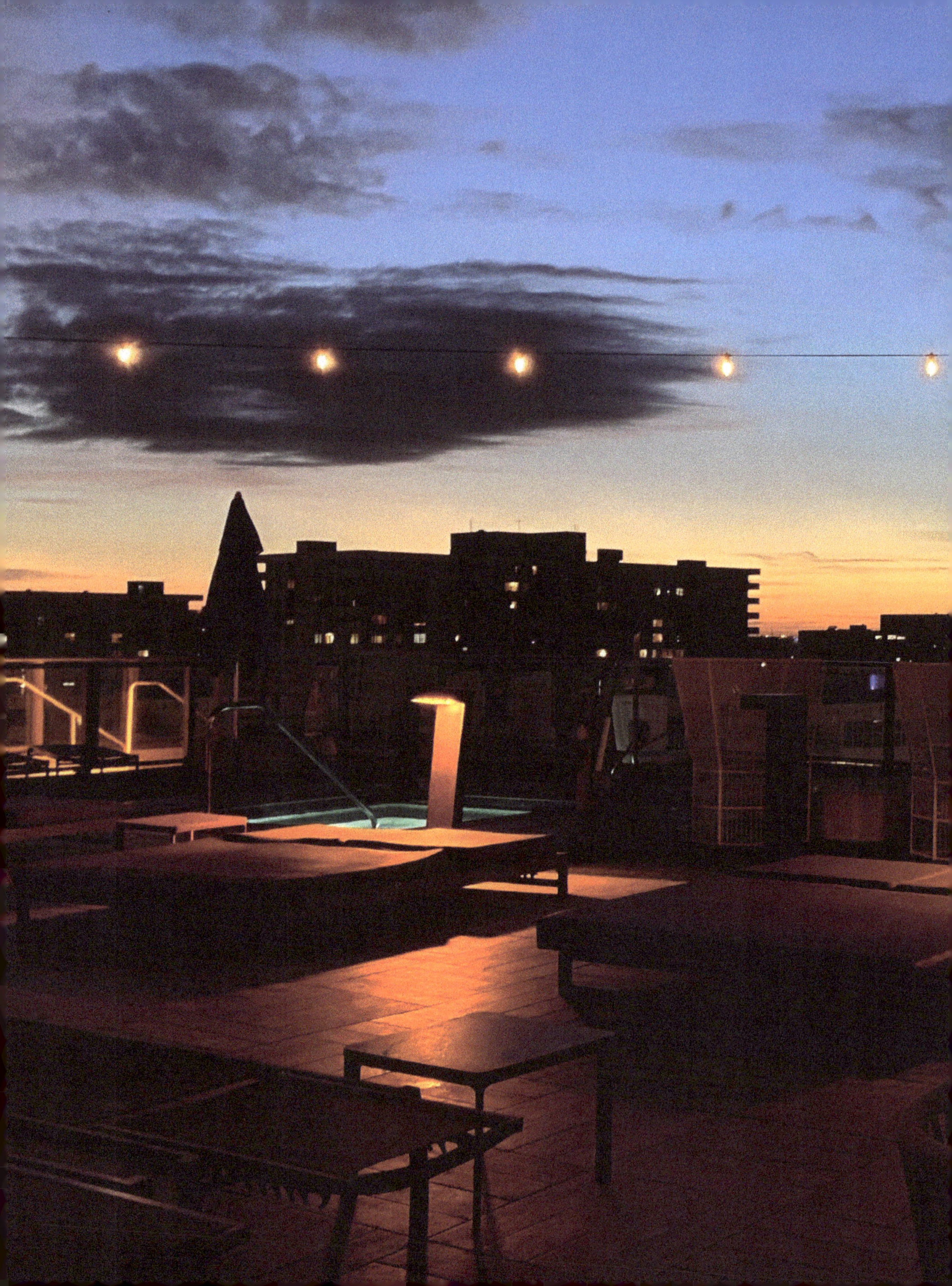

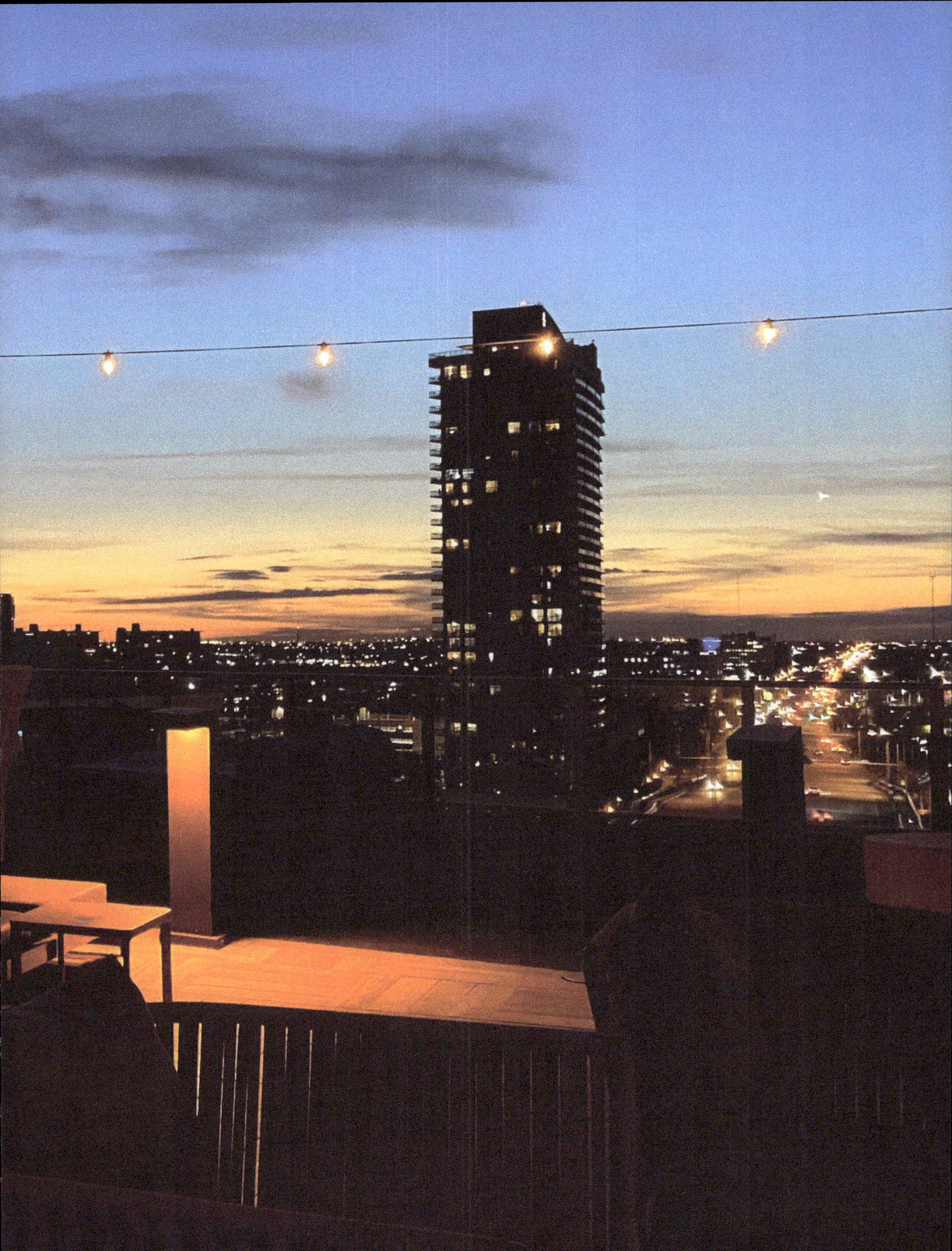

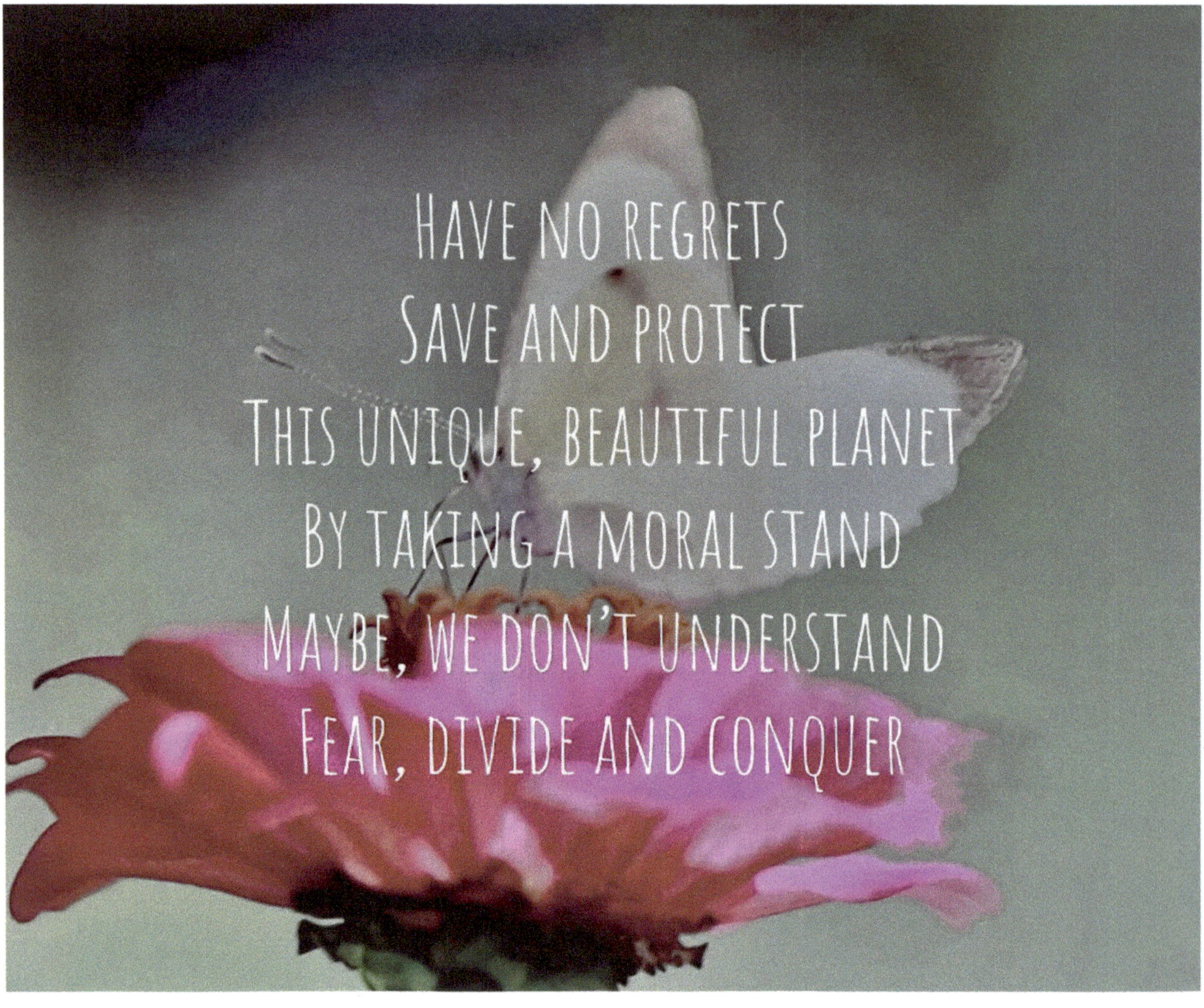

Have no regrets
Save and protect
This unique, beautiful planet
By taking a moral stand
Maybe, we don't understand
Fear, divide and conquer

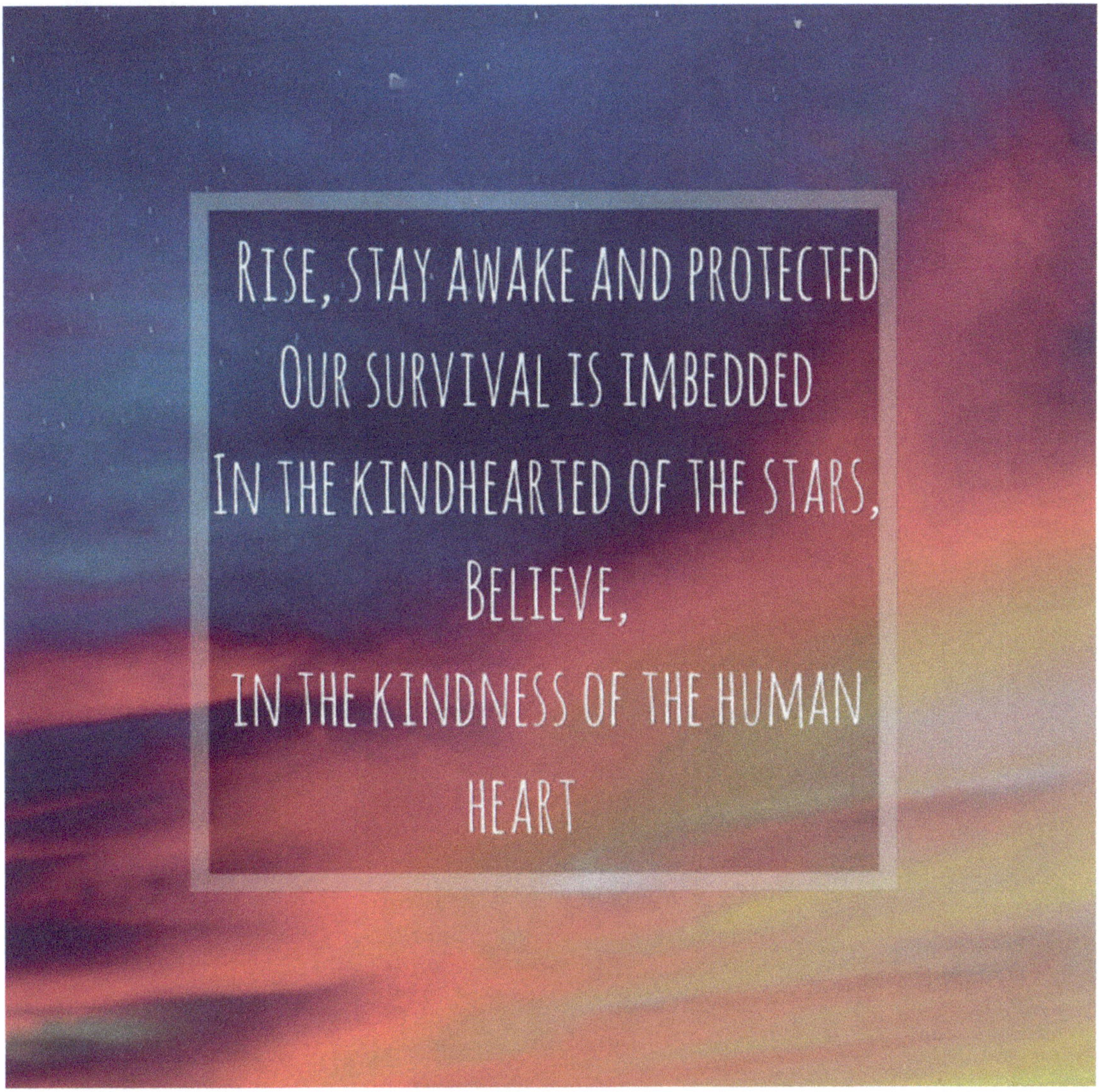

Rise, stay awake and protected
Our survival is imbedded
In the kindhearted of the stars,
Believe,
In the kindness of the human
heart

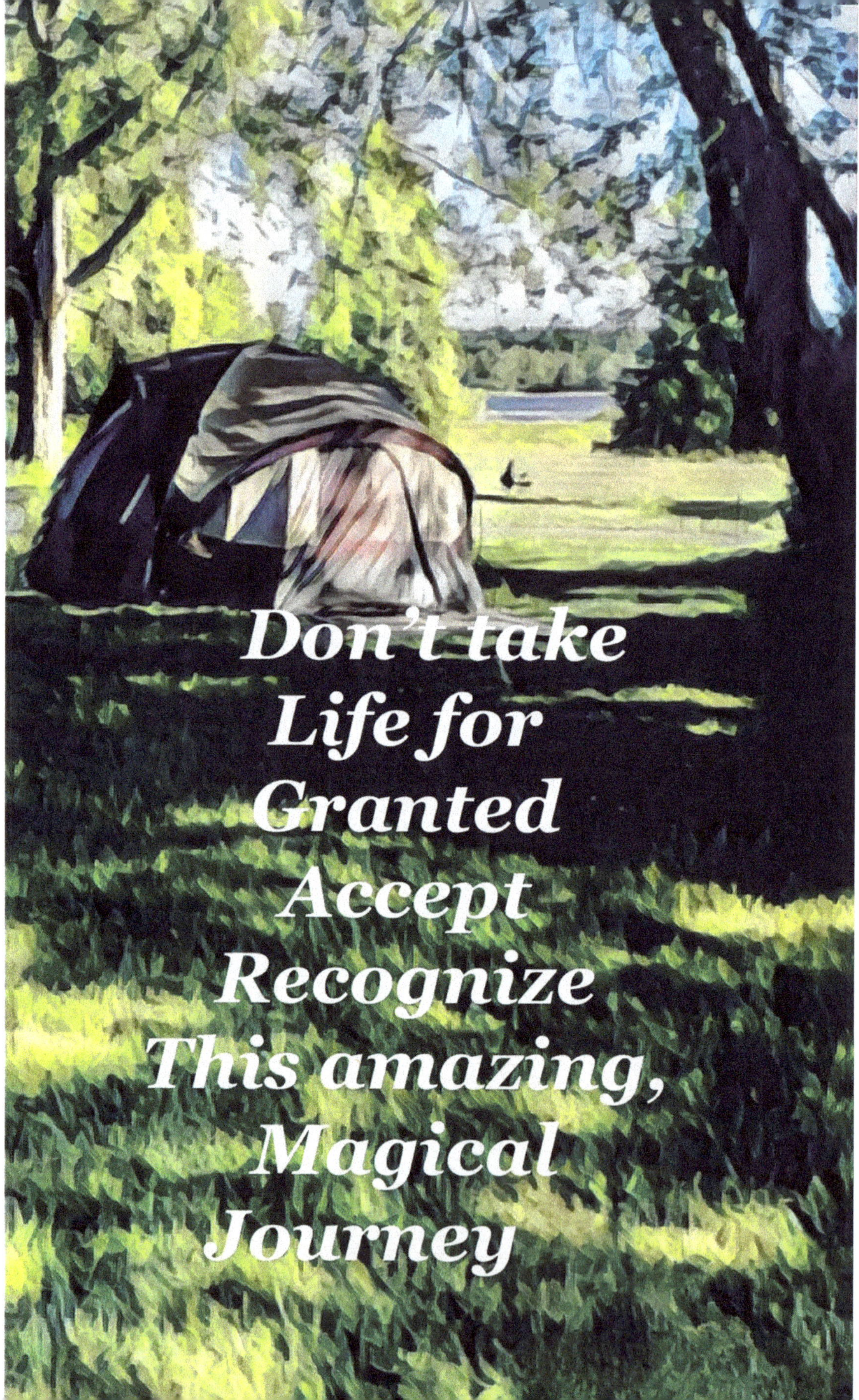
Don't take
Life for
Granted
Accept
Recognize
This amazing,
Magical
Journey

Changing

People change
People range
From loving
To revolving
Talk of promises
Act like compromises
Winds unsettle
Flowing dismantle
No planned future
Make us so insecure
Nobody knows with certainty
What a couple years
Changes happily
Immense possibility
Unimaginable infinity
Different affinity
Independence
If so preference
Afraid of commitment
Later implement
Family values
Need revalues
Older no order
Nobody offers
Flowering colors
New birth odors
Lets imagine
A world engine

If all immature
Don't settle, nurture
She's changing
Like tornado blowing
Round and round
Taking me up and down
Merry-go-round
Leave me on sure ground
Take your time
Hope of being mine
Change your ways
Learn you may
Patience, understanding
Qualities of meanings
Met for inspiring
Long for lasting
Please stay
Stop going astray
Change for stability
All will be easy
Only if you may
Natures calm and pray
We might just find our way

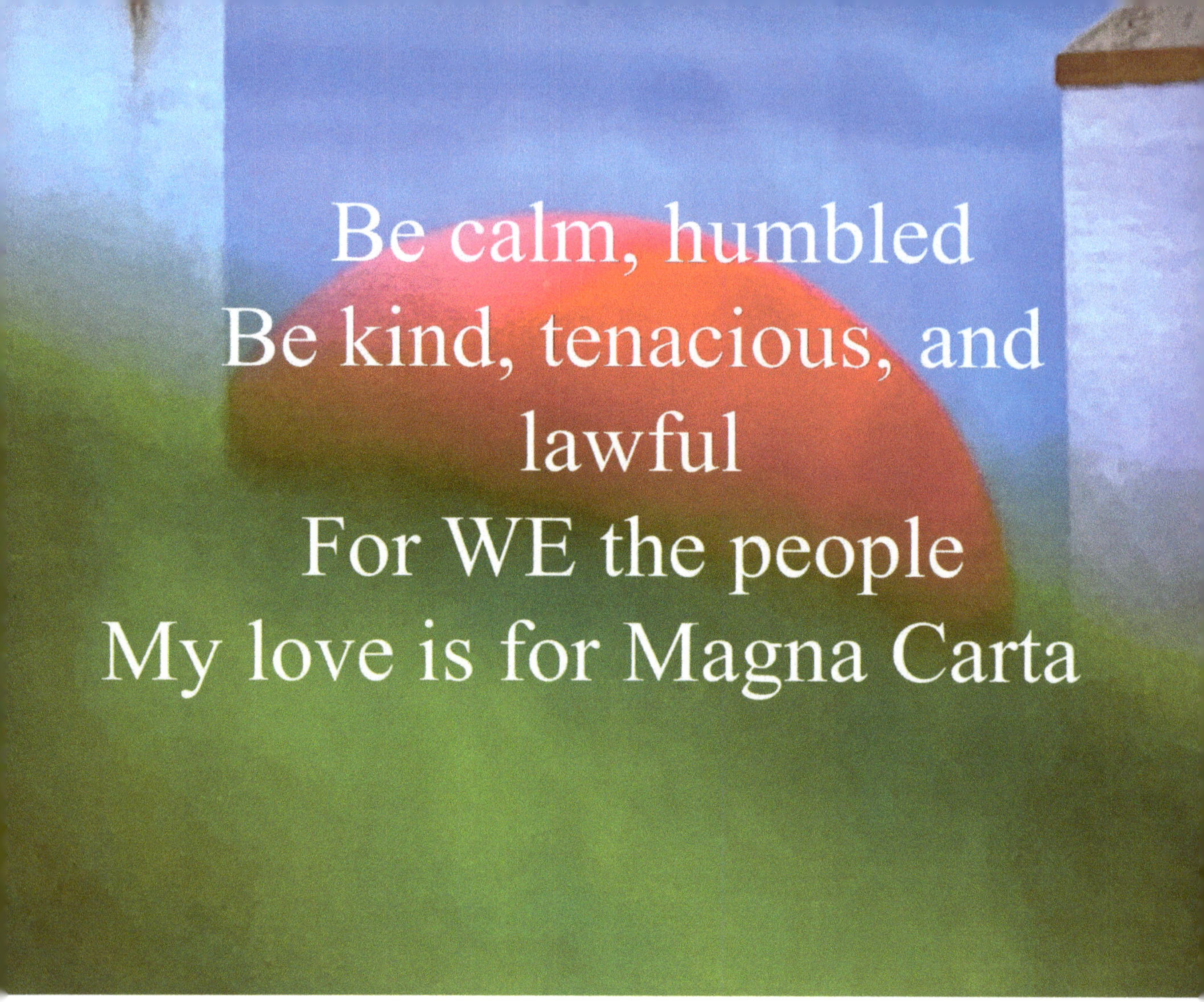

Be calm, humbled
Be kind, tenacious, and
lawful
For WE the people
My love is for Magna Carta

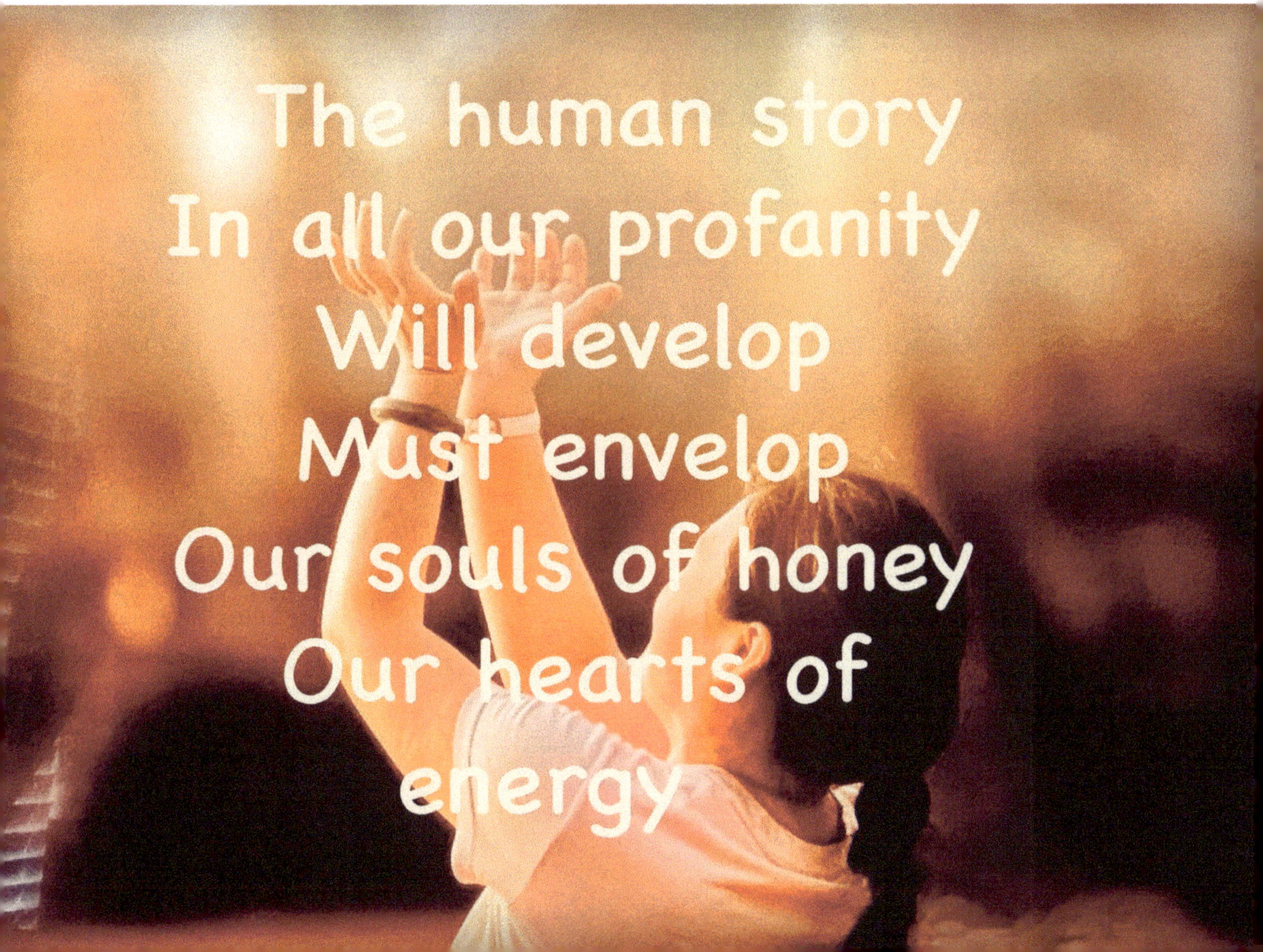

The human story
In all our profanity
Will develop
Must envelop
Our souls of honey
Our hearts of
energy

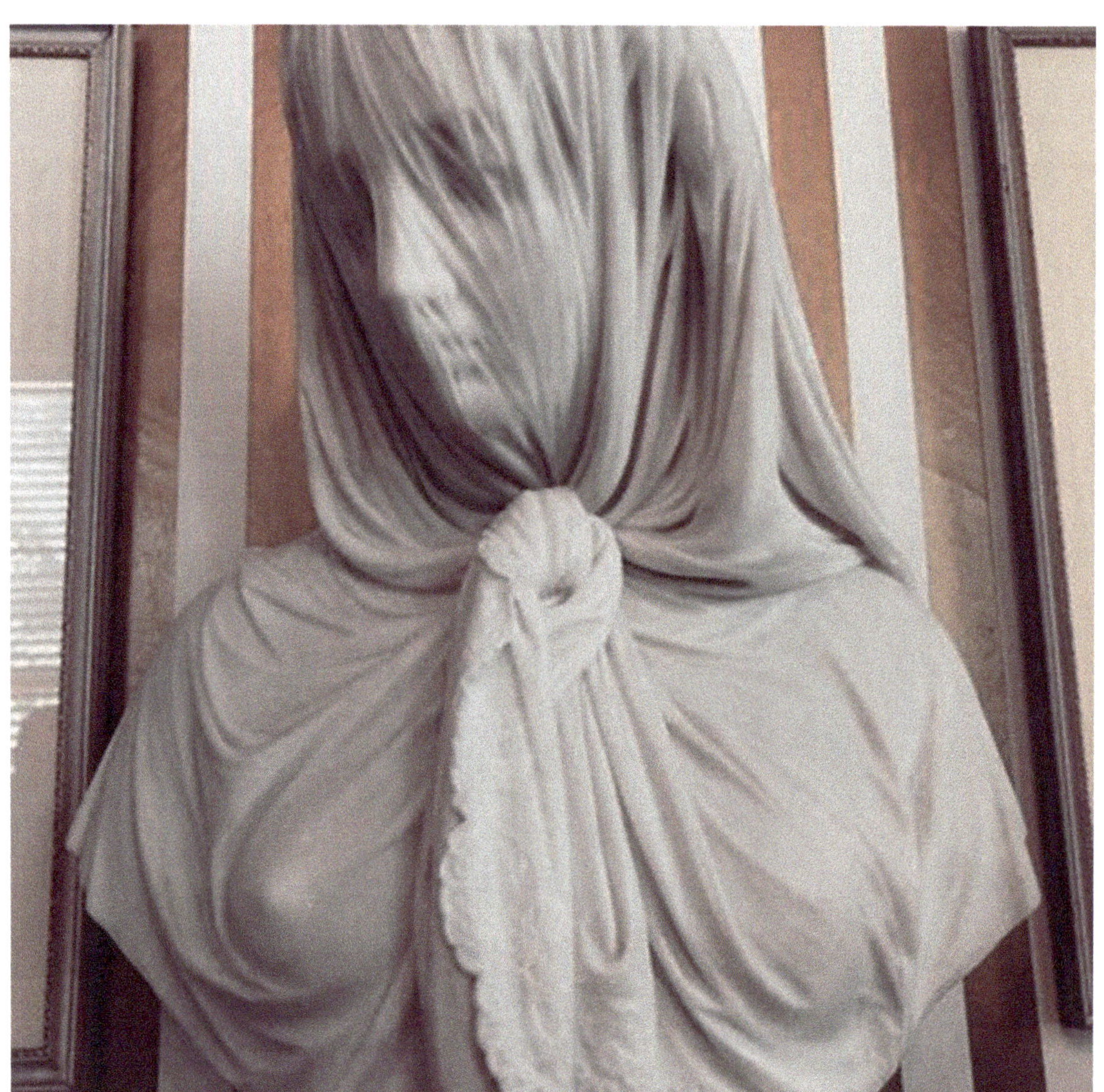

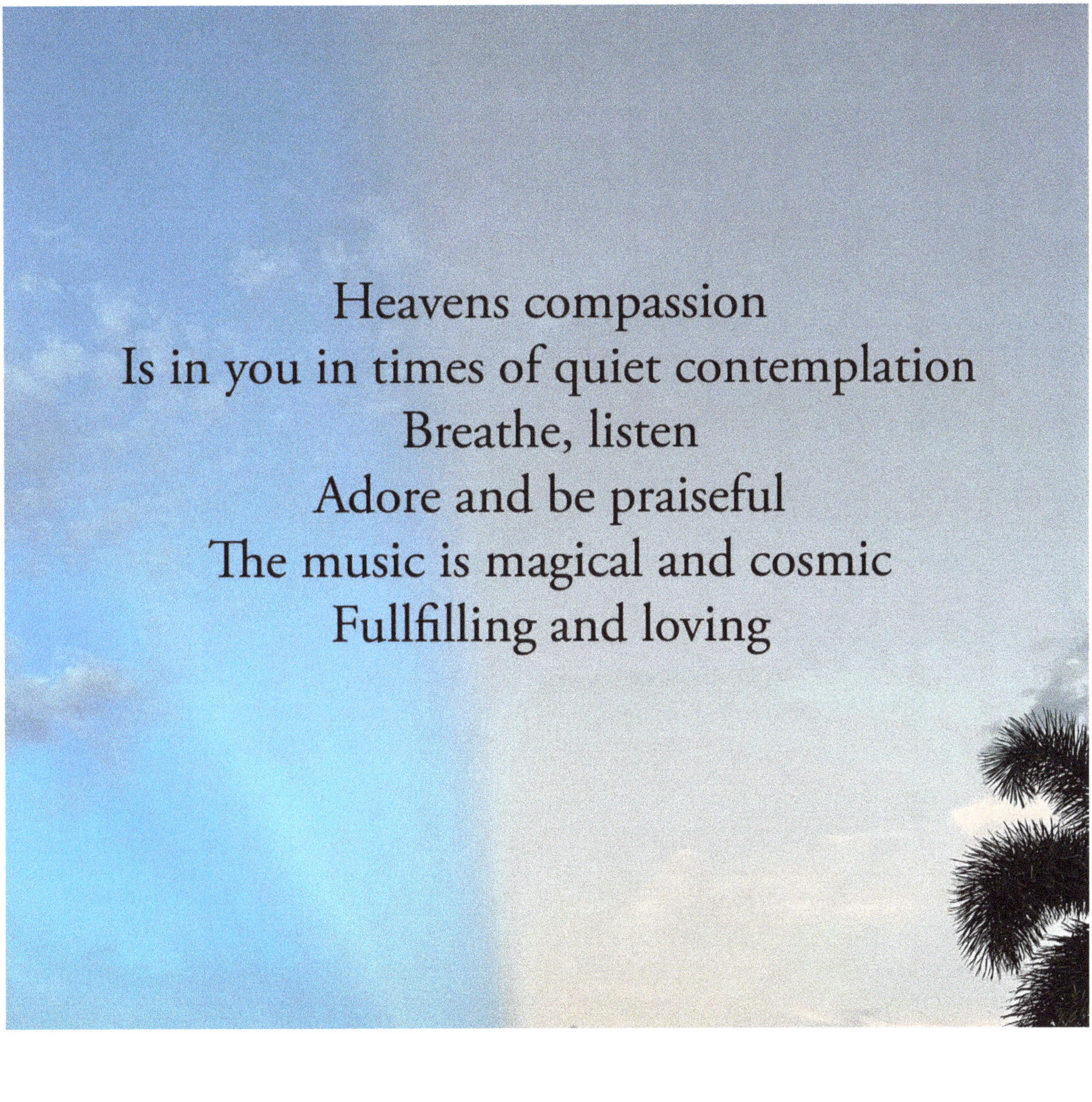

Heavens compassion
Is in you in times of quiet contemplation
Breathe, listen
Adore and be praiseful
The music is magical and cosmic
Fullfilling and loving

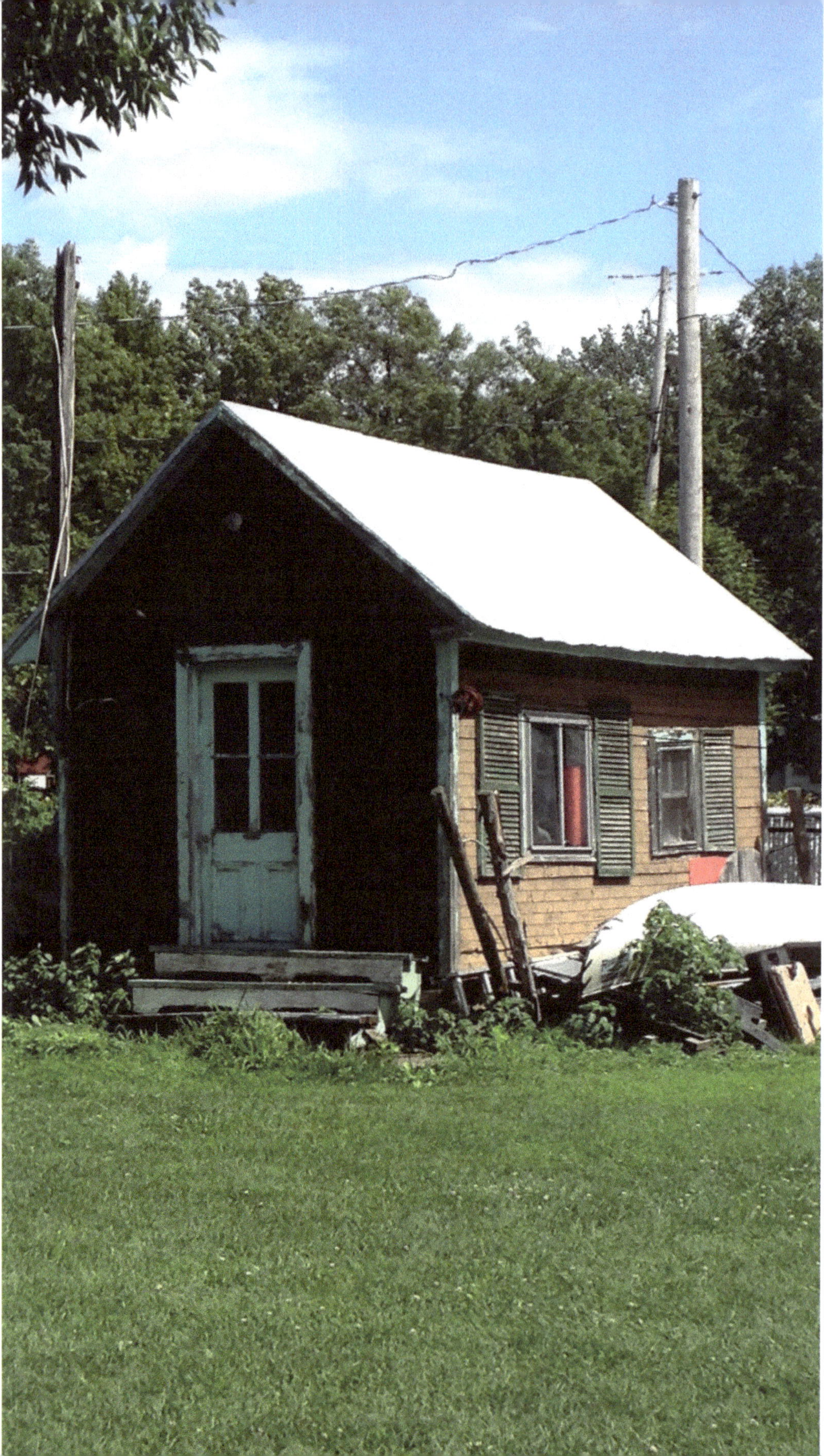

Technology

Technology happy
Beautiful women
Software worry
Smells of sweet heaven
Are we people closer
Drifting even further
Would it be safer
Keep distance under
Different, age, younger
Generation application
Smartphone revolution
Distant relation
Texts appreciation
Manners, none existence
Seems like arrogance
Why not even talk
See what sparks
Young appearance
A lot of I pretend
Much more admire
Subtitles of images
Attires for differences
No need of knowledge
Nobody has the edge
All gone for generation
Technology degeneration
Touched impossible
Screen irresistible

Work hard rewards
Might win award
Lasting long feeling
Ever more taking
Real human touching
She's for real loving
People seems awkward
Yet she tries real hard
Fabulous and outward
Personality forward
Touching me deep
For she is to keep
Remember agreed
Time if read
Let's erupt passion
That's the situation
Reading no occasion
My woman oblivion

The Flower Named Love

If you love a flower
Wouldn't you give her water
Wouldn't you point her out to the sun
So don't put her in the shade or under a cover
Vitamins and nutrients is what she needs
Or she will, find the smallest breach
Pull out, expend beyond your reach
Help her find her true colors
Find her individuality
To fulfill your personality
Let her keep her roots
Allow her to grow and become
The way she IS
Don't be overcome
By her happiness
By her wiseness

She will expend
She will become only her true beauty
The one she was meant to be
Only she knows, where her garden lies
The place where her heart will not die
Beside you
Honoring you
Thanking you
Loving you
Blooming and chanting
While reaching for her truth
In the glory of the light
Shining so pure and so bright
Just let her Be... she will flourish
This is, what love is meant to be
Free...

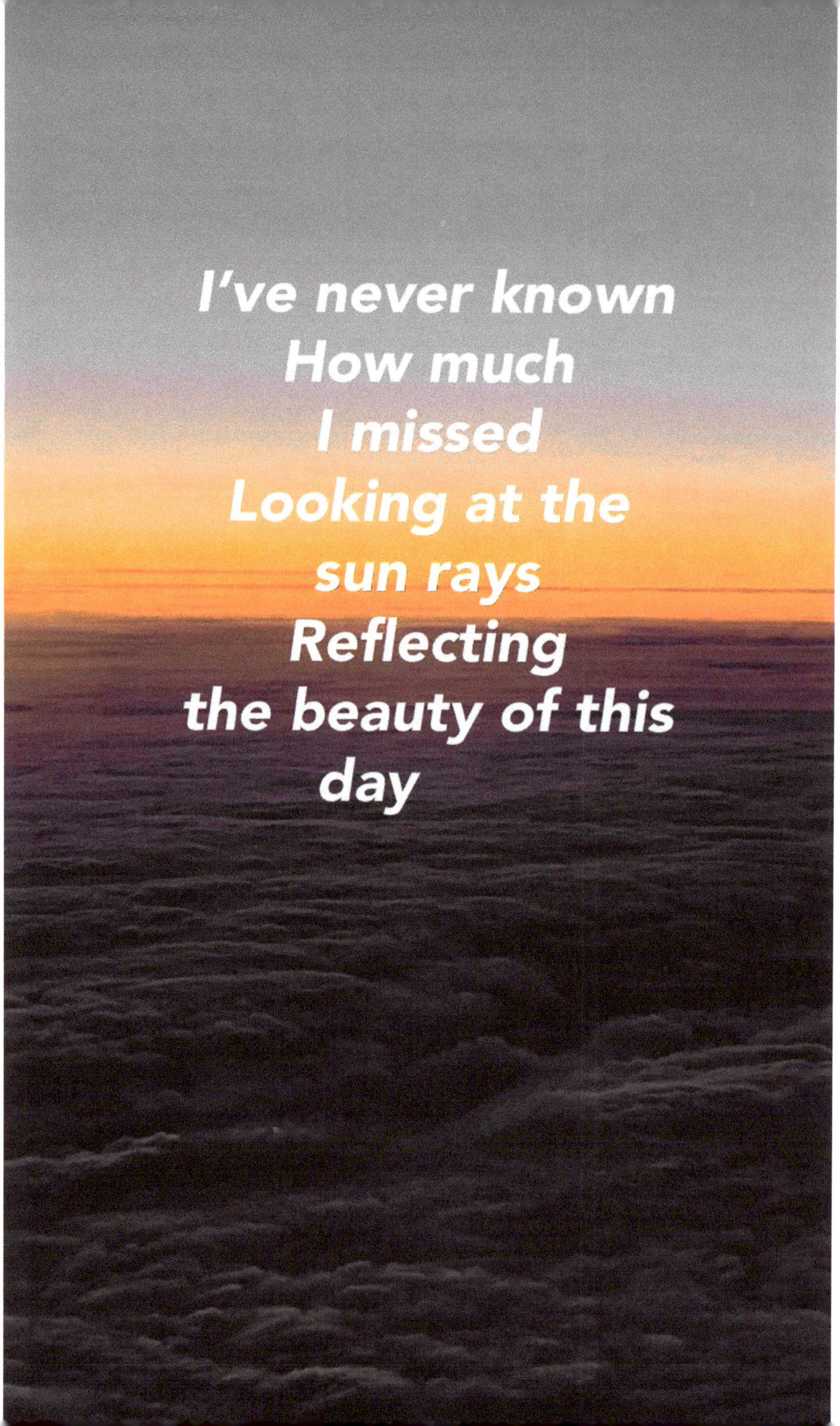

I've never known
How much
I missed
Looking at the
sun rays
Reflecting
the beauty of this
day

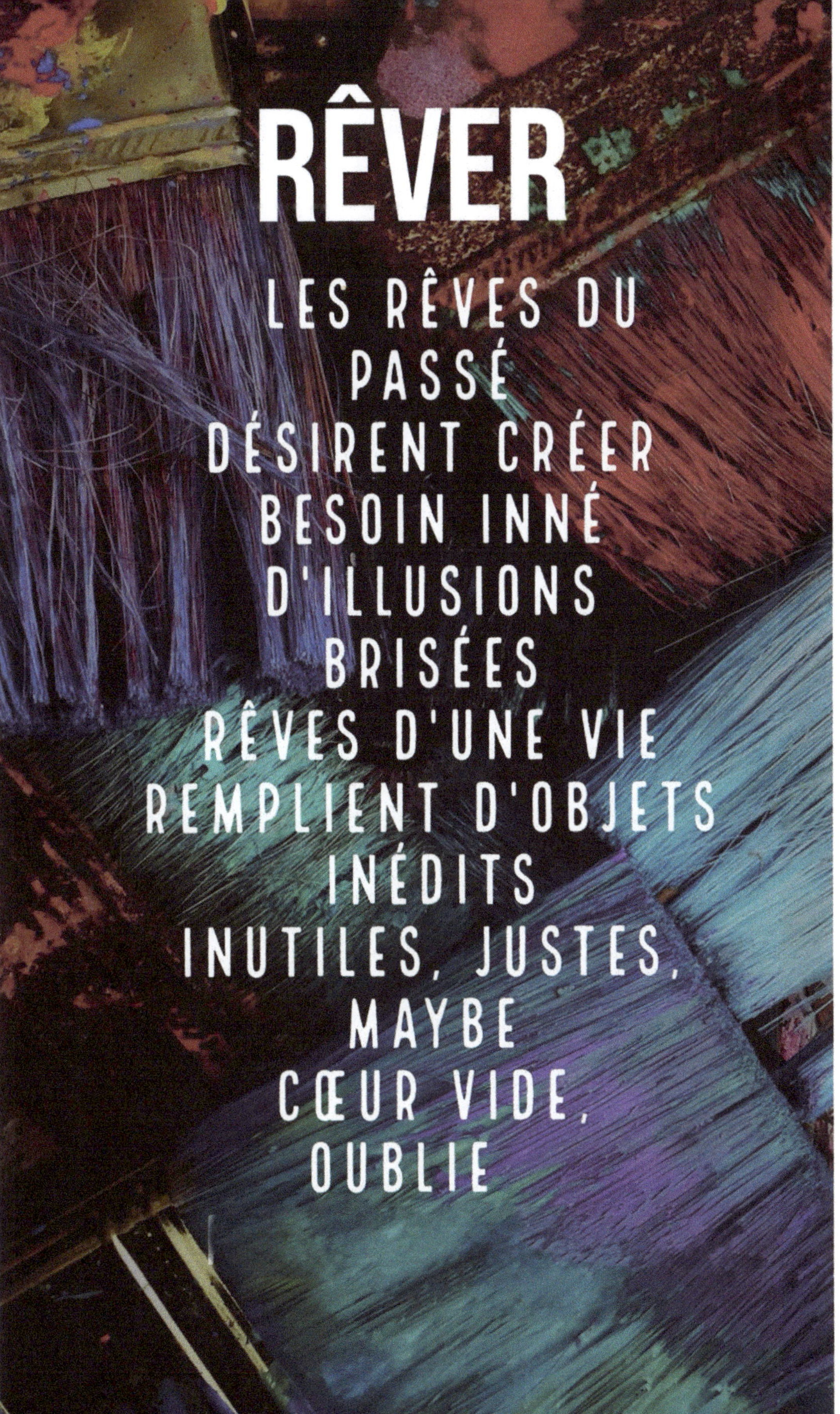

RÊVER
LES RÊVES DU
PASSÉ
DÉSIRENT CRÉER
BESOIN INNÉ
D'ILLUSIONS
BRISÉES
RÊVES D'UNE VIE
REMPLIENT D'OBJETS
INÉDITS
INUTILES, JUSTES,
MAYBE
CŒUR VIDE,
OUBLIE

If I offered you a dream
Would you wake up to redeem
This reality and your power
To shape and perceive this, Our
Into a brighter enlightened unity
A better world of human destiny

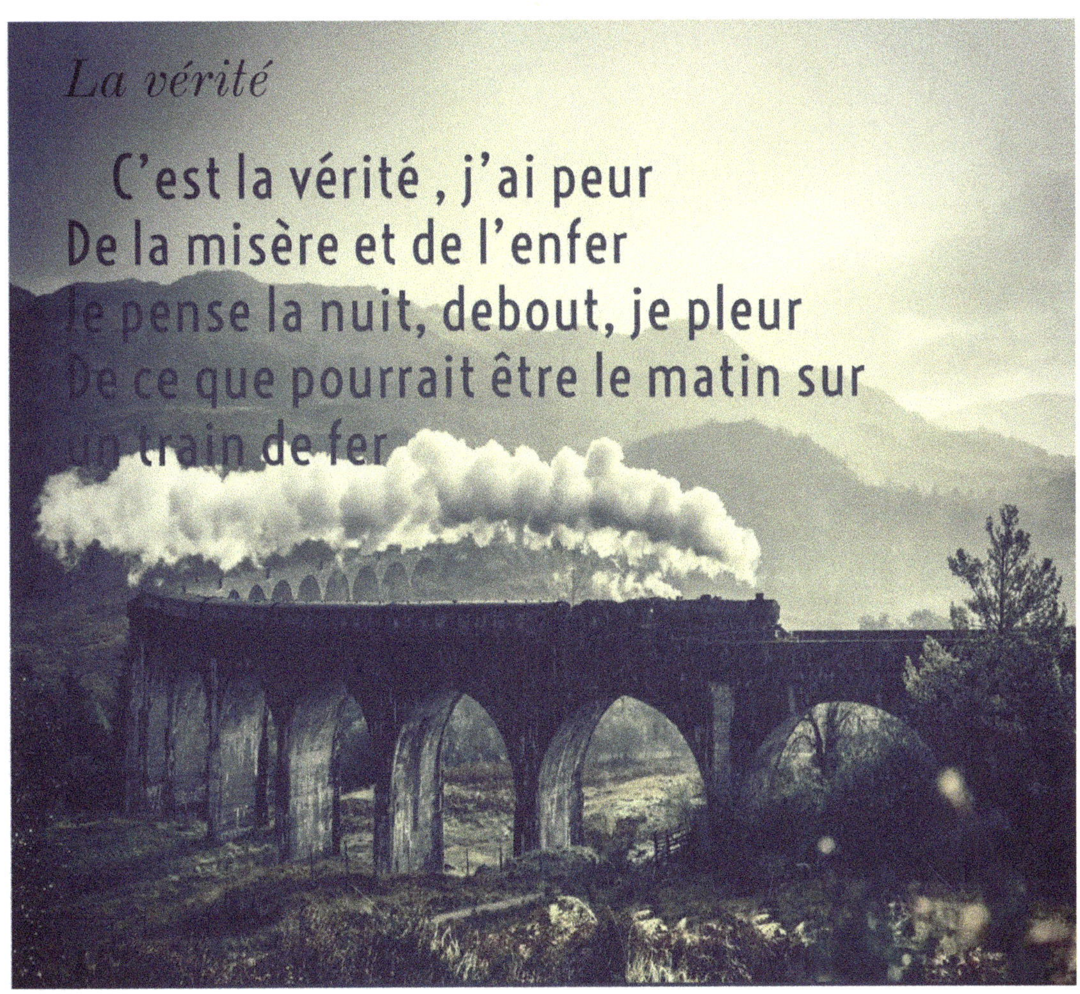
La vérité

C'est la vérité , j'ai peur
De la misère et de l'enfer
Je pense la nuit, debout, je pleur
De ce que pourrait être le matin sur
un train de fer

Seasons

Sunshine be mine
Rays of light so shine
Seasons change
My mind ranges
Up and down
Head, heart, drown
In the smell of rain
Loving with no refrain
Beautiful like the spring
Youthful she bring
Me closer, lover
Every day with her
Trust me summer
Is here soon, hummer
Songs of love
You're my beloved
Minds alike
Path I like
See her every day
Takes my blues away
Be my partner, forever
Would you be ever
You're my dream
In high esteem
Forming future
Together I ensure
Trying my best
Forming our nest
Philosopher
Poet and lover
Hope you love
Me, as I love you
Life bring us this way
A new path, we may
Life's never the same
I can't seem to shame
I will love you no matter
Will you be forever
Never be scared little princesse
Feelings deep priceless
Give me my chance
Really I'm a prince

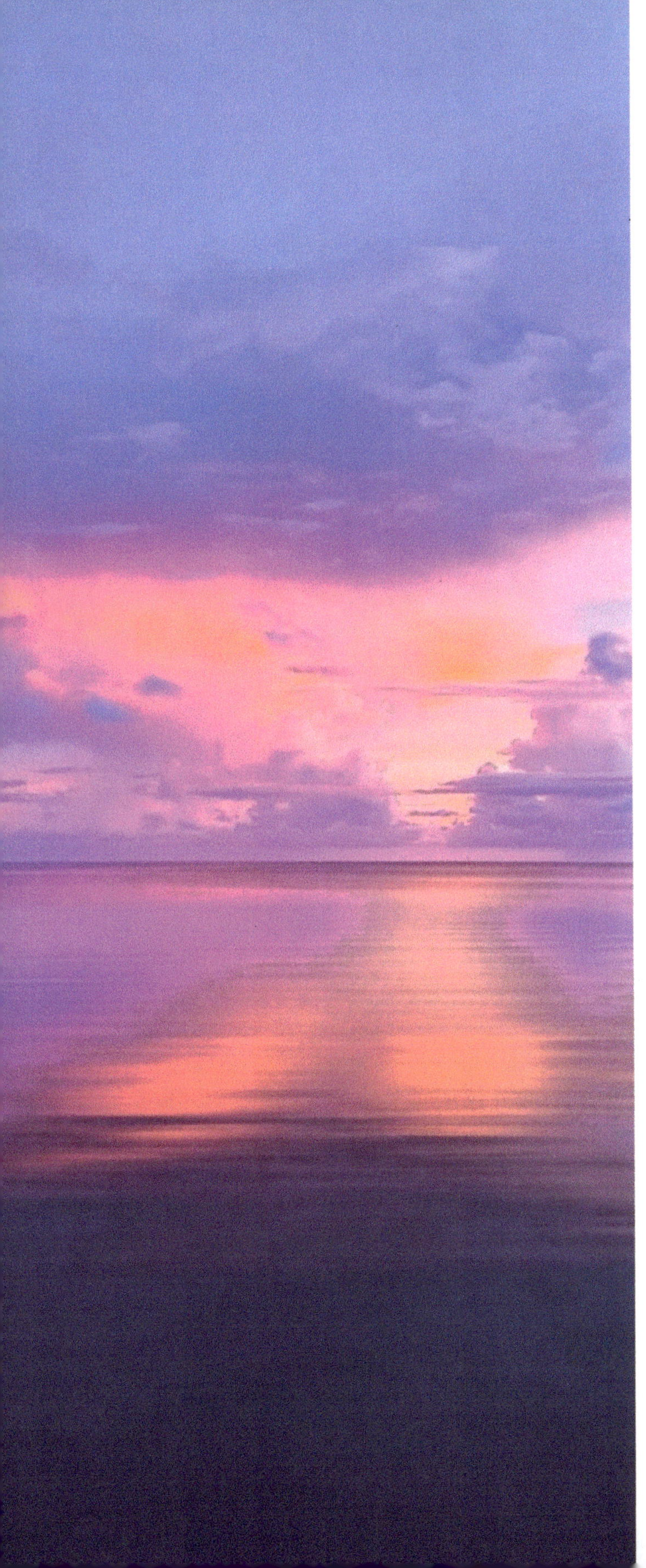

In the making.. sure
Help me mature
Autumn will fall
Red, orange, yellow, in all
Passion is nature's brush
So why should we rush
Cold, windy storms
Will happen in all forms
Freezing, icy weather
Only makes stronger
Unions made to last
Always survive wind's blast
I'm always thinking
Beautiful is the spring
Exactly like her, naturally
Owning me completely
Never stop the seasons
Change, there is no reason
We wouldn't be together
Lifetime, lovers forever

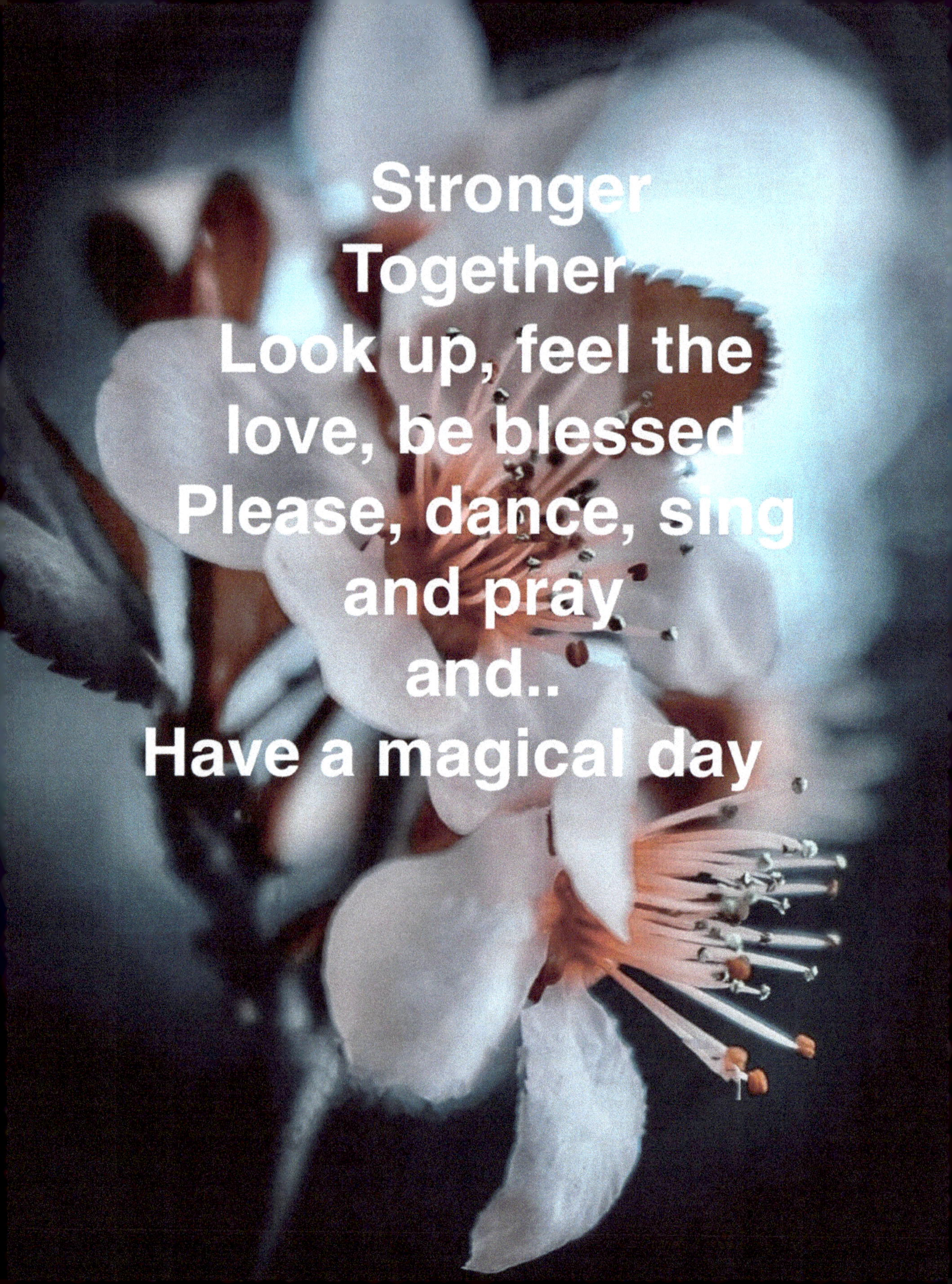

Stronger
Together
Look up, feel the
love, be blessed
Please, dance, sing
and pray
and..
Have a magical day

Memory

Memory losing
Smile fading
Time passing
Just wandering
Should I go
Reach out slow
See her, just say hello
Most would say no
Too much, too low
I would give anything
To see her smiling
Hold her warming
My heart shining
So much unsaid
Would see her led
To explanation
Or exaltation
Hope no condemnation
Only good intention
Sing under her balcony
Would be much irony
Not the time only
Wrong century
Materialist
No more romanticist
Poetry books
Cheques hooks
So I stay waiting

Wandering
Probably never
See her figure
Disappeared forever
Did she go away
She might just may
Coming back ready
For more fantasy
Life is easy
When you peacefully
Respect the needs
Allow the freed
Time to breathe
Follow her speed
Her return reunion
Chat with reason
Natural sensation
Two persons unison
Dreams are made
Think hard aid
Make reality,
Hopefully

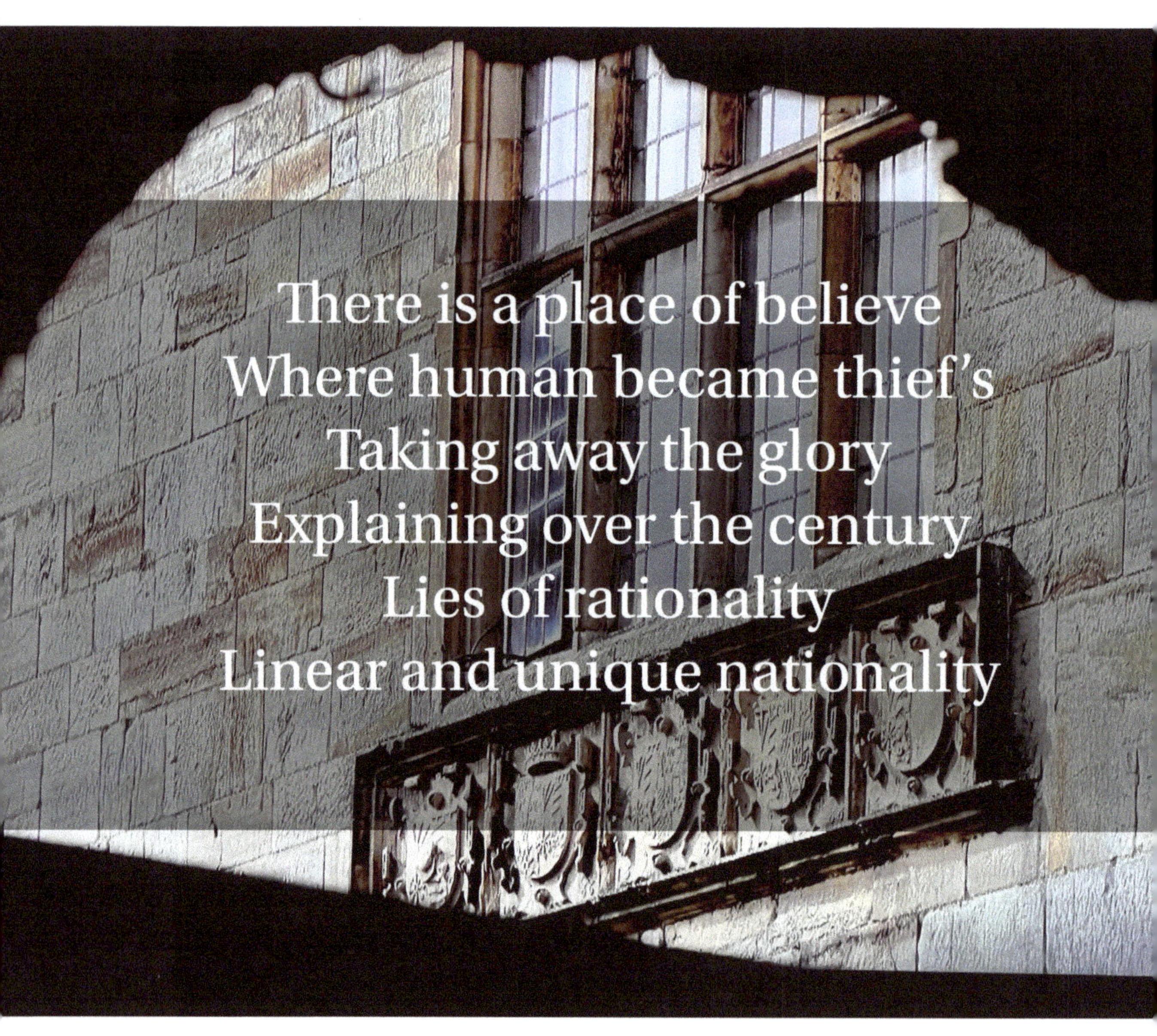
There is a place of believe
Where human became thief's
Taking away the glory
Explaining over the century
Lies of rationality
Linear and unique nationality

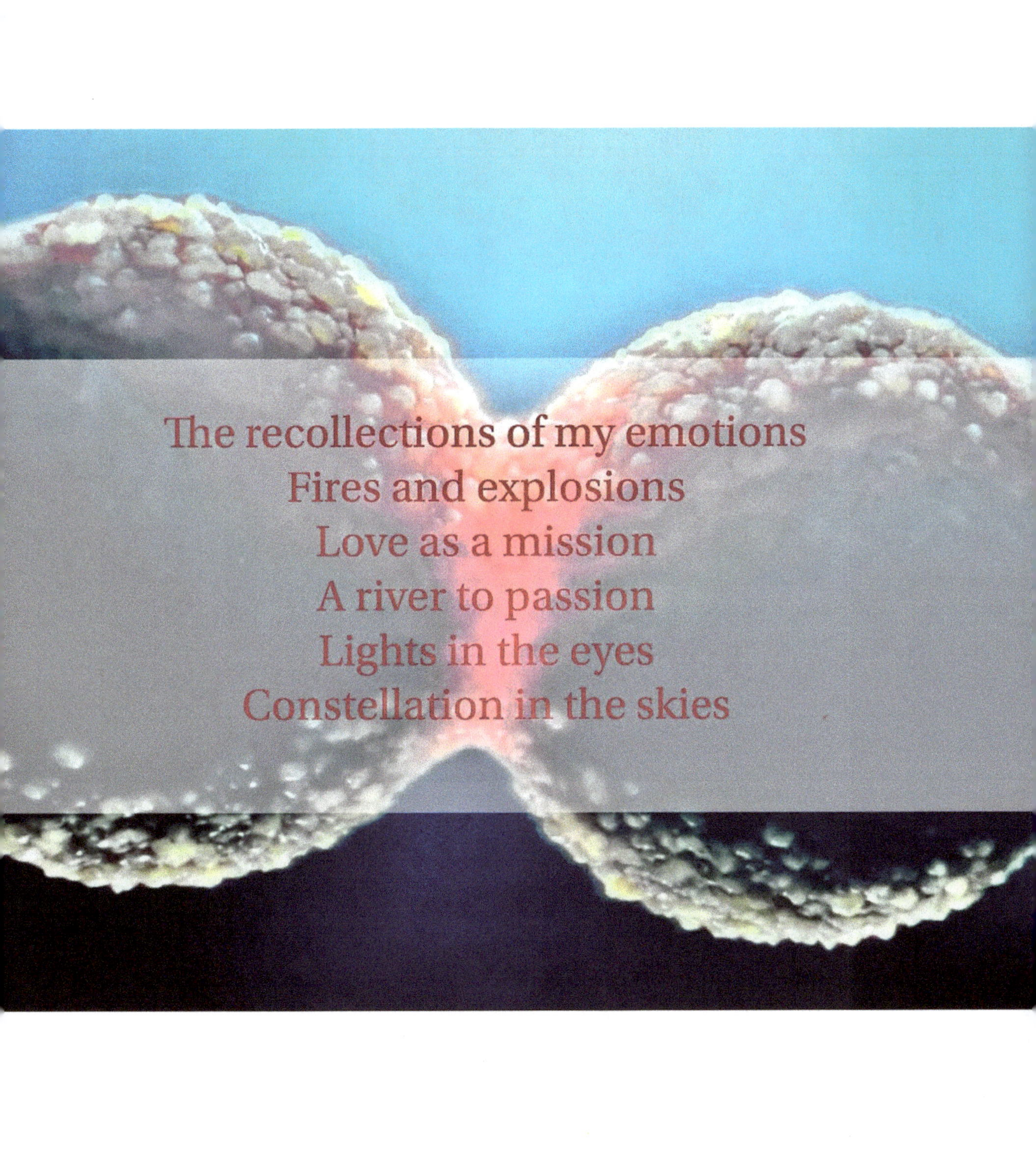

The recollections of my emotions
Fires and explosions
Love as a mission
A river to passion
Lights in the eyes
Constellation in the skies

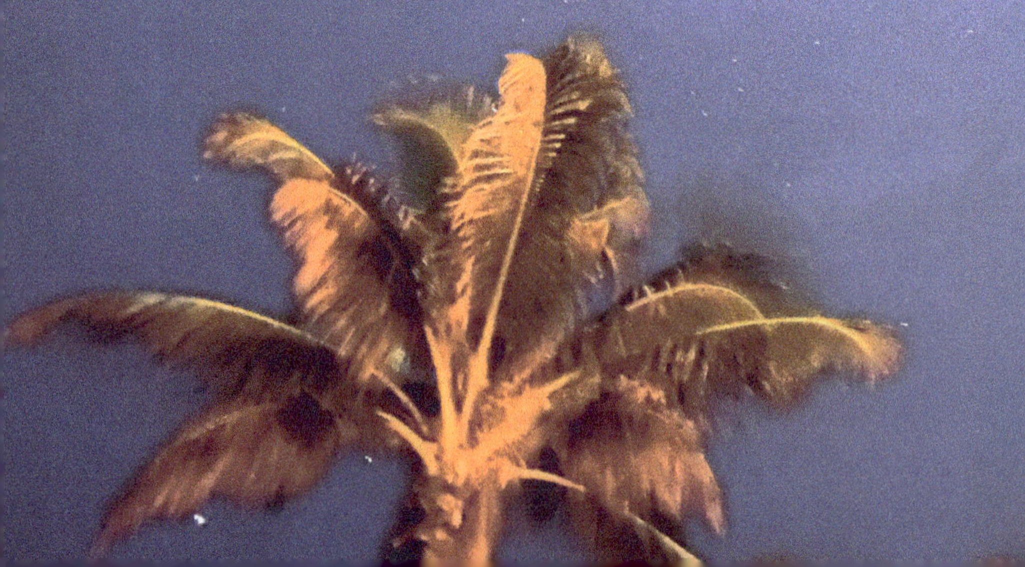

Our eyes will eventually open
to humanity
The nightmare, dissipated in its
absurdity
Passions, admirations, love,
respect
Will reveal our true identity
Of a real honest, evolving
society
I love you, kiss you, embrace
you, wake up .. to a wonderful
new reality

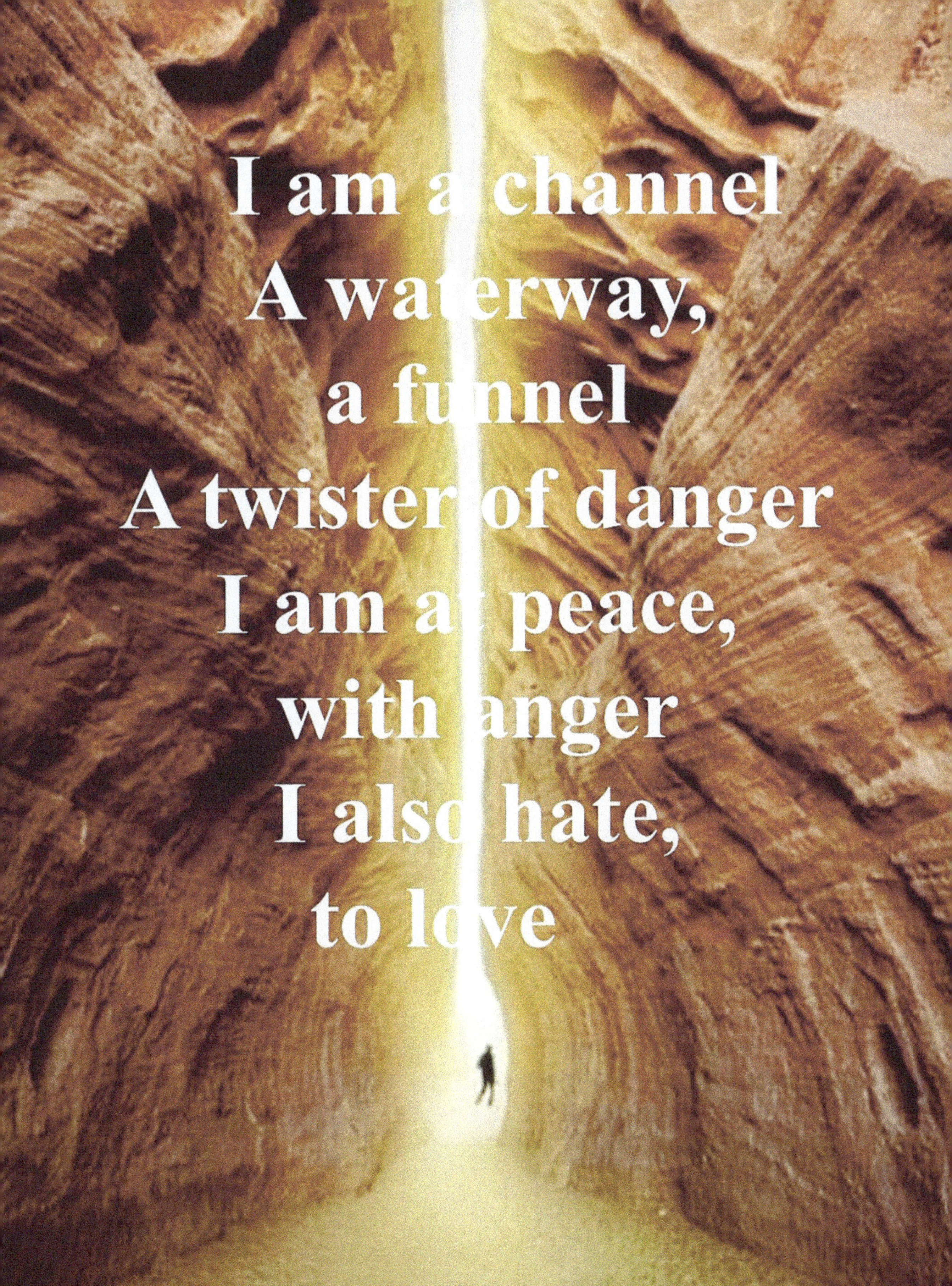

I am a channel
A waterway,
a funnel
A twister of danger
I am at peace,
with anger
I also hate,
to love

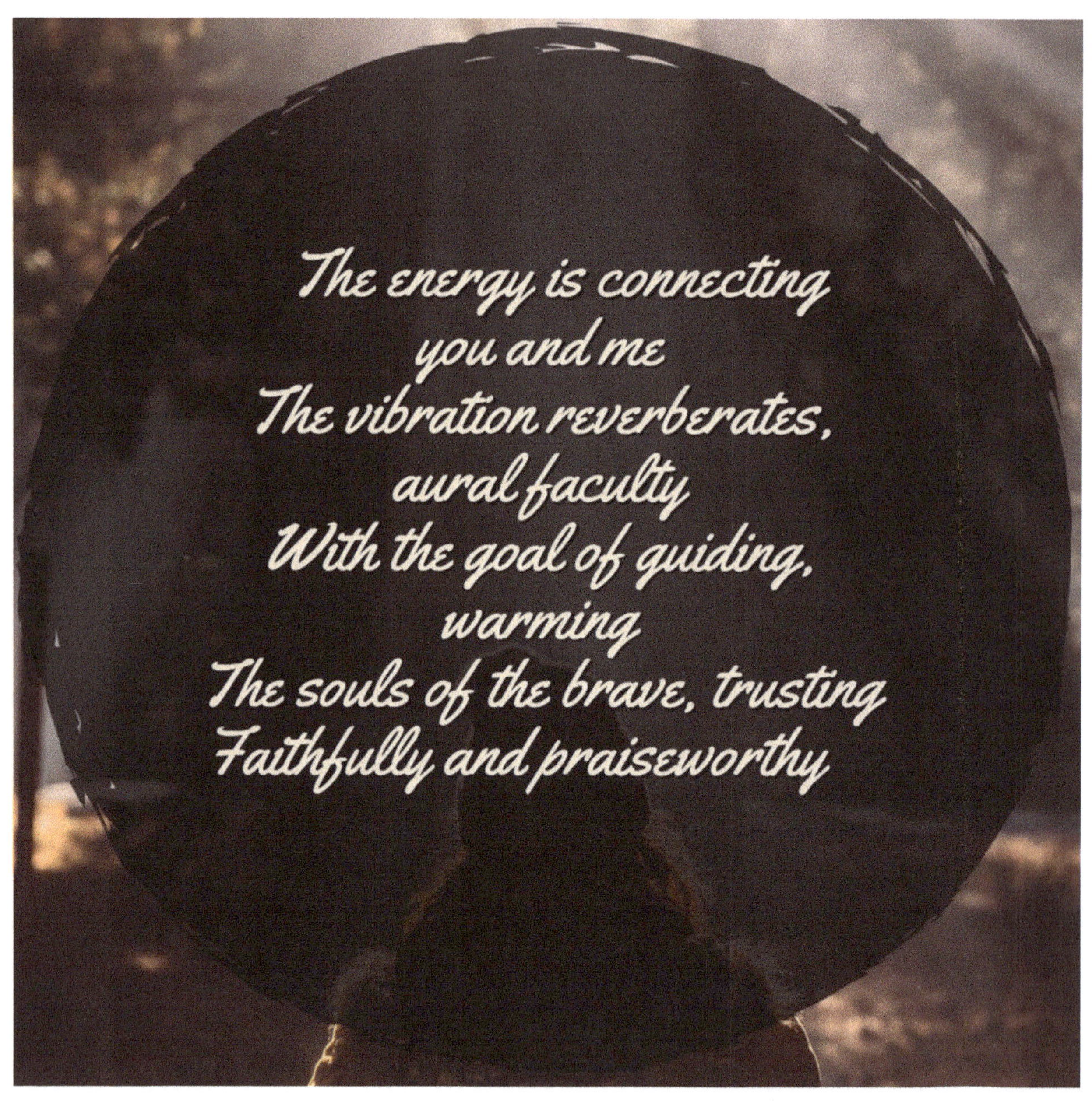

The energy is connecting
you and me
The vibration reverberates,
aural faculty
With the goal of guiding,
warming
The souls of the brave, trusting
Faithfully and praiseworthy

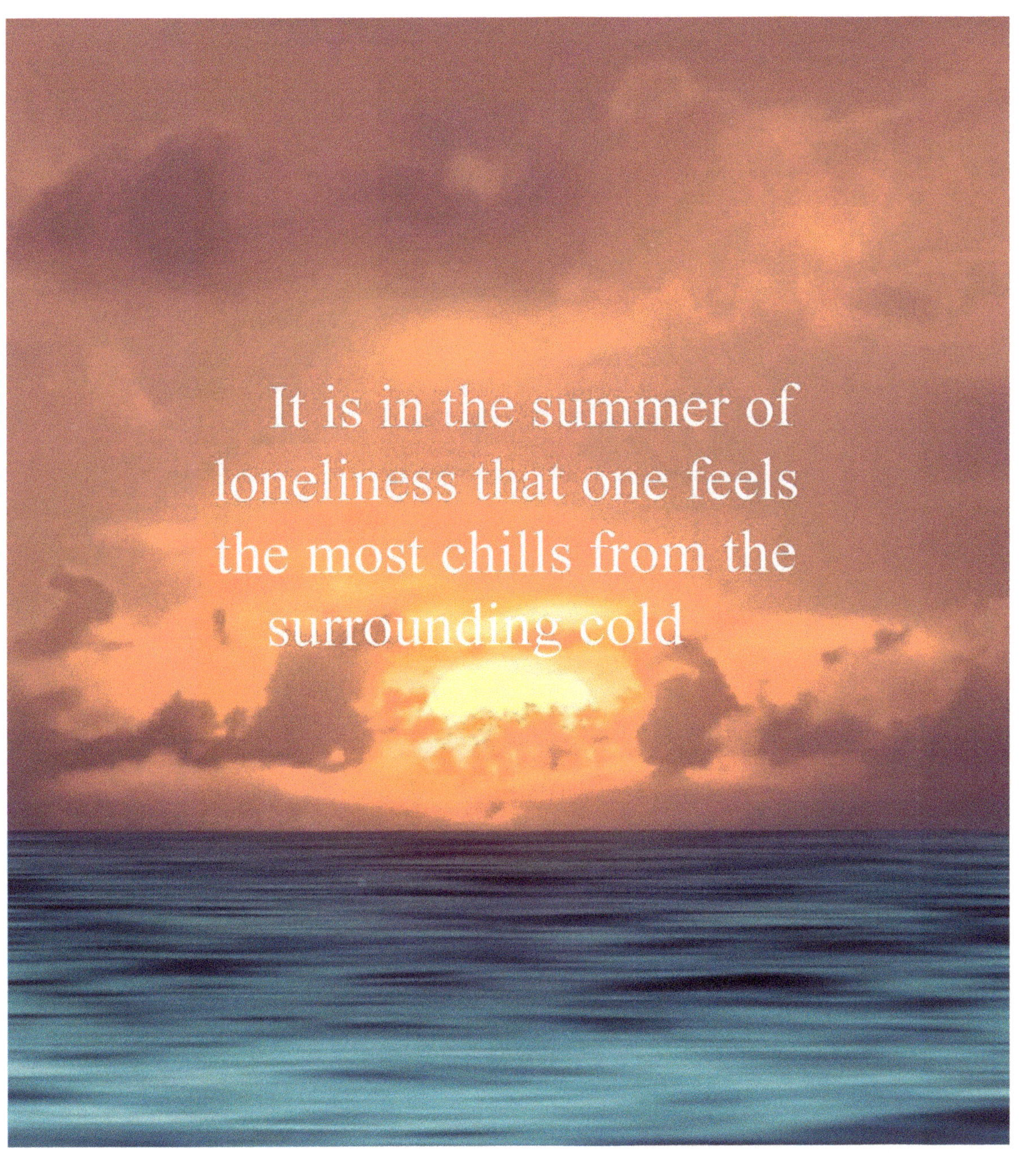

It is in the summer of
loneliness that one feels
the most chills from the
surrounding cold

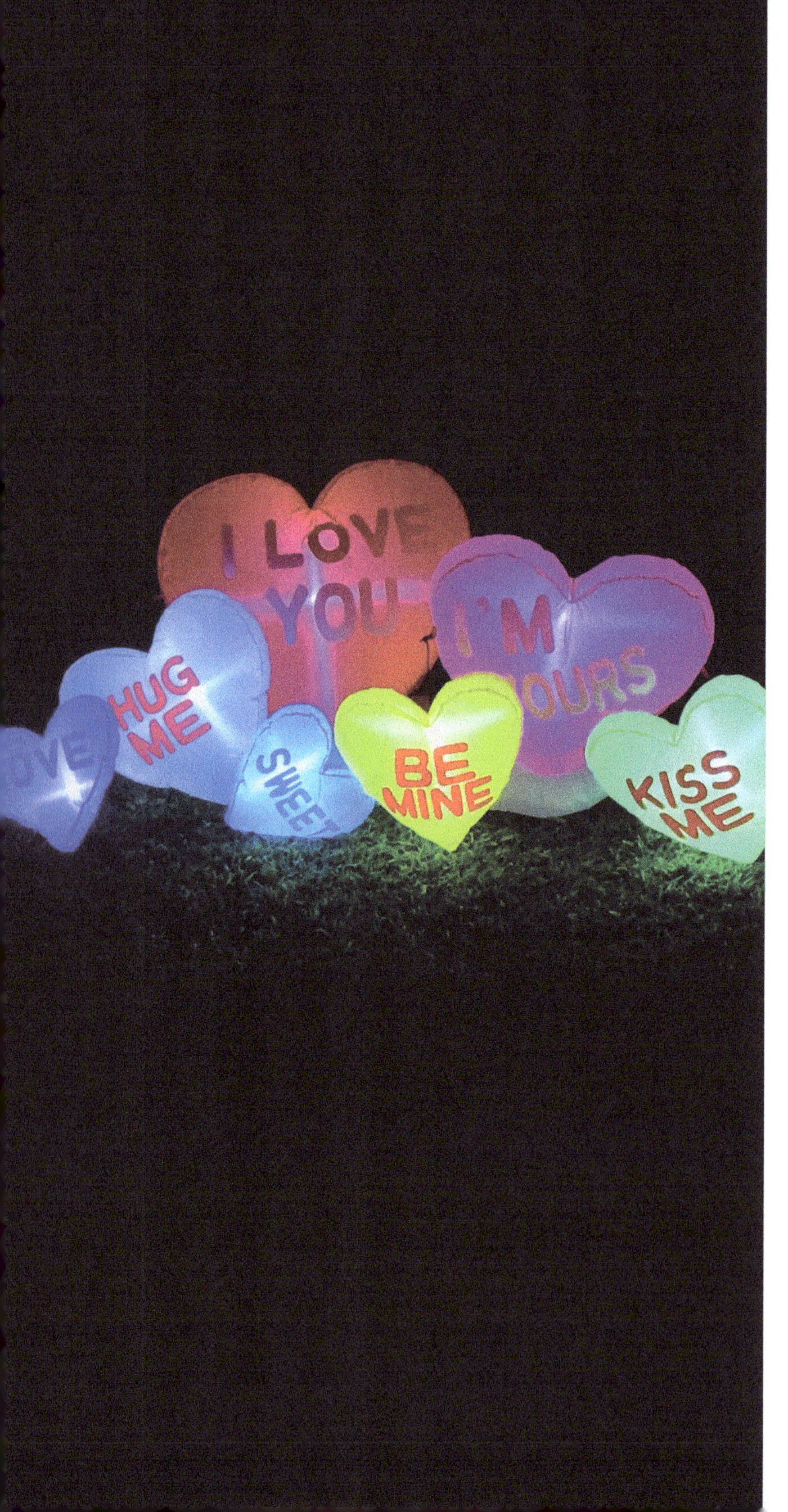
I LOVE YOU
I'M YOURS
HUG ME
BE MINE
SWEET
KISS ME
LOVE

Out of Words

I'm out of words
There is someone unattainable
Yet so close and unbelievable
Feeling so real
Yet so unreal
I feel like running
With feelings
Of always returning
Where I belong
Like the greatest song
No words can describe
Her beauty, controls me
Her soul understands me
So attracted
Physically distracted
Mind at ease
Speechless, I freeze
Wanting to see her
Day after day, warmer
In her arms holding
Until light awakens the morning
Smooth skin
Gentle scents of sin
Losing morality
Fighting against reality
Wishing
Everlasting, singing
In such harmony

Rewrite all poetry
So far, but attainable
Or is it, even possible
Nothing's impossible
Tear down barricades
Go through like hurricanes
Storms, winds, cascading
Being, believable
Understanding
Stay away
Might be the way
For the moment
To secure enjoyment
Storms pass by
Wishing for an alibi
Stay with me for a while
Don't ask me why
No words, no sounds
Sweet touch of clouds
Sleeping alone
Would be long gone
Caring, sharing
Ever adoring
Redefine our future
Together, be so pure
Taking on this endeavor
Wishing to gain her favor
Uniting, bodies and minds

Sweat is intertwined
Nothing undisclosed
All over exposed
Growing old, weak
Reaching our peak
Me supporting her
She always nurtures
Life's being a bliss
Unattainable
Indescribable
Or perfectly suitable and absolutely comfortable
And so desirable, so incredible
I ask you
Is it for you

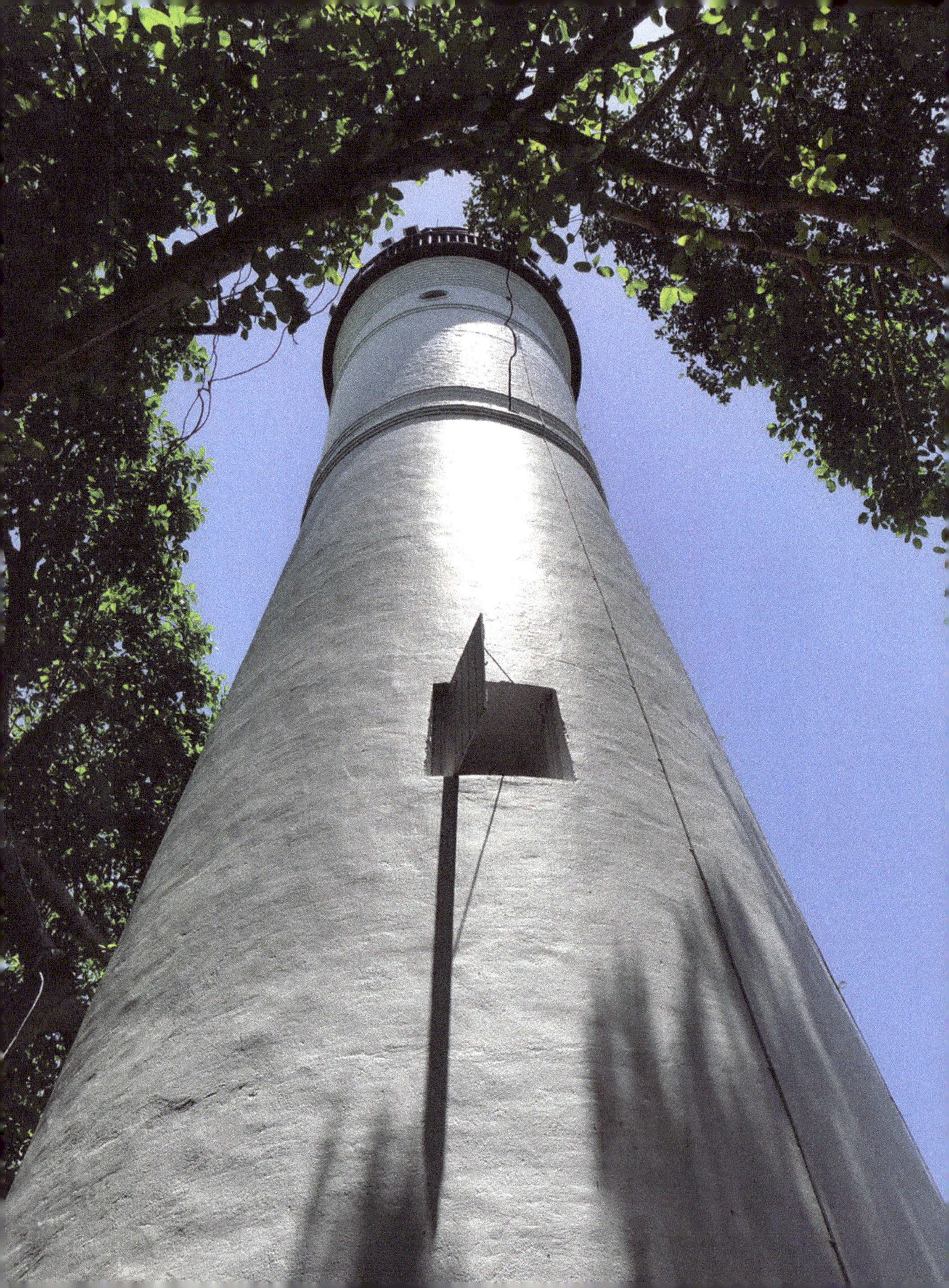

Music

Quiet all alone
Listening to the tone
Music bursting
Sounds trilling
Thoughts of better day
Guitar rhythm astray
Words of wisdom
Waves centrum
Love brings epiphany
Loneliness guaranty
Where do you stand
In moving sand
Slipping, descending
Slowly but surely
Cast me a rope
I will try to cope
Tunes of blues
They have no clues
Liquor in my veins
Nobody's to blame
Singer screaming
Gone in a stream
Fluid moving flow
Beat this solo
Music blowing
Sounds trilling
Indecent proposal
Soul's renewal

Incense smoking
Smells appealing
Traveling minds
Notes grind
Harmony faery
Music stop
Back to the spot
Quiet all alone
Silence on my own
Silence surrender
Really sad it's over
She moved me
Like a grand symphony

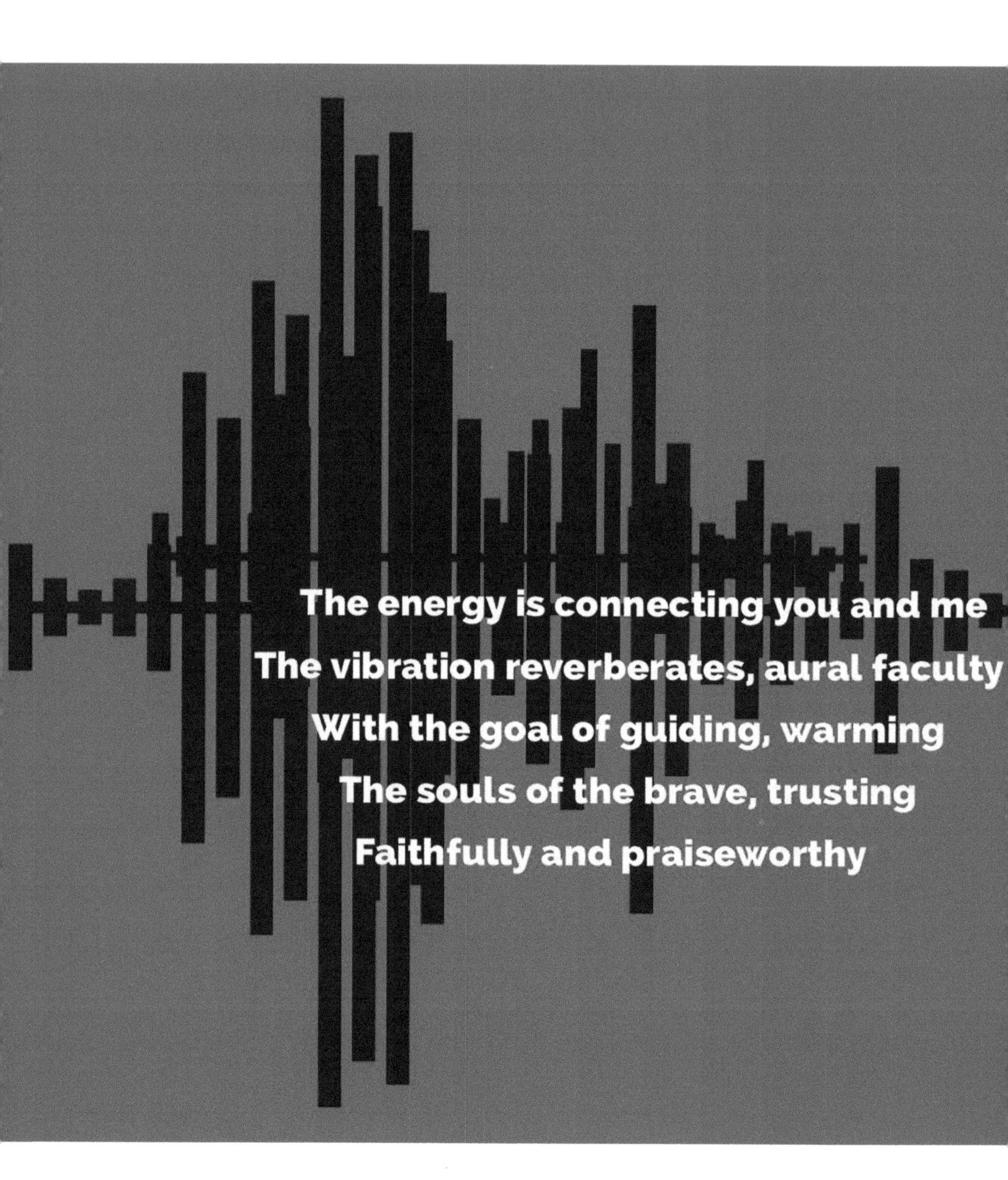
The energy is connecting you and me
The vibration reverberates, aural faculty
With the goal of guiding, warming
The souls of the brave, trusting
Faithfully and praiseworthy

Matrix

Is it the Matrix
That's playing tricks
A glitch in the fabric
Of space, in time, cosmic
Change your mind
As an effect through time
Ripples of our kind
Shining out, be fine
Echoes in a distance
Reflects of a instance
Resonating softly
Out creating gently
Our existence
Flowing by insistence
Forming or dreaming
Reality, beauty, streaming
Shades, clouds, and pains
Is it all that remains
In your mind reside
The truth from inside
Turning, forming, the outside
Most outcomes are sublime
With a connection to the divine
Or tormented pieces
Of an emotional release
Different lives
Learn how to thrive
Ancient and deep experiences

Evolving in real differences
Love God
Return to basics
Find and applaud
Your movie in transit
Will be made
Cared
Caressed
Fully transformed
In all density and forms
Mysterious
Glamorous
Marvelous
Revealed and praised
You will be amazed
And truly experience
The greatness of His
Magnificence
Release the restraints
Of your brains
Human feelings
Relieve and believe
It will be created
A chef d'œuvre
A masterpiece
Which, will match, only your beliefs

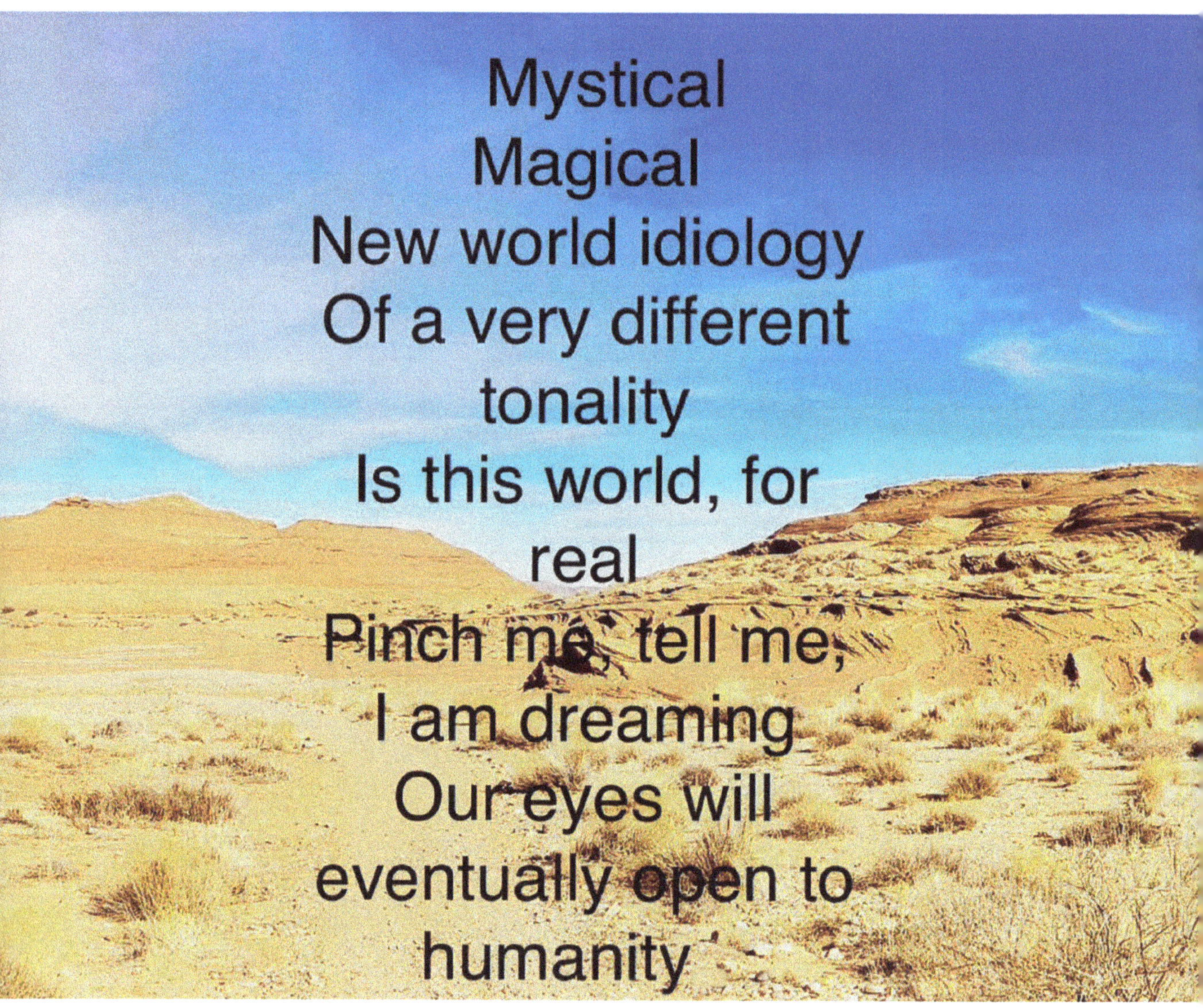

Mystical
Magical
New world idiology
Of a very different
tonality
Is this world, for
real
Pinch me, tell me,
I am dreaming
Our eyes will
eventually open to
humanity

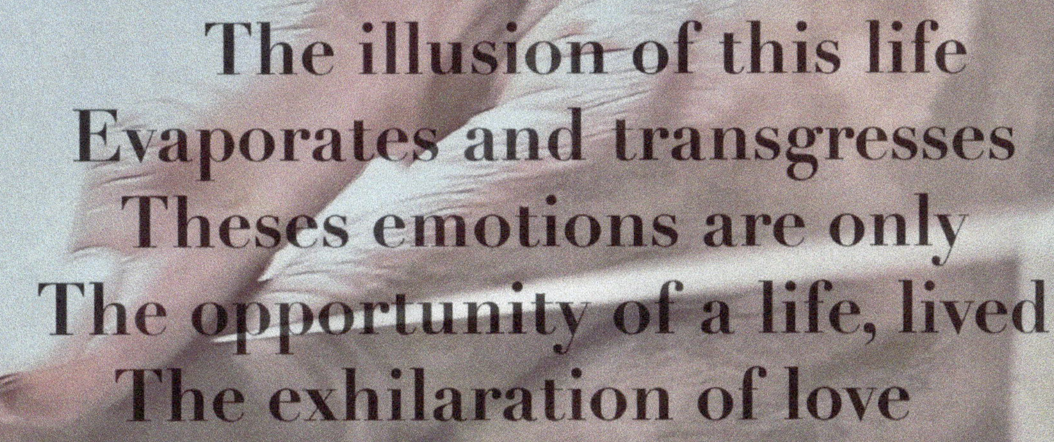
The illusion of this life
Evaporates and transgresses
Theses emotions are only
The opportunity of a life, lived
The exhilaration of love

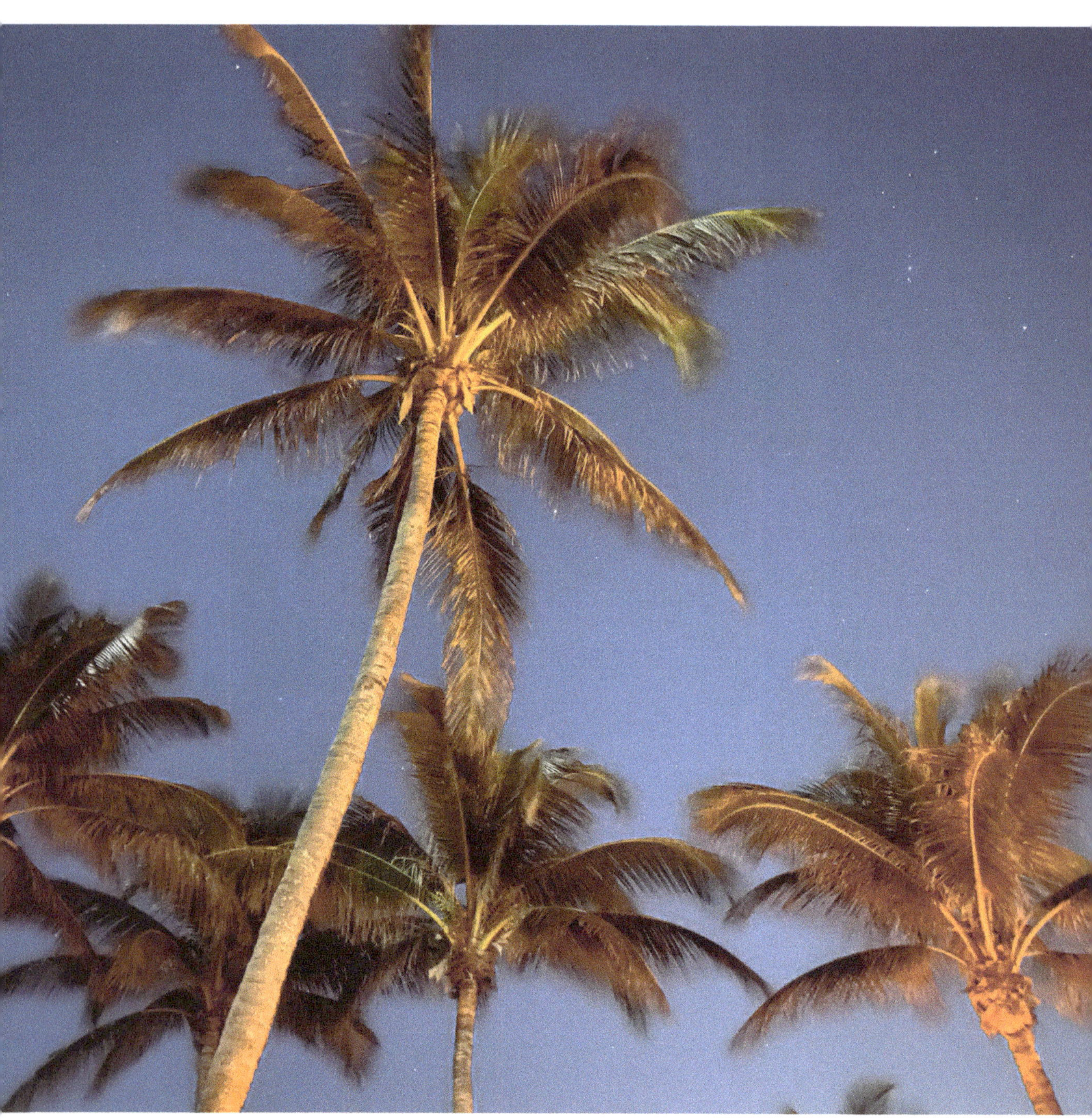

Night Sky

It's getting darker
I'm getting lighter
Life is good, I suppose
Finding purpose
People streaming
All sort, pretending
Two, just meeting
Soft winds unsettle
Lives unravel
Relaxing, absorbing
Time passing
Let's not assume
Anything unconsumed
Bed early
Nothing crazy
The sun will rise again
Everything will remain
Tomorrow might
Be the same
Palm trees agree
Let's all be free
I'm a little lost
Without her, I feel a frost
Down my spine, chilling

Lovers passing
Remind me a direction
Where to pay attention
Forward attribution
Stars in motion
Thunder sounds
Lighting grounds
Illuminating the sky
Like her deep eyes
Hunted me
Morning sky, hurry
Reminds me, to be happy
If only, she sees
She's got me
Kept under key
Give a try to happiness
In a bliss
Partners exploring
Experience sharing
Looking back
Holding, nothing
Life's full and filling
Bright skies forever

I Have to Tell You a Dream

I dream of peace
I dream of unity
I dream to live in a world free of jealousy
Where humans would live in harmony
I dream to be painted in colors living quietly side by side
I dream to love and be loved
I dream of whispering to all, wake up
If it is true that some people love
If children are all the same
We will have to say, it's easy to do a little bit more than the ordinary
Just a little more love
For less emptiness
I would love to say the words that I receive
Are like a perfume we breathe
Just a small look would mean more than the extraordinary
Just a little more love
For less tears, for more life
For less winters
Since we all live in the cup of a dream
Since we all leave in the same light
Even if there are colors, that we prefer
I would love to say
Love just a little more
For less tears
For less emptiness
For less winters
Breathe, it's easy to do a little more
The color in your eyes

Reminds me of blue skies
Still I dream of unity
I dream of whispering in her ears
If you think you know about love
Breathe and smell the flowers
Look, open your mind to see
The power of eternity
Loves you more than me
The good news is here around you
I dream of whispering to all, wake up
I am the guy with sparkles of joy
Speaking of love in black and white
Life is giving me what I need of her
Follow me in the twist and turns
Do not run, help me dream of peace
Let's paint the canvas of love
In colors from above
(Inspired by translated Francis Cabrel Il faudra leur dire)

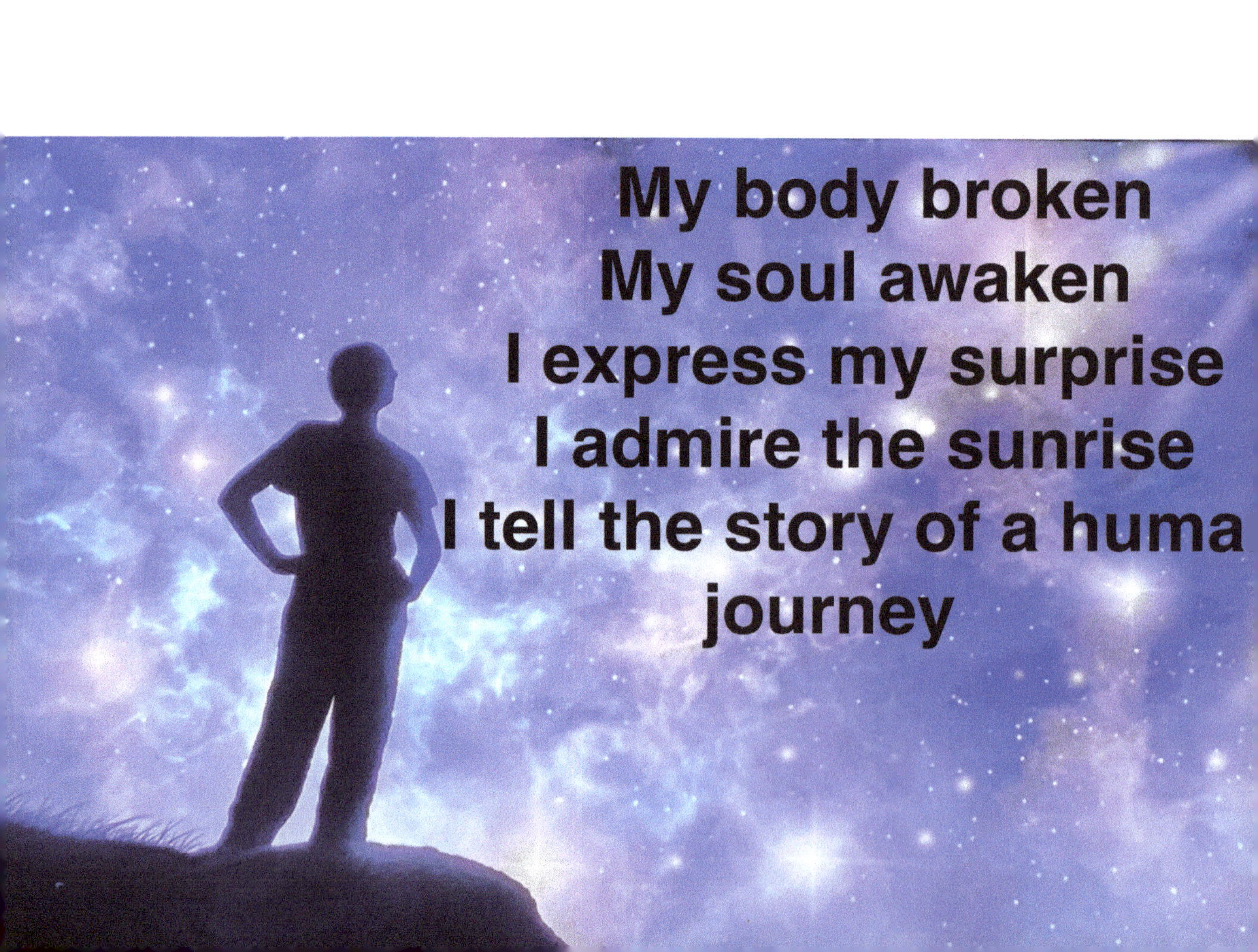

My body broken
My soul awaken
I express my surprise
I admire the sunrise
I tell the story of a huma
journey

Late Night

Late nights
All is lost
Music is loud
Impersonal, proud
Lies around
To many believe
Relation eve
No solid base
Nothing will last
Figures, age
Nothing but image
What they have to say
Nobody really worries
Animal's sex
Why are you perplexed
Future base, assets
Make child offset
Young beliefs
Affection
Connection
Parent's separation
Affects generation
What were you thinking
Stop pretending
Look for real
Keep the Lord's deal
Image fraud
Morals, immoral

Lead not to immortal
Destiny is made
When the heart is revealed
Honestly and peacefully
Sometimes fooled
Guard down overruled
Someone rule
Emotions overturned
Follow this pattern
Sometimes miracles
Often disgrace
Only the Lord knows
Time only shows
Light from dark
Listen to your heart

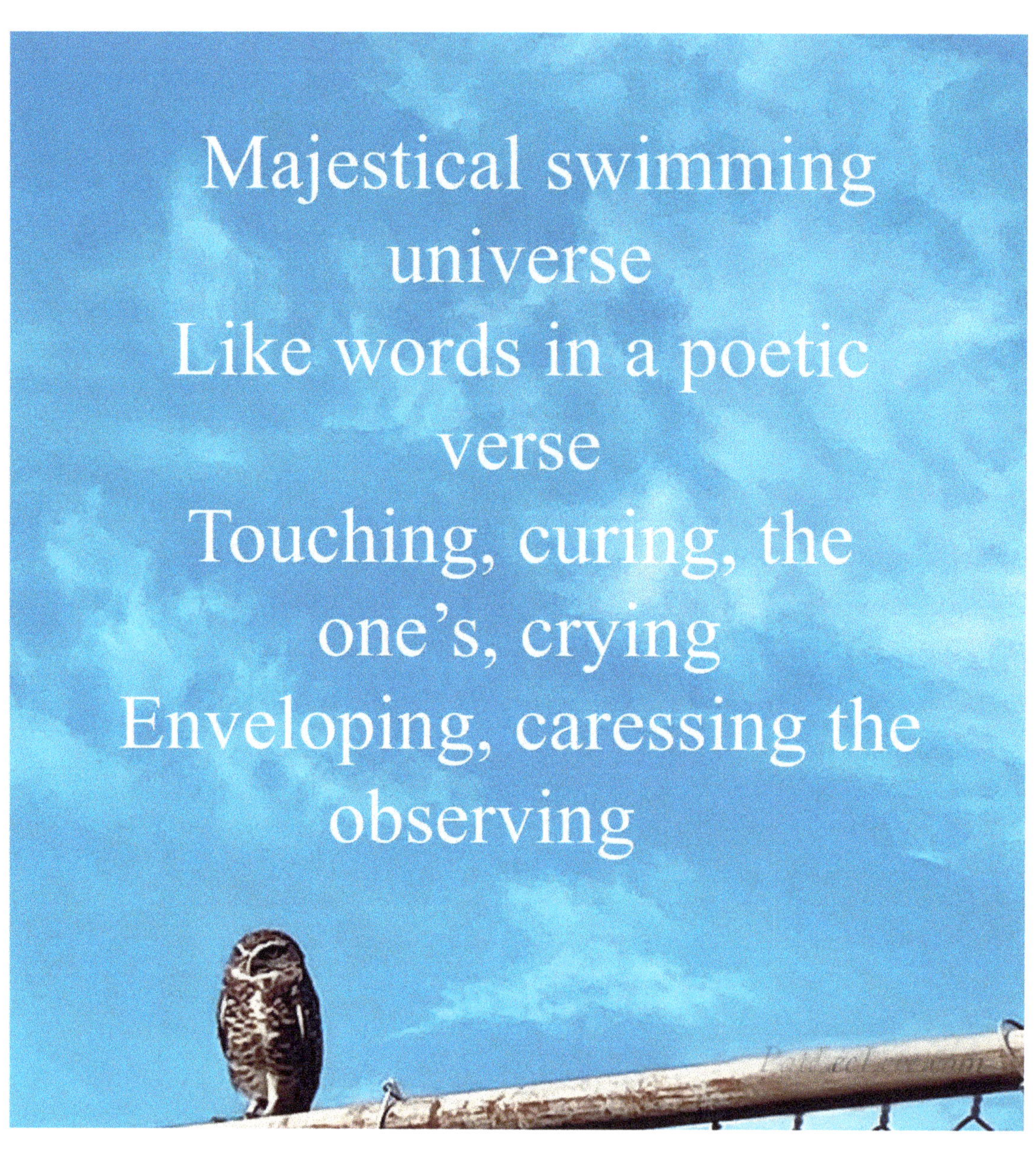
Majestical swimming
universe
Like words in a poetic
verse
Touching, curing, the
one's, crying
Enveloping, caressing the
observing

Love is not
measured
But vastly abundant
Limitless and vibrant
Don't be defined
By their minds

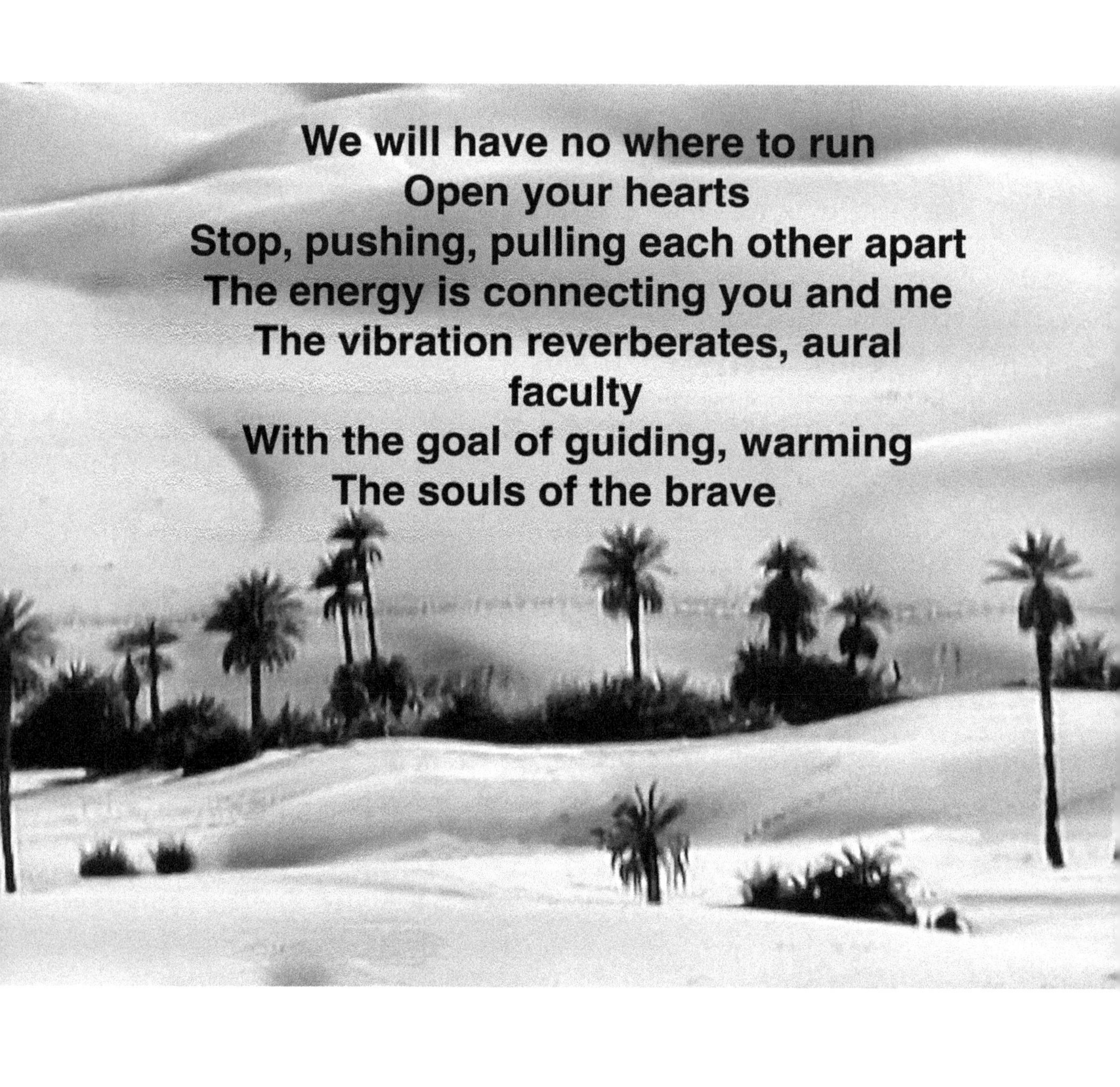

We will have no where to run
Open your hearts
Stop, pushing, pulling each other apart
The energy is connecting you and me
The vibration reverberates, aural
faculty
With the goal of guiding, warming
The souls of the brave

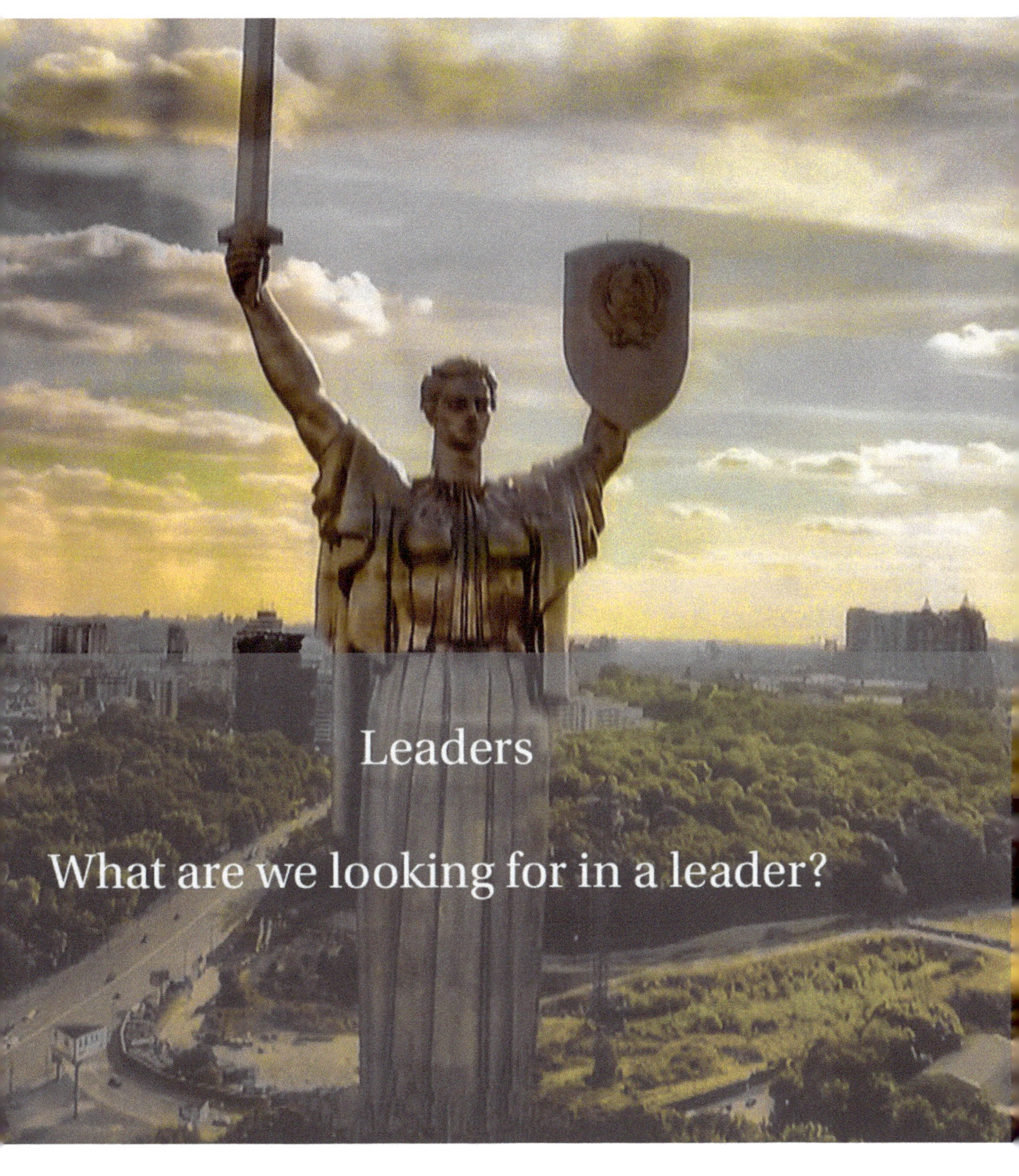
Leaders

What are we looking for in a leader?

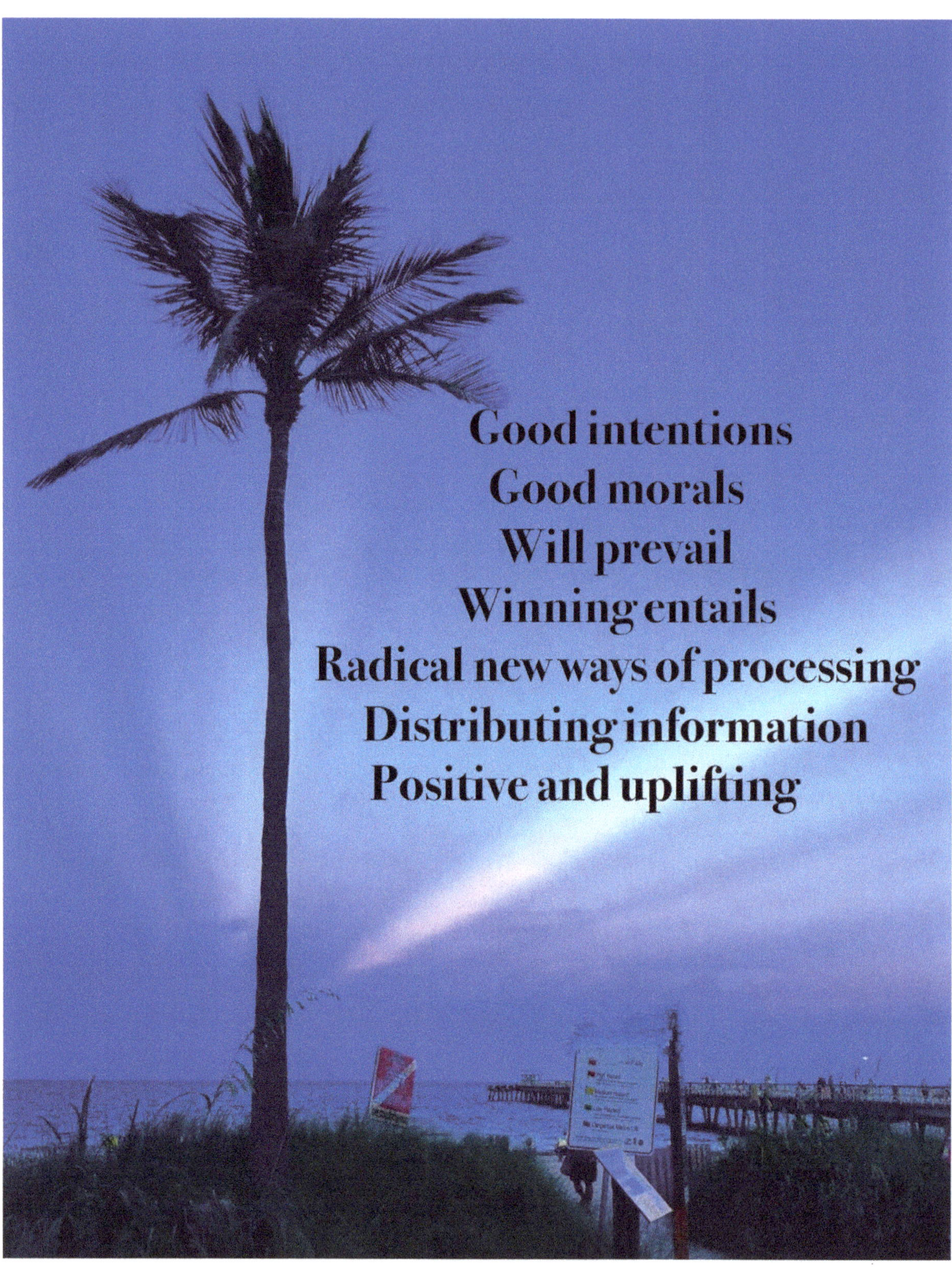

Good intentions
Good morals
Will prevail
Winning entails
Radical new ways of processing
Distributing information
Positive and uplifting

Cosmic Appeal

Only a mind at peace
Can surely live at ease
Soft, smooth music
With an eye on the optic
Of illusions
Is passion
A vibration
Of emotions
Or a sound
So profound
One can only imagine
The cadence of our origin
The remembrance of heaven
The love of children
The laugh of joy
Innocence of a boy
Like the notes of fragrance
Uplifting the soul in a trance
Remembering peace
Of a mind at ease
Hearing our torment
Suffering and ascent
Ignoring life's beauty
Passing over its glory
Life and its beautiful small moments
Inspiring
Uplifting
An upsurge

Of strength
Observing and nurturing
See it and believe it
Heaven's compassion
Is in you in times of quiet contem-
plation
Breathe, listen
Adore and be praiseful
The music is magical and cosmic
Fulfilling and loving

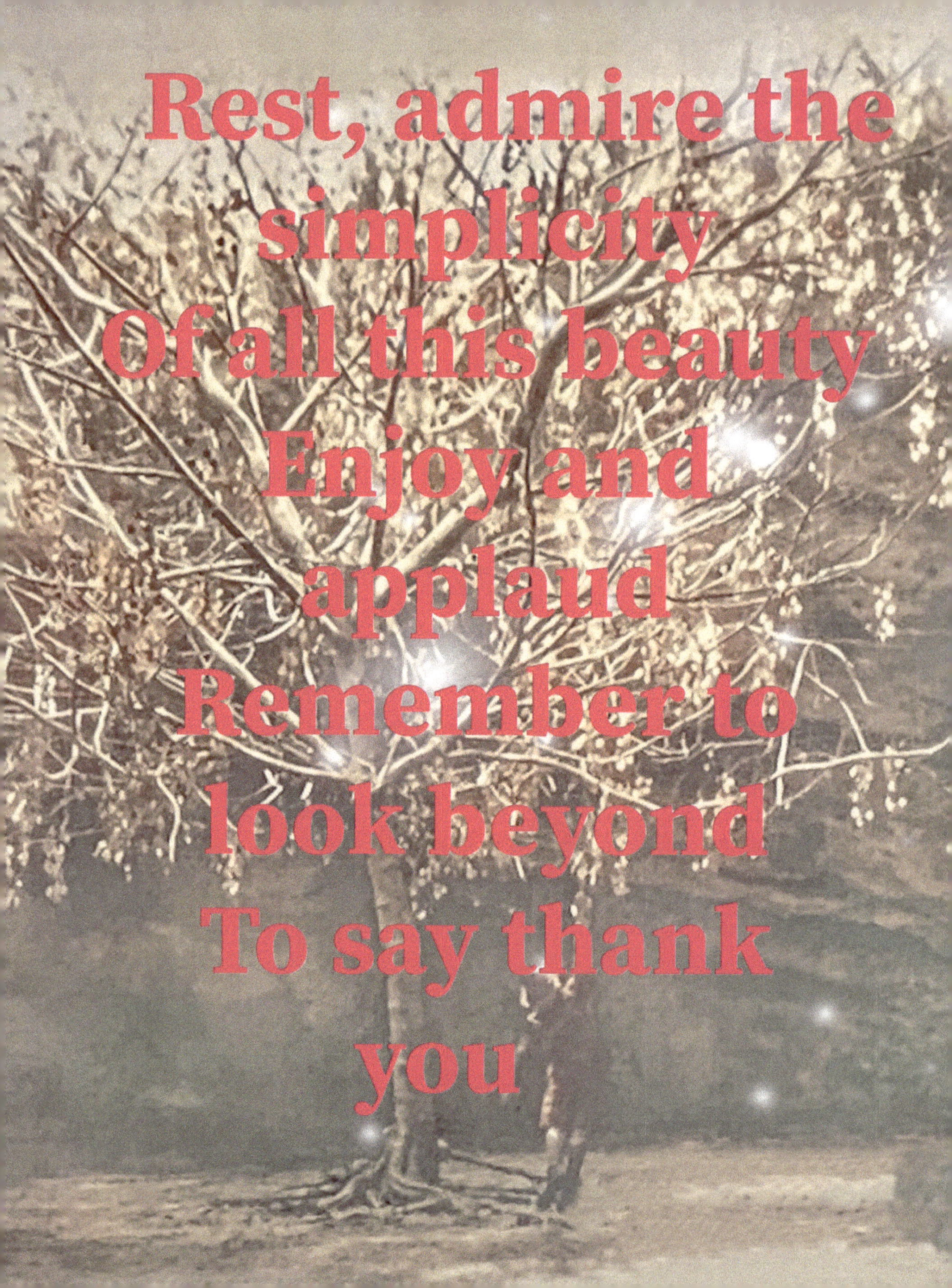

Rest, admire the
simplicity
Of all this beauty
Enjoy and
applaud
Remember to
look beyond
To say thank
you

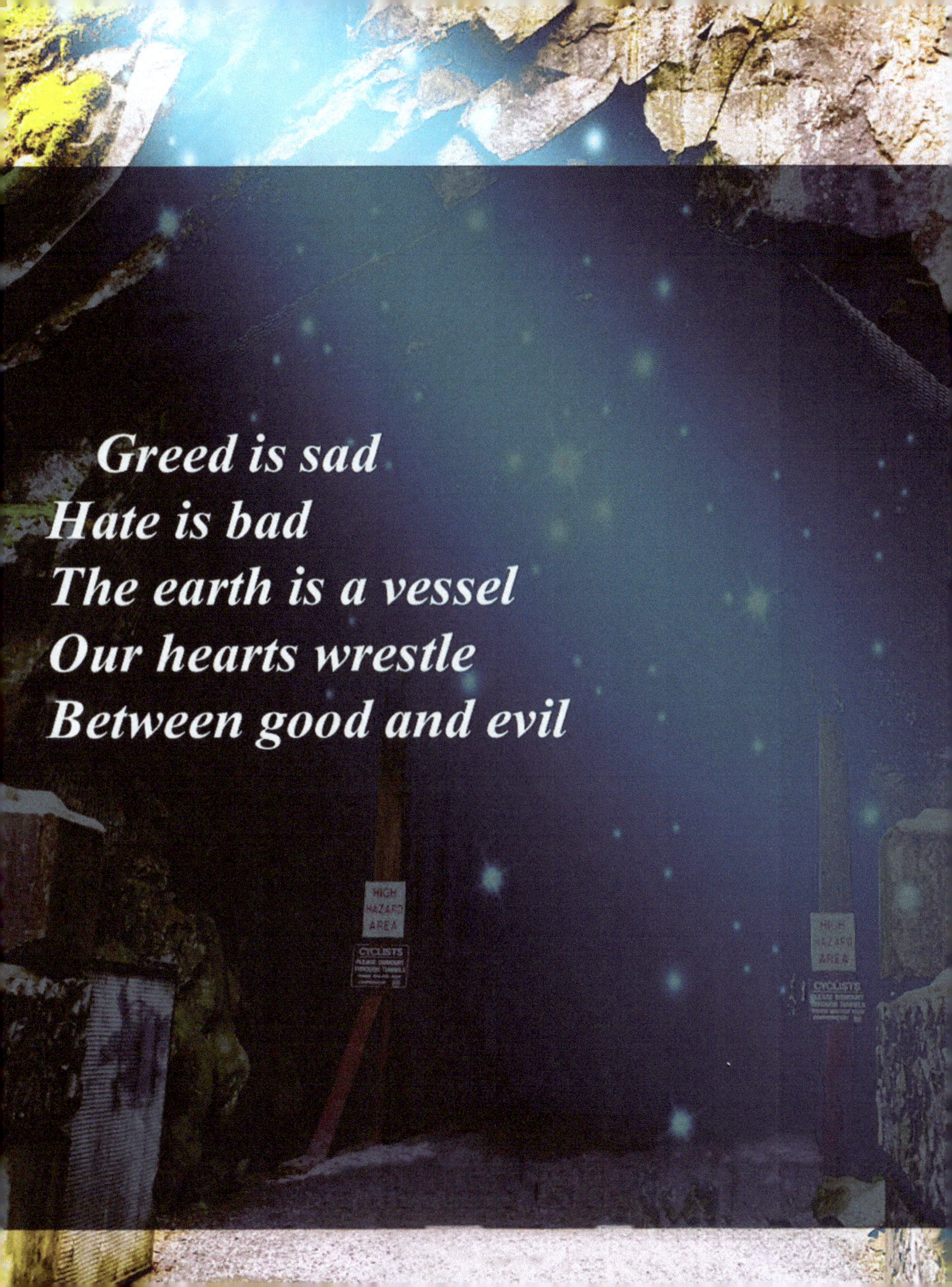

Greed is sad
Hate is bad
The earth is a vessel
Our hearts wrestle
Between good and evil

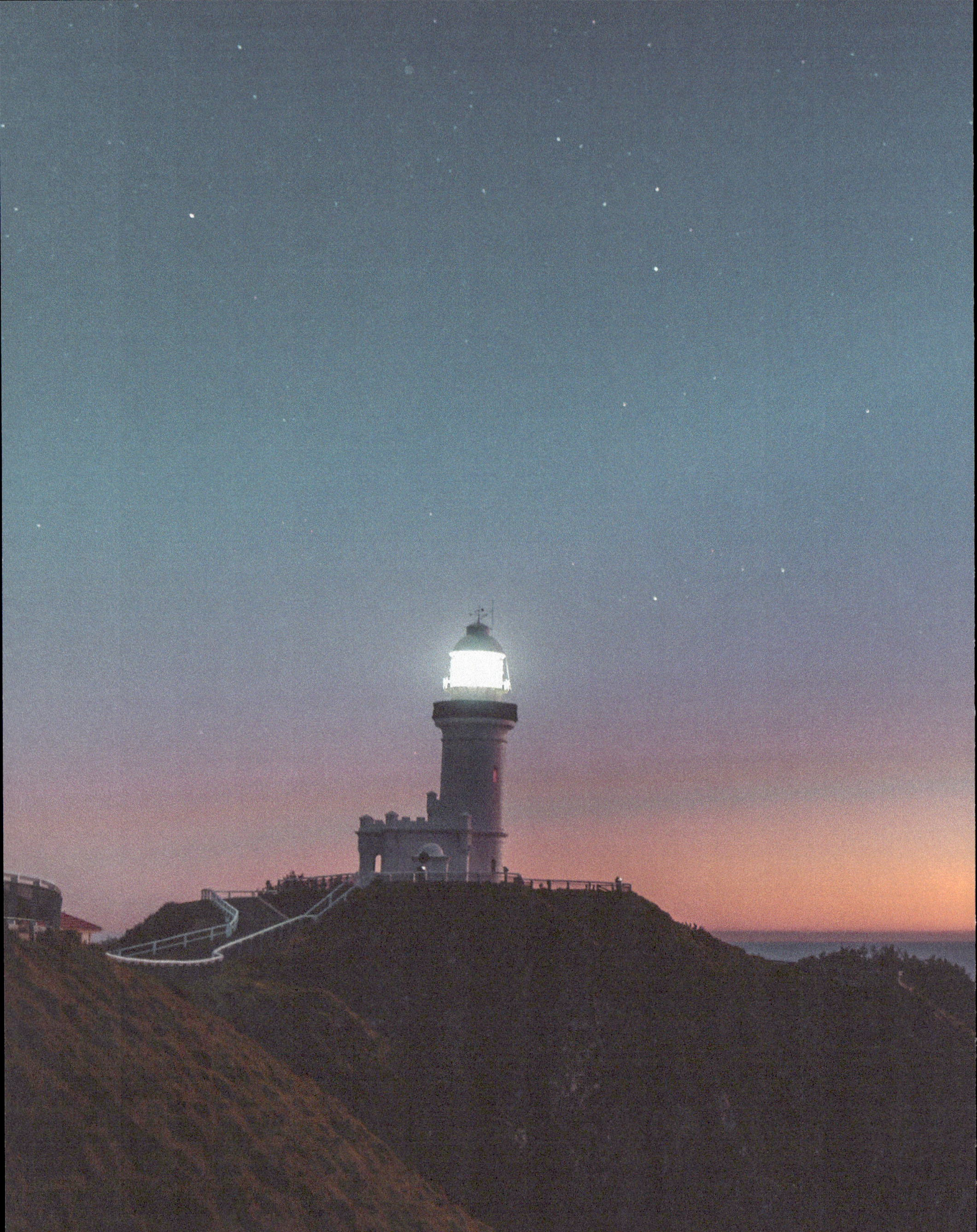

I Am Not "Pre-Tending"

I am preempting
I do not pretend to be a scholar
I do not pretend to be a star
I write with my heart
I cry, with my art
My body broken
My soul awaken
I express my surprises
I admire the sunrise
I tell the story of a human journey
Thrifty, loving, at times happy
Upset by humanity and its idiocy
Praying.. for peace and harmony
Imploring.. for the end of tyranny
Asking, for fairness in diplomacy
Could we all live in harmony
Stop, all these monstrous atrocities
Greed is sad
Hate is bad
The earth is a vessel
Our hearts wrestle
Between good and evil
Separating beauty in people
Differences sorted and disliked
Appreciating life, is all right

Only to those who can separate
Darkness from the light
In His name, be humble
It's ok to stumble
Lift your head up high
Look out and admire
This beautiful creation
Nature and its ambition
See the nectar of flowers
The birds and their colors
The enticing smells
The light in those who are blind
The beating heart in those you dislike
Feel the wind, hear the rain
Take away their pain
Be brave, sing praise
I do not pretend to be a scholar
I just love my fellows and our Father
I live my journey, trying to enlighten
In our time, the skies have darkened
Stronger
Together
Look up, feel the love, be blessed
Please, dance, sing and pray
...and, have a magical day

Photo by Dylan

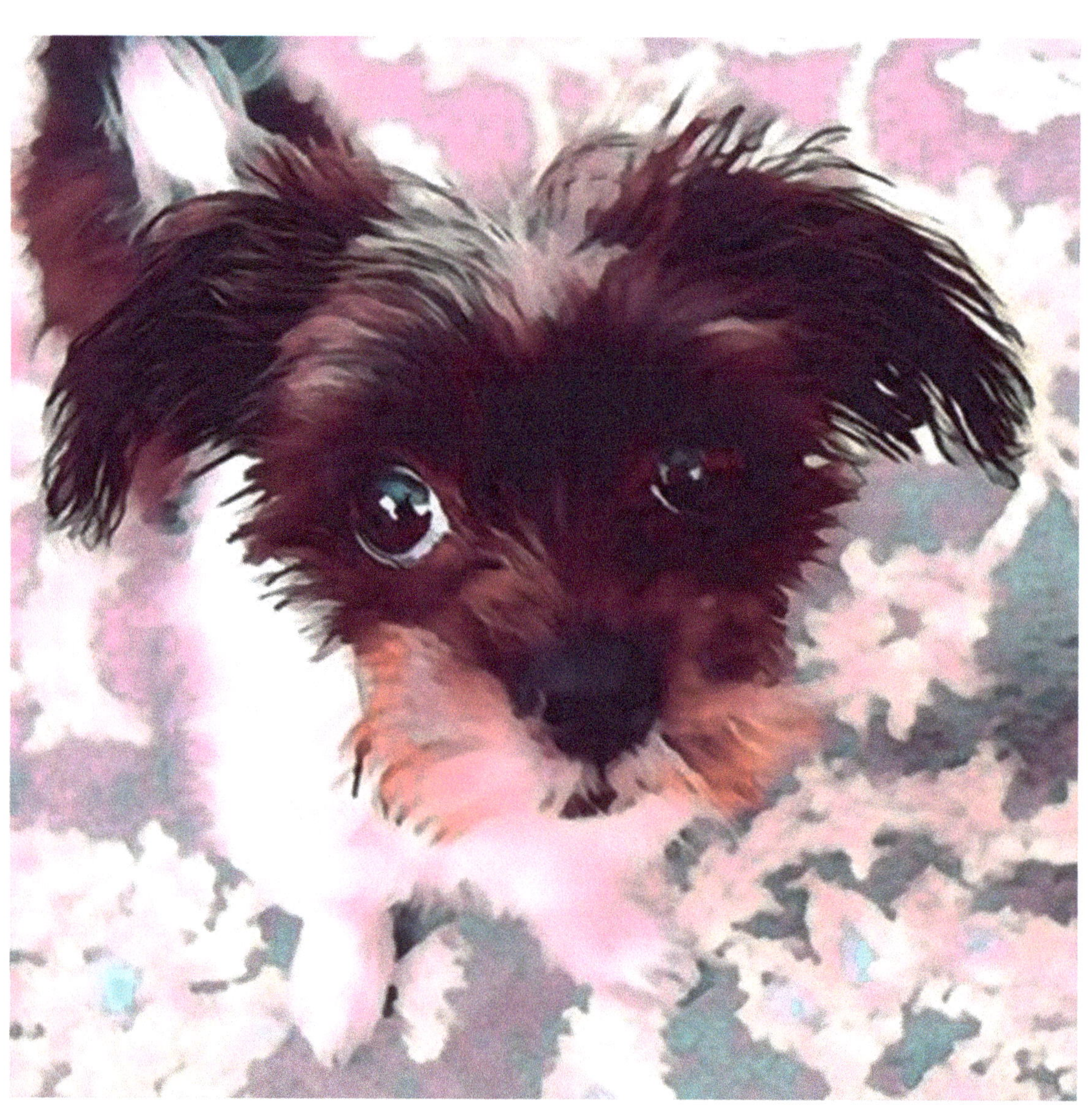

Future, Pass

Future with who, unsure
Reassure, help for sure
Everyone needs love
Even us fragile doves
Loving, embracing
Child reinventing
Personality insecure
Facing life's pressures
Someone's love
Support, you above
Insanity of crowds
Reporting clowns
Gives me ground
Away from around
Beautiful she is
Heart full, his
Hope for a future
Unsure, insecure
Children are pure
Parents be sure
Listen, carry no worry
There will always be
You and me
Best, worst, no hurry
Love forever
Being together
Loving her laughter
Best option after
It might be...
Please reassure me

The thought, of we
She should see in me
I would glance at she
All past
So fast
In a sounding hurry
Founding my family
Looking back, hold
Growing wiser and old
A story behold
My life being told
Past, future, hurry
Our, we, progeny
Would be prodigy
Beautiful, mildly
Pass life's sure
Knowing, reassure
Help was measure
Love is pure
Doves fly above
Our life in a cove
Toward future prose
Backward rove
Easy decision
Uneasy prediction
Will she be sure
I can tell my cure
Love I need
Dove I plead

Are we part of the same family?
Or ego's and individuality
If I offered you a dream
Would you wake up to redeem
This reality and your power

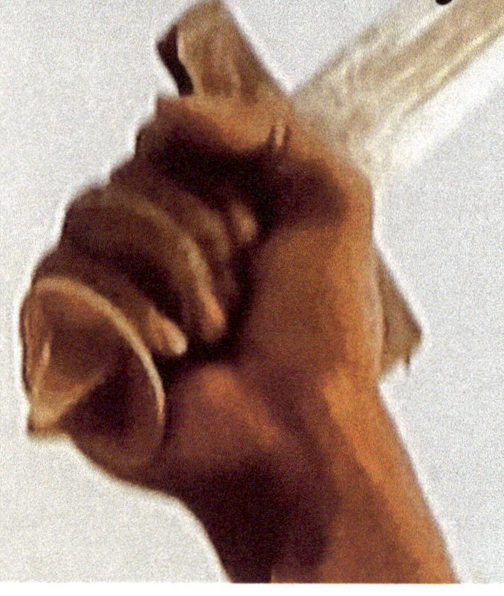

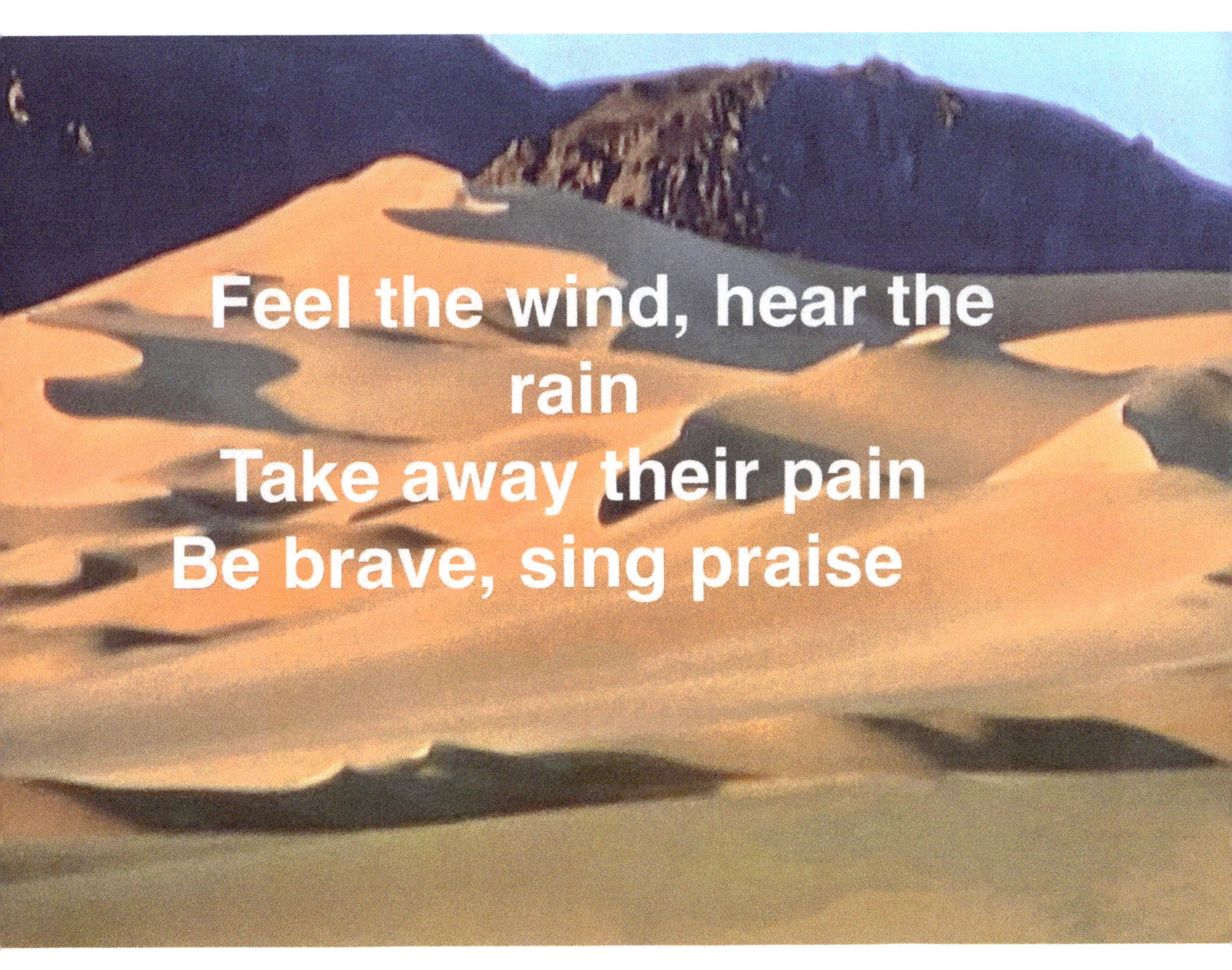

Feel the wind, hear the rain
Take away their pain
Be brave, sing praise

See the nectar of
flowers
The birds and their
colors
The enticing smells
The light in those who
are blinds
The beating heart in
those you dislike

Isn't Safe to Say

For the good of the country
We should have peace and unity
Pass on to our children
Stories of wisdom, of success
Over folly of proudness
People with reason
Not treason
Fighting for the cause of iniquity
Giving up on guns and violence
To pray on art and confidence
Isn't it brave to say
You love your neighbors
No matter what their colors
Create security
Not scrutiny
Love of music
Note symphonic
Purifying our hearts
With what really matters
Respect, honestly embraced
Love, nurture, and nature
The human soul open
Connected to the source
Understanding its characteristics
Love, blessings, and energetic
Violence and deaths
Only diminish the wealth
The uplifting possibilities

Of the strong, caring
Mother of our land bearing
Proud, beautiful, and free
To be made great again
Is to treat the Constitution with a stubborn
Obsession of justice through peace
Nationality through unity
Isn't hard to say
Mistakes were made
Lies were told
Pardons were issued as a pass foretold
Of a dynasty fighting for power and glory
Without character, but for misery
Money after all, only, fills the pockets
Not the hearts of the ones not able to
Correlate with God
Father ancestor of this unique
Strength of our consciousness
As a free, honest, and passionate
Young population
Isn't fair to command
Without the ability to comprehend
Put a stop to the idiocy
Regain our social authenticity
Respect

Her

I feel sorry we haven't met before
Talks, seem so much better...
Than ever before
I want to be close to you
Melt our skins together
All the way till later
Way much later
Where are you
Why I haven't met you
Way before..
Talks, seems so much better..
If we grew together
Could you wonder
Of better times
Talks, seem so much better
I don't have to explain myself
My dreams are your dreams
My life is yourself
Sleepless nights away from love
Wandering, why
I haven't met you
Way before
Talks, seem so much better...
Than ever before

I want to touch you all over
You make me feel, all so younger
Dreams of your every-way
Keep me wondering all day
Why I haven't met you before
Nights are so much more
Fulfilling every desire
Everyday, my pleasure
Your beautiful
Mind, true and blissful
Away from you feels cold
Way more than any other before
I ever hold
Your precious hearth
I was lost in my ways
Winters freezing always
Why I haven't met you before
Seems like a test
Was I ever ready to rest
In your arms
Laying down my arms
Let go to the flow
The discussion is so
Making me feel anew

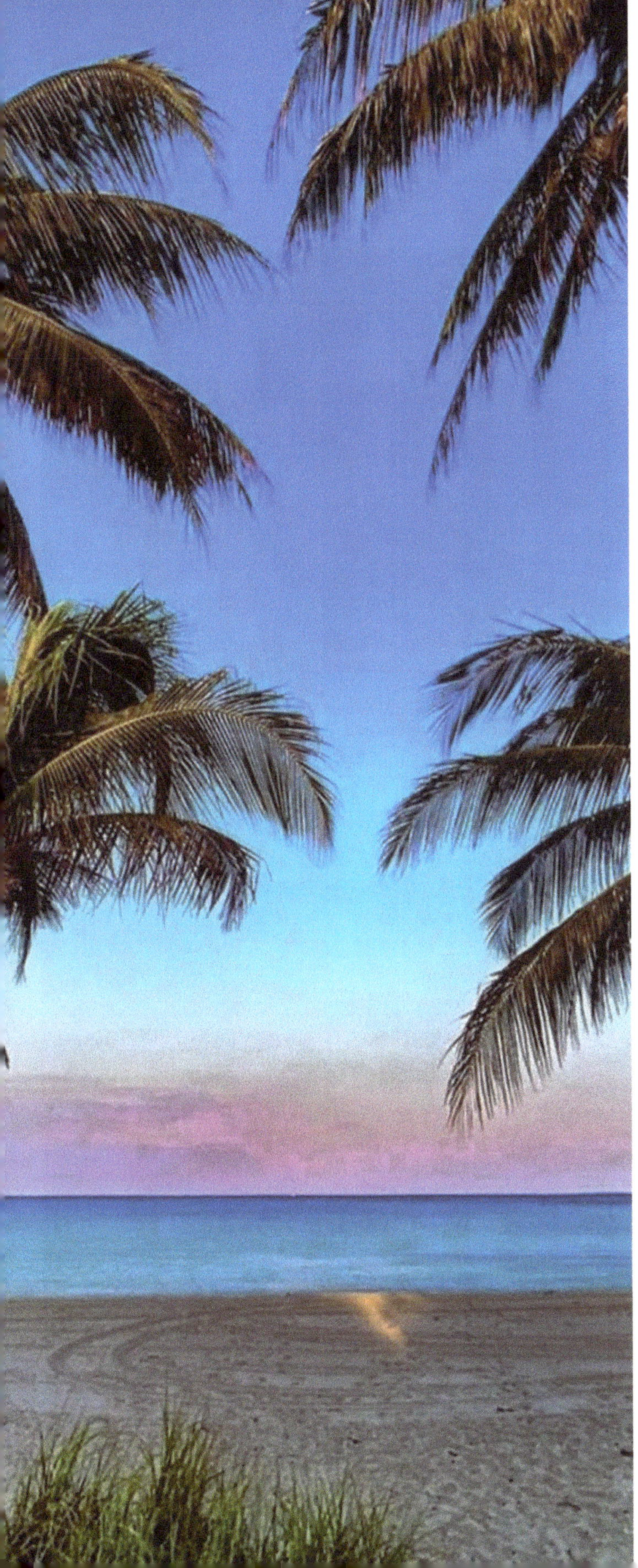

Like I knew
We would meet one day
I have nothing to hide, to hold on
Other than you, day after day
Talks, seem so much better...
Than ever before
Knowing you, makes my life
So much better
Could I love you forever
And ever
Hold you closer
And closer
Feel your heart, your mind
Would you mind, being mine
Talks, seem so much better...
Than ever before
I wish, to talk on the pillow
Hold on, highs and lows
Love, would you, let me
Talk to you, evermore
Every day
Kiss me, hold me, love me
Don't ever let go

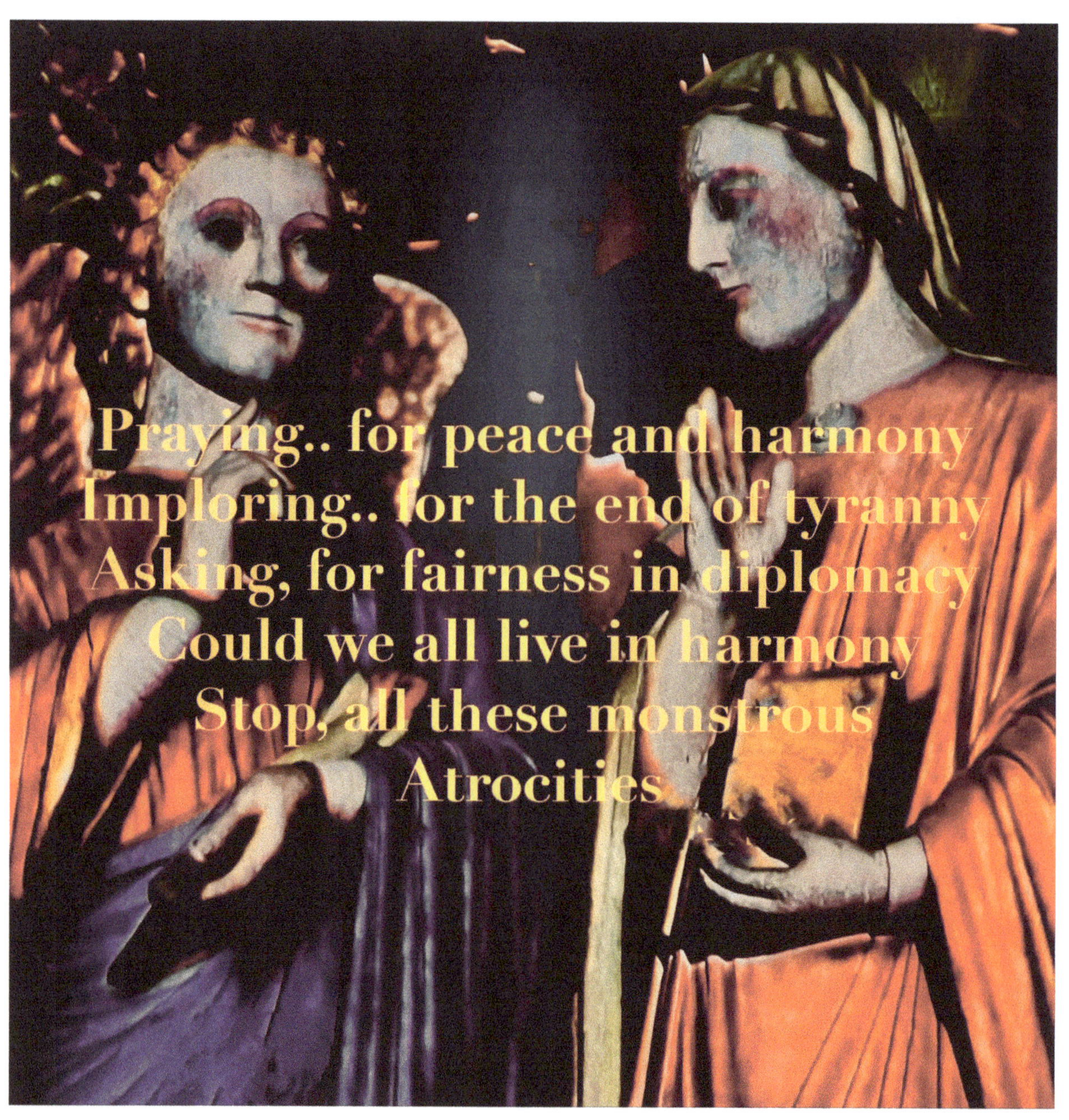

Praying.. for peace and harmony
Imploring.. for the end of tyranny
Asking, for fairness in diplomacy
Could we all live in harmony
Stop, all these monstrous
Atrocities

Future

If life went our way
Would you really throw it away
Or stay if you could play
There's a lot that doesn't work
Also seems, no one to report
The wild is a safe place
If you understand their faces
Overthinking creates anxiety
Moments softly created with facility
We're probably meant to be
Understand the probability
Never anything happens
Like it, or not, we all depend
Faith, fatality, or destiny
It's at the end all poetry
Life seems like a wave
Up around and down, crave
Follow the water flow
Should we know
Bend, contour, detours
Why wouldn't it be yours
Wise would say
We all live under the same day
Different time, age, and space
Together in the same race
Slow down, agree
Your neighbor is also free
Competition belongs nowhere

Newer intention requires, we wear
Our brothers and sisters
Make it seems like lovers
Gentle, soft, good manners
Opens the door to laughters
Soothing, believing, sharing
Would be amazing acquiring
Reformat neurons
Reboot our belongs
Sing harmony, be happy
Earth is the only
Place we all have
Bounding everybody
Why is it a mystery
Listen our hearts are wire
It's all there consider hire
Take care, work for the good
We all have our part, if we only would
Please, I personally ask
Priority make your task
To help, share goodness
We all need softness
Create a new earth
We have to stop the hurt
Where is it going
If there's no remaking
Let's all be honest
May we progress

Evolve, time comes
It's not out of range
Needed new reality
If only finding our priority
We will, things will change
Generations later, rearrange
Good purpose gladly
Presented openly
What if we all had our way
Would we remake it the same way....

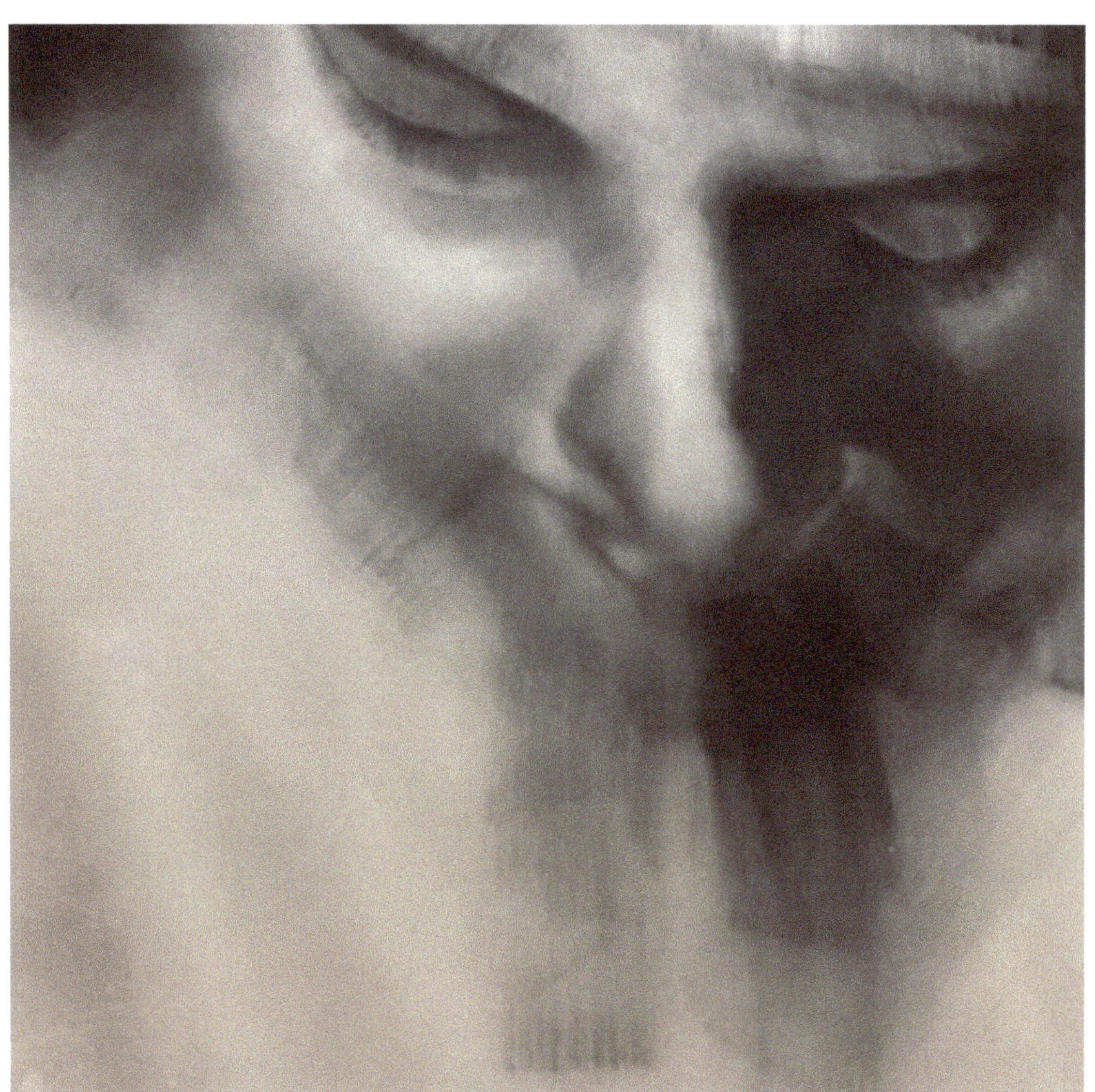

Future Under Weather

Distant of a future
Tonight seems unsure
Far distance apart
Seeing her heart
Unwilling, giving
Makes me freezing
Cold times
Weather rhymes
Stay so warm
Baby no harm
Open the door
Fire me more
There's a line
Very, very fine
Ice, brings flames
No one is to blame
Missing you
It is, so true
Her voice warming
For me warning
Not mine, be kind
One day remind
Complicity never match
Let me, catch you
Under watch
Watching over you, angel
Stay away
It's fine, you may

Still, I will care
Until you dare
Maybe one day
You might just lay
In my arms
I mean you no harm
A future together
Different than any other
Surely outlast
Past all currents
Let's be real
So suppose, we do heal
You are a beauty
I love you crazy
Where's the end
Without your hand
I'm lost, roaming
To my own roaring
Help me, help you
Let's be real...
Help you, helping me
Healing could only be
Completed when you see me
Future turning chills
Into your high hills

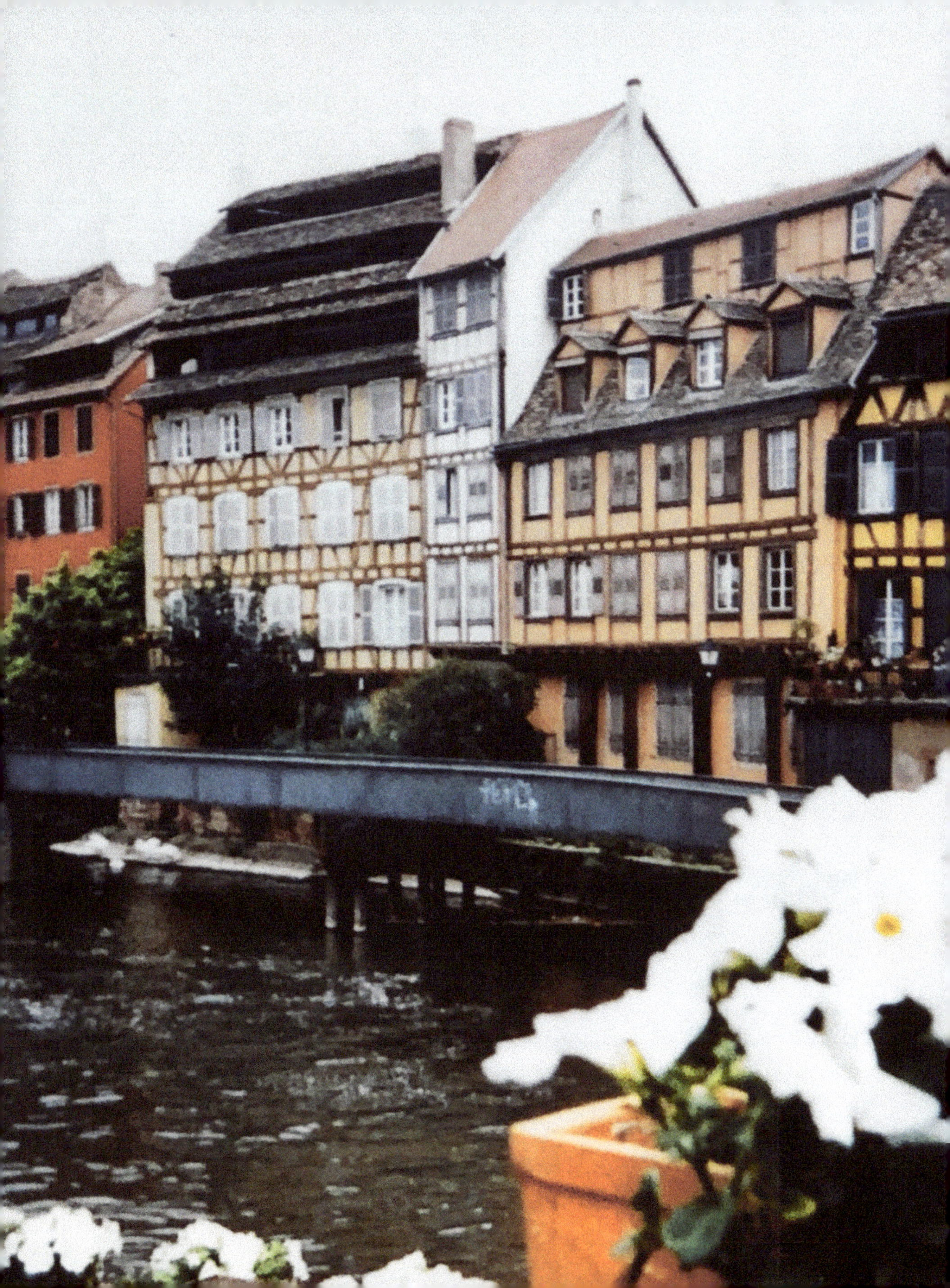

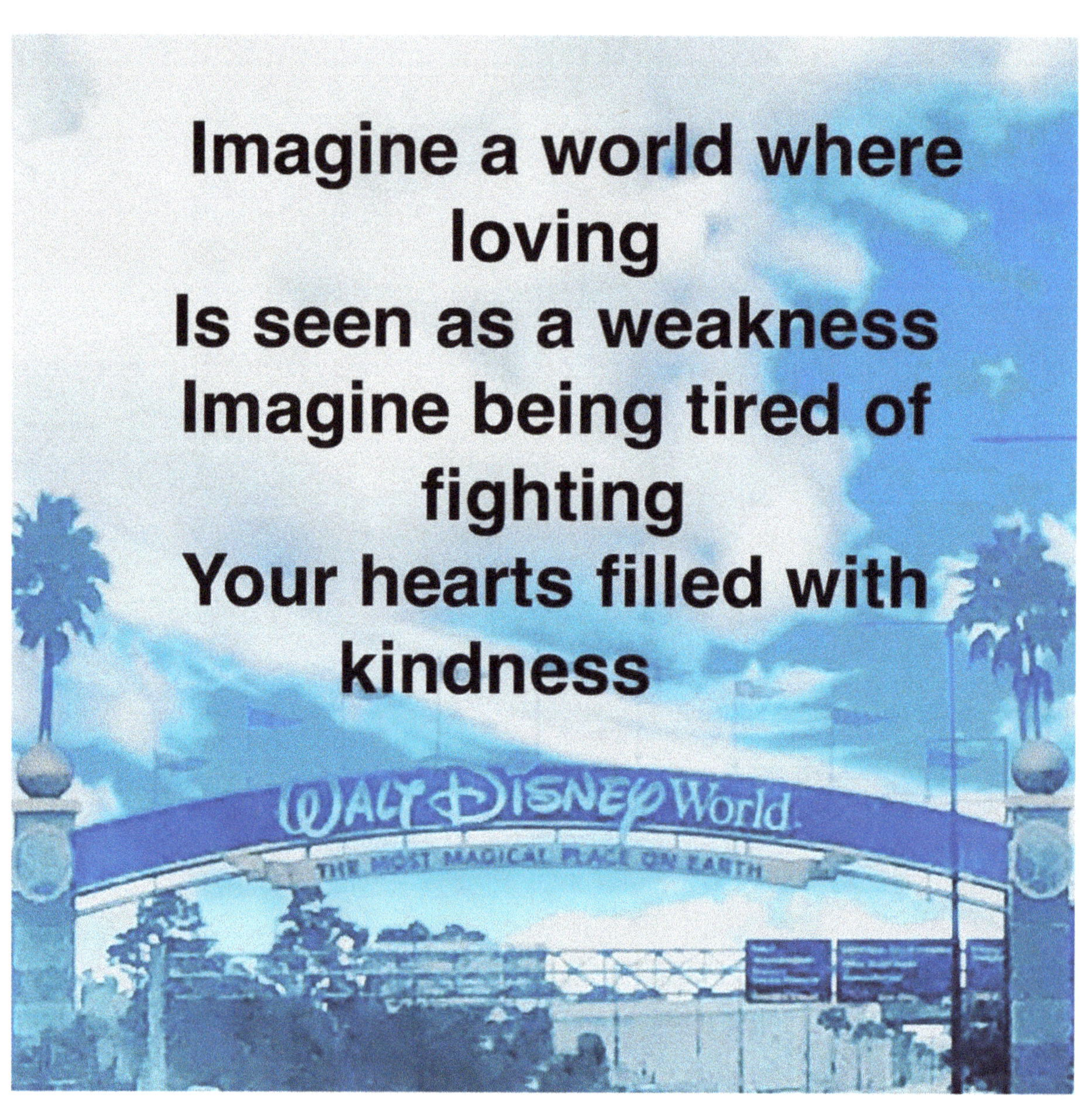
Imagine a world where loving
Is seen as a weakness
Imagine being tired of fighting
Your hearts filled with kindness
WALT DISNEP World.
THE MOST MAGICAL PLACE ON EARTH

Paradise is simple you see
Love and compassion
Naturally
Flowing into the sea
Honestly and Free

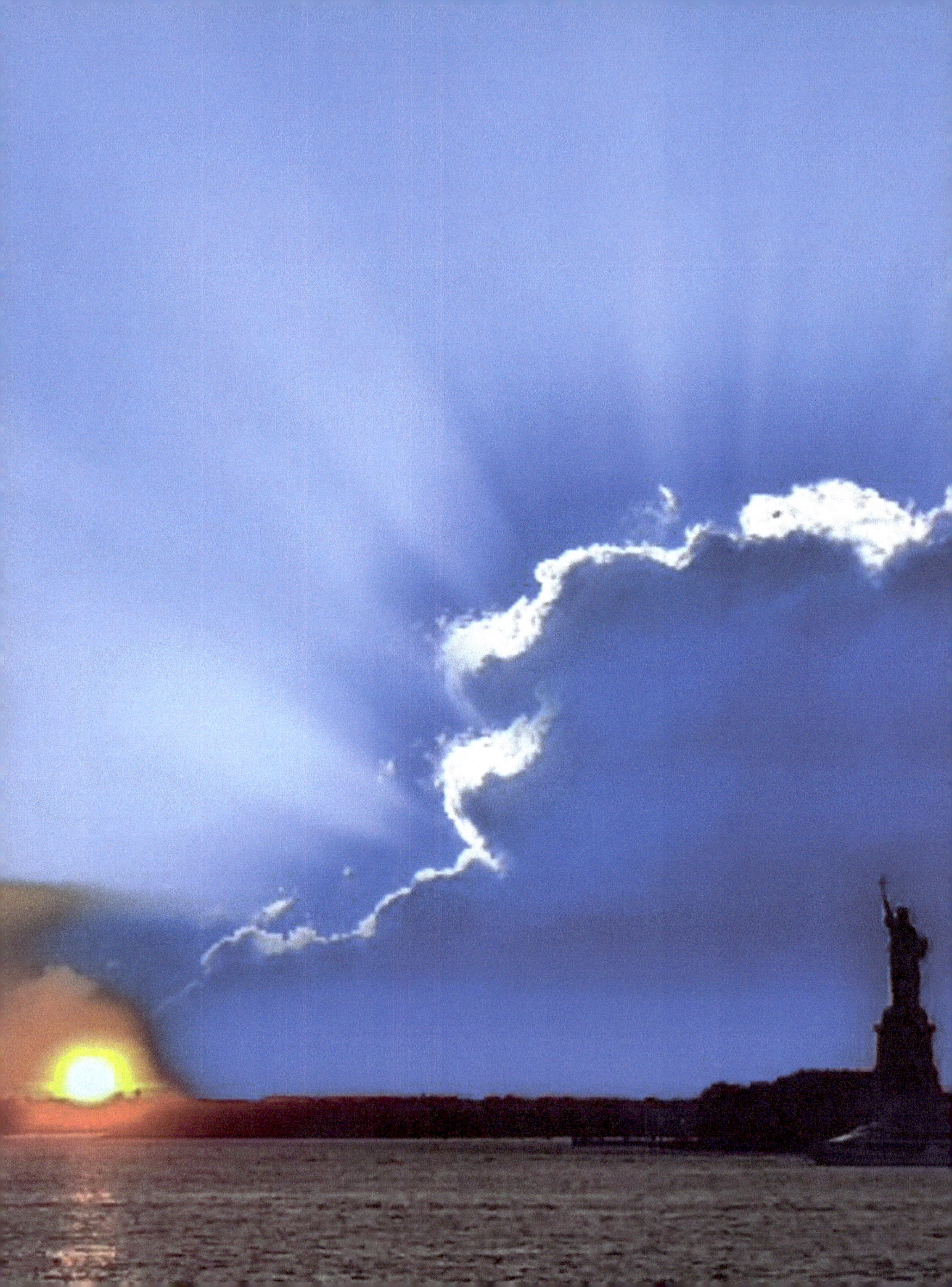

Dreams

Sheep's
Dreams are deep
They prefer to let go
Follow, follow
Life is made of every day
Keep on, day by day
Break the lines
Don't realign
Find the child inside
As time flies
Don't let it say goodbye
Pick up your bags
Take off
Far off
Your destiny might be
Somewhere else, you ought to be
Distant shores
Cultural scores
Anything but follow
Days after days
Same old pay
Don't worry baby
The world is ready
Destiny is out there
Adventures elsewhere

Sheep's
Dreams are deep
They prefer to let go
Follow, follow
Ready, ready, let's go
I always know
When it's time to glow
Distant ethnicity
Is where the electricity
Pumps in the veins
Inflames the brain
Dreams are meant to follow
Projects, prospects
All with respect
Forward ambitions
Be full of aspirations
Discover what is under your cover
Your true beautiful nature
Follow your allure
Sheep's
Dreams are deep
They prefer to lie low
I scream and say no
Come, come, let's go

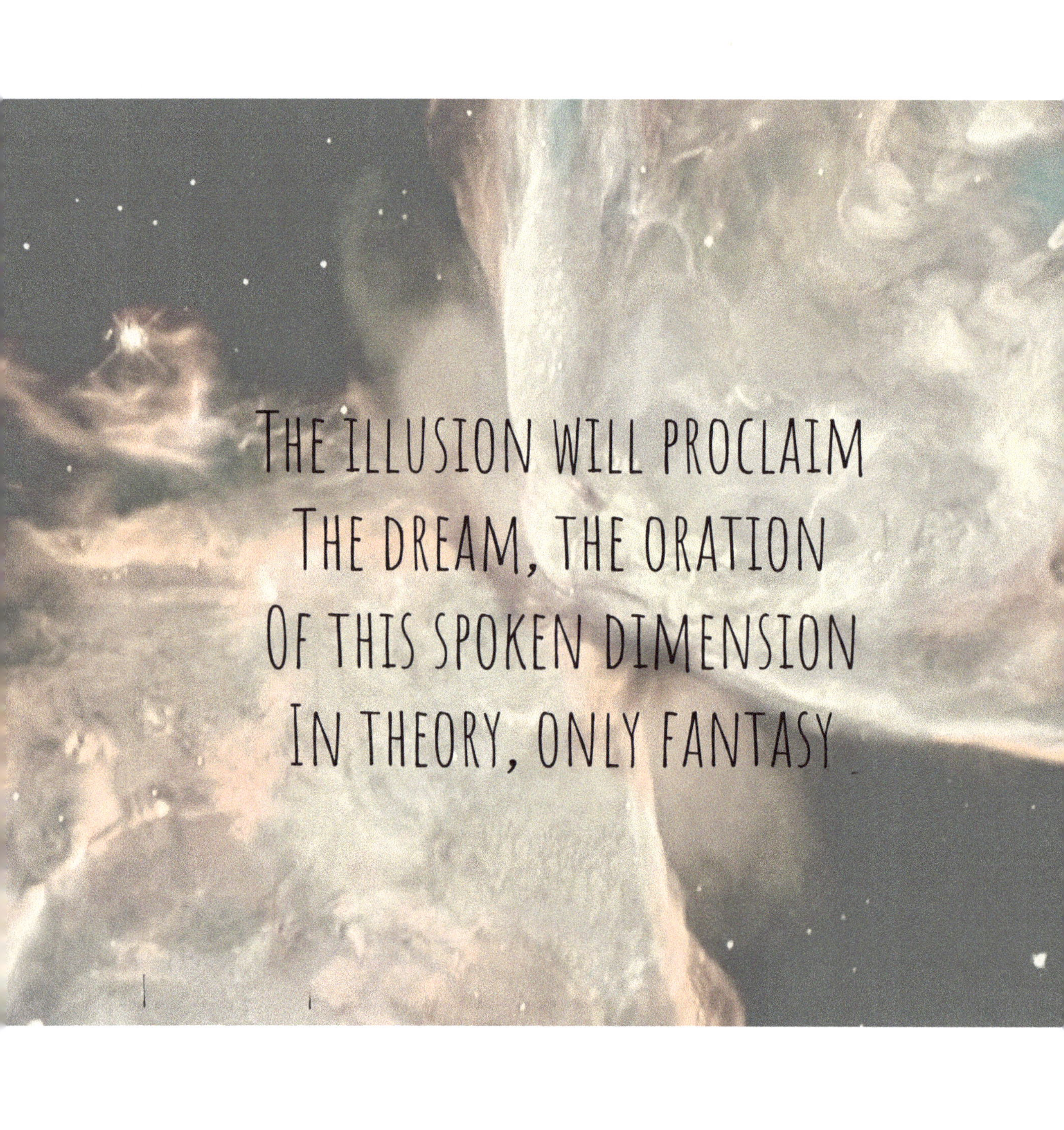
The illusion will proclaim
The dream, the oration
Of this spoken dimension
In theory, only fantasy

Crazy

I am going crazy
Am I, I'm dreaming
Of the possibility
Of the transforming
Capability of the butterfly
As a design for humanity
Cocoon, ugly darkness, why?
So many different personalities
Evolving
Expending
Our wings and fly
Listen to the vibrations
Feel the energy of transformation
Let it be, multicolors
Seamless, without effort
Be light
Be bright
Elevate and soar
Hope for more
Peace and justice
The end of prejudice
No more madness of wars
Thoughts could soar
Light explored
Life implored
I am, going crazy
With this simple fantasy
Is it really a utopia?
Paradise you see
Is in our reach
Let's teach
Our minds, purified

Our souls, amplified
By love
And above
Compassions
Passions
For kindness
Our deepest
Concerns for others
Like nothing else matters
No more shame of ridicule
In sharing our particles
Emotions and concerns
Self preservation
Is not justification
Be more aware
Out of nowhere
Create
Do not abdicate
To the temptations
Without redemption
I am, going crazy
Open your wings
Take flight, honey
Show your colors
Discover the splendors
Hidden inside the chrysalis
Is our metamorphosis
Into the new world
Come with me
Let's go crazy
You and me
And follow Thee

Drinking Anguish

Drinks, drinks, help you are to me
Sitting here dreaming
Calming emotions are rising
I'm only thinking of the stars
Why, I don't understand what she is doing to me
How it happened, I can't see
I just can't deal with the feeling of being lonely
I'm missing my beautiful lady
Should I stay and drink? I'll have another...
The bartender, the next one is on me
Forget, move on, look around
There are so many lovely
But she's my lady
He doesn't understand, just like me
Why her, why now, it keeps me wondering
Always day dreaming
Drinks, drinks, making me feel loose and happy
Tomorrow is another day, but if only
Forget it, don't be sorry
Life goes on understand
Your head in the sand
She would be just a memory
Tonight, drinks keep me happy
I'm just alone amid the lonely
All looking to forgive, be content
That's what's important
The next one is on me
We are all broken, torn eagerly

Skip my turn
I only wish she kept me
Bartender please another
My mind is still... with her
Where, why, isn't she with me
I can't take a hold of me
Let it be
Another drink, I'll feel drowsy
Tomorrow is another day if only
Let her go and hope she is happy
Tonight my soul wishes she stayed
My body, in the morning, will suffer
What if I was richer
I will pray
I could've had it my way
Lord if you may
Drinks, drinks, tonight I think I'll stay...

Disc "Over" Me

Discover, who
You want me to be
Who do you want, to see?
Images of heroes
Deeper than marrow
Hurting the soul
Frustrated by this role
Of the magnificent giants
Made up by false suppliant
Augmented
Marketed
By the media
Fed by acedia
Wouldn't it be easier
To love by touching, softer
The hearts
The arts
The colors of passions
The fear of hesitations
Innocence of relinquish
Facades and barricades
Trumpets and blockades
Harmony and symphony
Of two bodies
Warming up
Flaring up
In the heat of instinctivness
Feelings often destructive

Of souls recovered
Of passions discovered
In the rare uniqueness
In individuality, romanesque
Dream, awake
Rest in my wake
Understanding
Remembering
Life without fear
Murmuring to my ear
Butterflies carried in the wind
A soft breeze intertwine
Of senses
Without pretense
Just being
Just caring
For love, for us
The Flight of the Albatros
Planning overseas
Feelings bringing me, to my knees
Imploring God for visions
Of a bright future without divisions
Are you sure you don't wish to see
Who I was meant to be...
The illusion of perfection
Might just be, a distraction
Reality is often our deepest prayer
In plain sight provided simply for lovers

Photo by Cottonbro

Accept yourself, to finally, be free
Ready, to recognize why, I am me
Delicate, dedicated, amant
Searching for the peace in your eyes
Finally, finding the truth of who
You are living to Be
Breathing and drumming, next to me...
Both free
Both in the melody
Of ecstasy

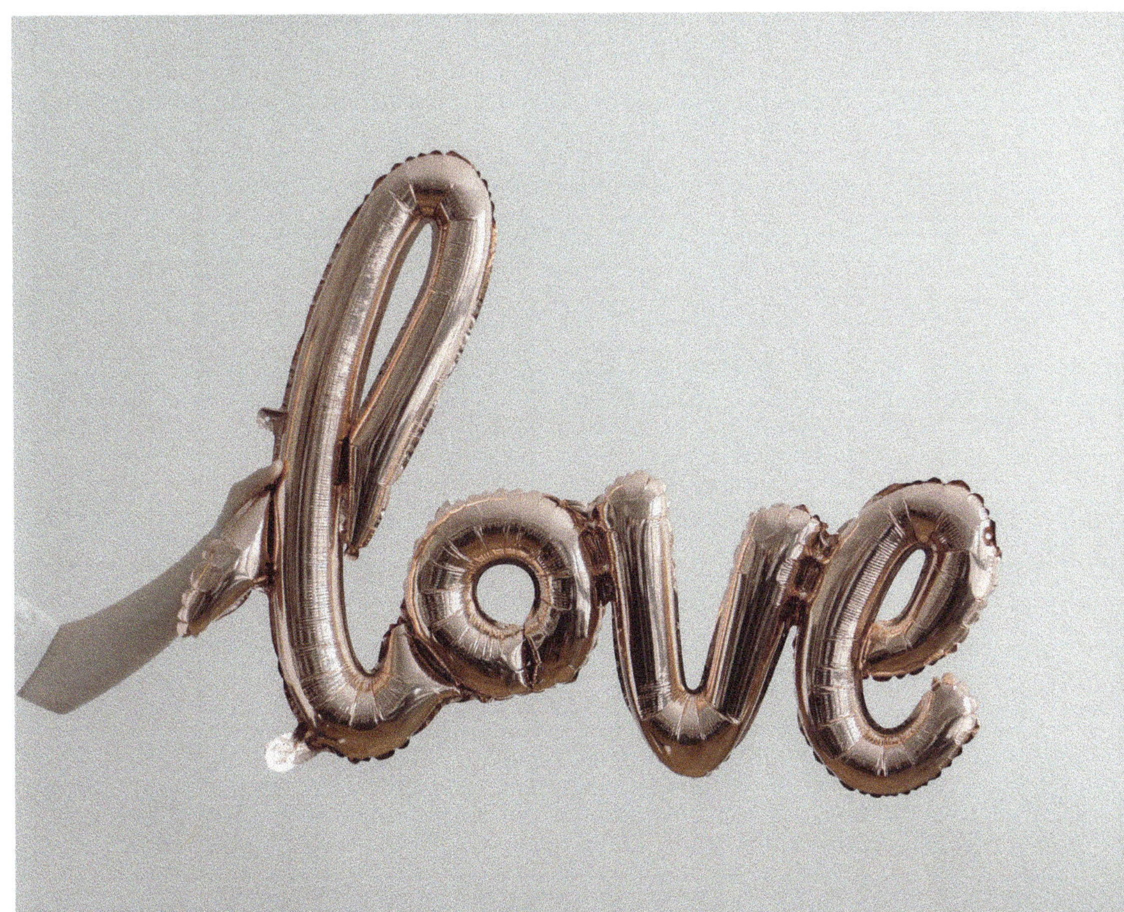

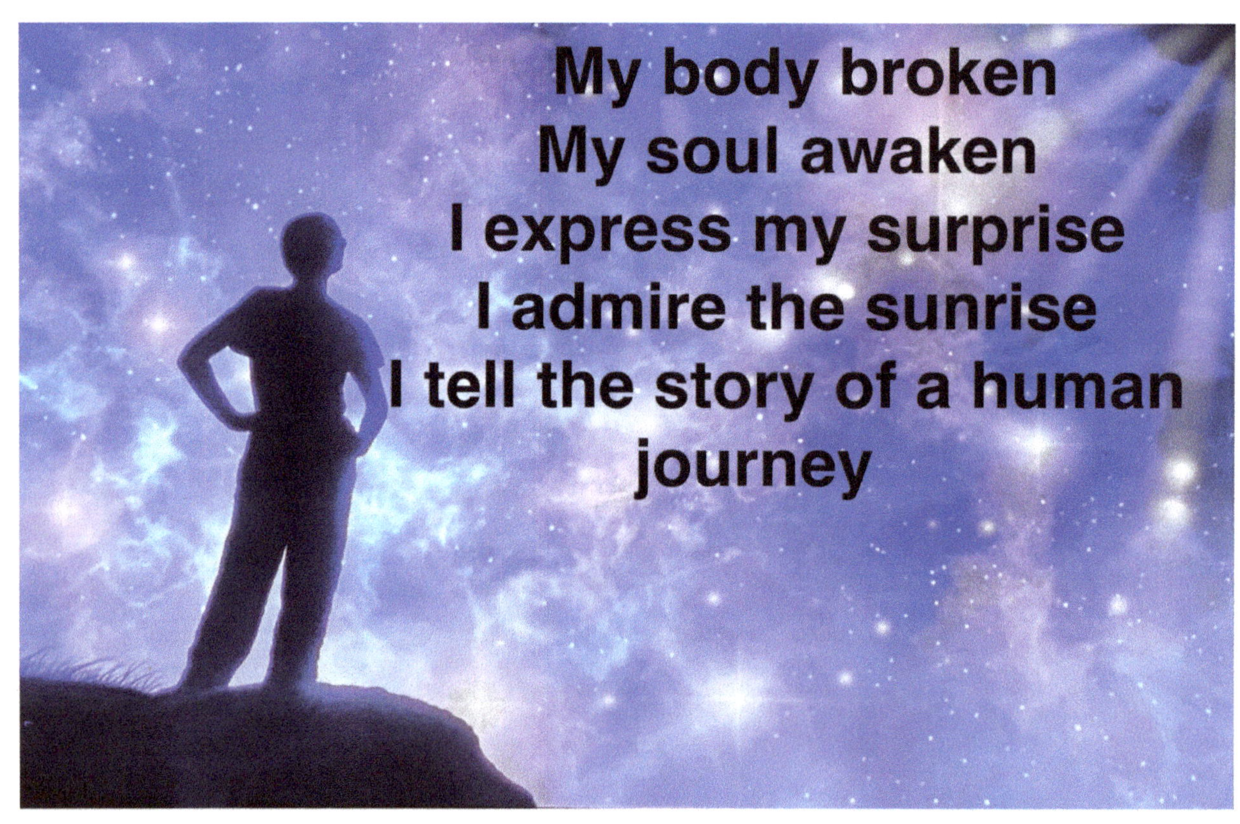
My body broken
My soul awaken
I express my surprise
I admire the sunrise
I tell the story of a human
journey

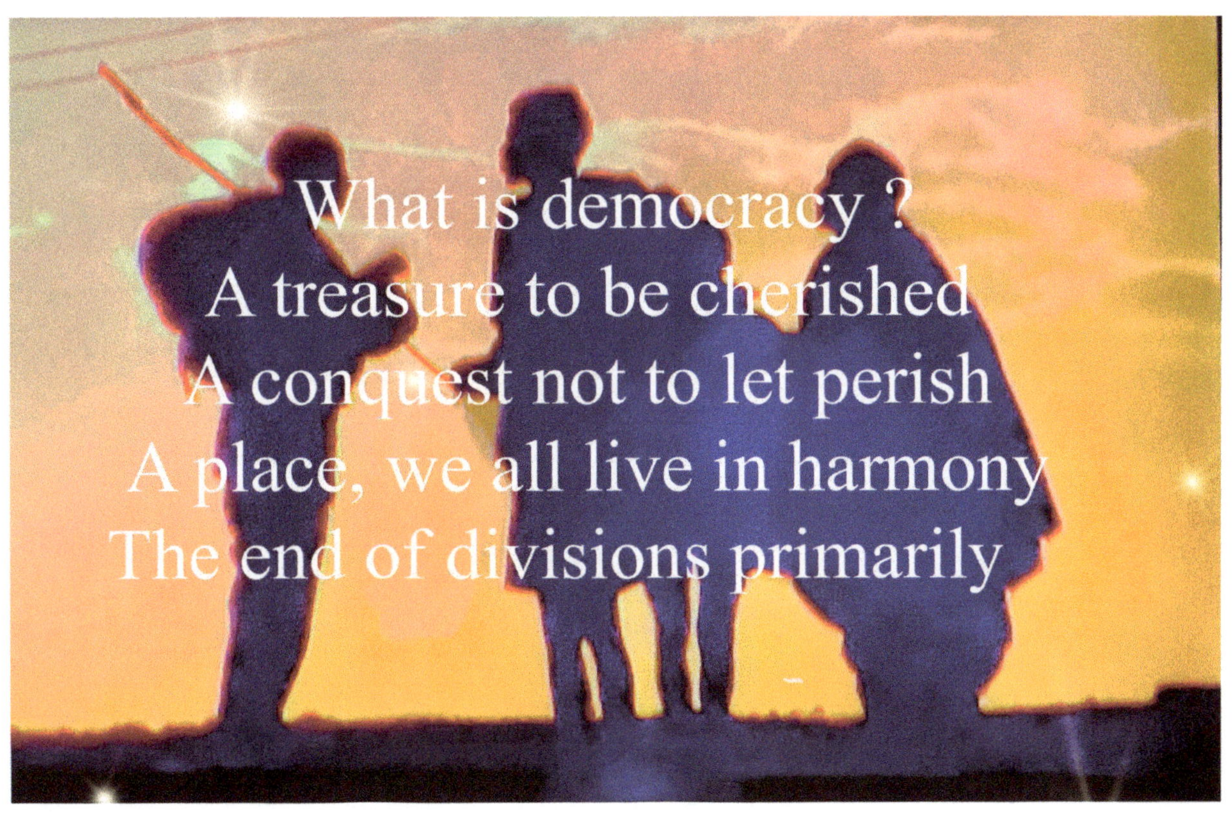

What is democracy ?
A treasure to be cherished
A conquest not to let perish
A place, we all live in harmony
The end of divisions primarily

I do not pretend to
be a scholar
I just love my fellows
and our Father
I live my journey,
trying to enlighten
In our time, the skies
have darken

Archways

Doors, fit in
Or stay out
Cold worry, sorry
There will be envy
Looking out from in
Seems warm within
Truth be told
Most of us hold
Images of fame, fortune
Disbeliefs and misfortune
Just be yourself
Mess with the rest
Turning doors
Sounding roars
Gateways to freedom
Pathways to unison
Individuality eventually
Produces unity
Breaking down wall
No doors for all
Safe and sound
No poverty around
Utopia or reality
Real, harmony
Will happen within
Individuals, hear in
We will grow old
All kinds of road

Leading to cautions
Most of opinions
Never realized
Potential revived
Live your life
Best to strive
Share, understand
Put out a hand
Look out, to look in
Look in, to look out
Don't worry about
The cold or the envy
Go for guts and glory
And share your story

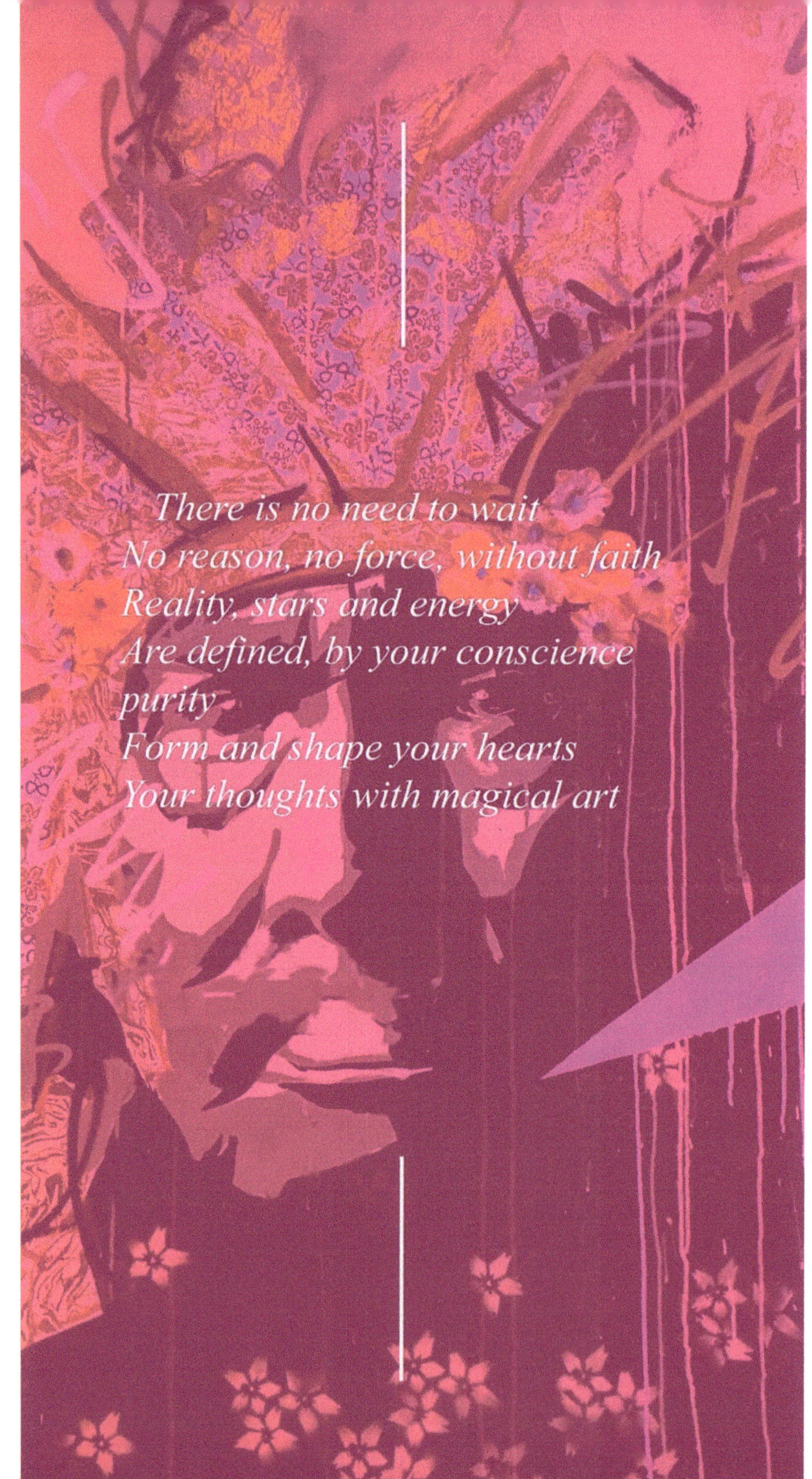

There is no need to wait
No reason, no force, without faith
Reality, stars and energy
Are defined, by your conscience
purity
Form and shape your hearts
Your thoughts with magical art

Bitterness

Why such bitterness
When offered tenderness
Pain in disbelief
Sadness to retrieve
Hope and dreams
Flowing like streams
Inspired and shared
But met with hatred
Soften your heart
Love, be part
Trust, recognize
Accept without precept
Blindness intercept
Messages
Passages
The reason
Like the season
Bring hope
Help, cope
All nations
One creation
I am that you are
Just a mirror
Live for eternity
For you and me
Accusations
Like weapons
Hurt, sorrows, and pain
Love must remain
Sweet tenderness
No more bitterness

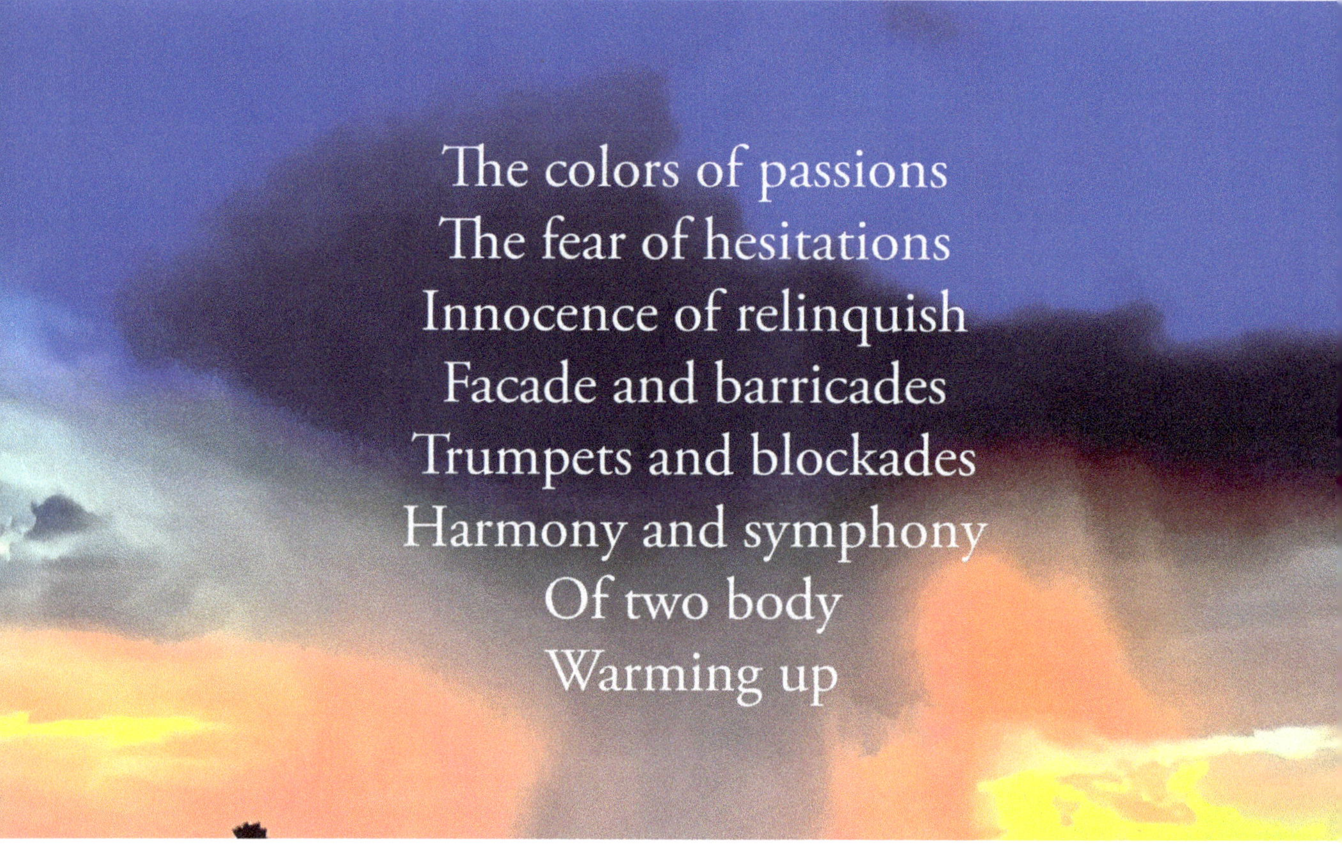
The colors of passions
The fear of hesitations
Innocence of relinquish
Facade and barricades
Trumpets and blockades
Harmony and symphony
Of two body
Warming up

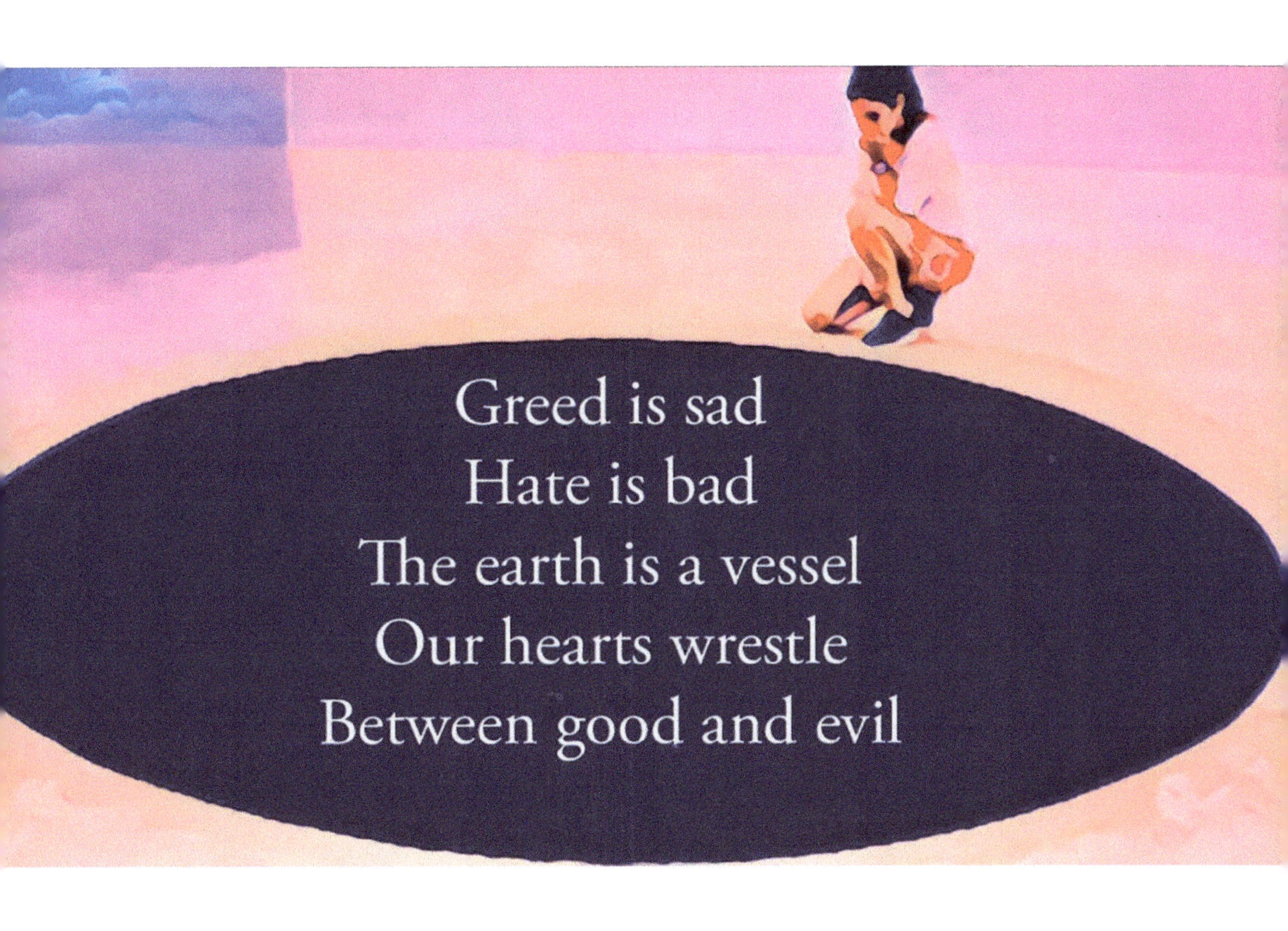

Greed is sad
Hate is bad
The earth is a vessel
Our hearts wrestle
Between good and evil

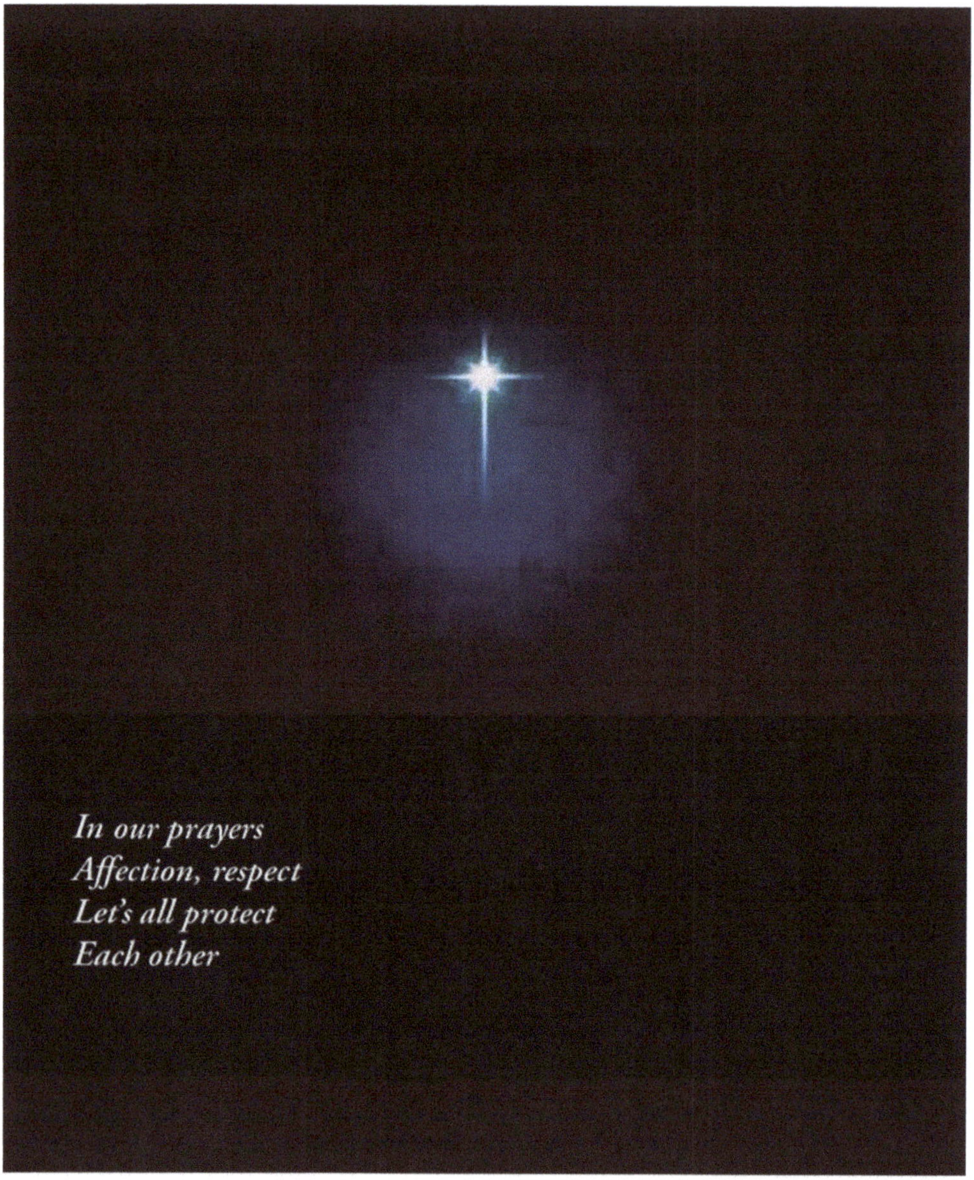

In our prayers
Affection, respect
Let's all protect
Each other

Angel

Beauty of an angel
Laugh so respectful
Before nightfall
Remember heart fall
Literally nonsense
Morally absent
Reality would be
Clean you see
Clearly I should
Fairly I could
Forget her
Mind over
Beautiful angel
Daunt get entangle
Storms of life
Bringing you alive
So far, yet so close
What's the purpose
After the rain
No pain remain
Life as it is, love
Remember, first dove
Sunshine calming
Souls reviving
Eternity in making
So fast dissolving
The facts of life
Renewing hive

Difference binds
Color blinds
Fight reminds
Humanity wins
No one knows
Really, how to grow
Expend your wings
There's no limit
To how high you fly
When set your eyes
Love only brings
Possibility of dreams
Life's forces
Bringing forward
Lovers as bees on flowers
Beauty upon angels
Before sunrise
Forgetful and heart full
Hopefully making sense
Literally enhance
The beauty of an angel
My heart being own
Completely

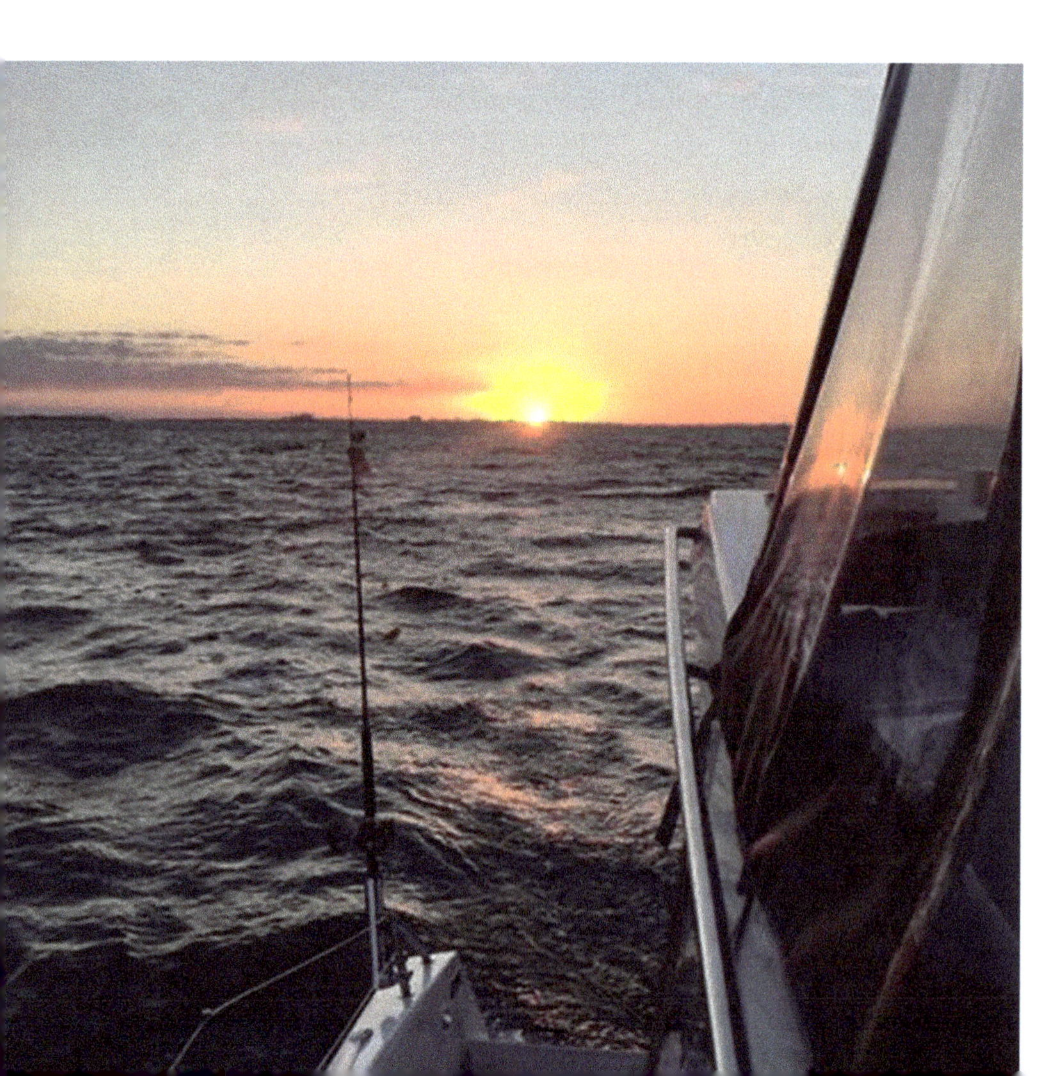

A Wish

I wish
I could, write
Something so bright
I could bring you
Very close, feeling bliss
Valentine's riches
Not to be fetch
Yet so etch
Cold night
Story story write
Forget the story
Rewrite our history
I'm sure our hearts
Pure as art
Finally let go our fears
Future is revere
I wish, I could
I don't know if I should
Sometimes so bright
Wouldn't be so right
The sun burns
The moon calms
Emotion earns
Sensations in our palms
I really wish
I could...

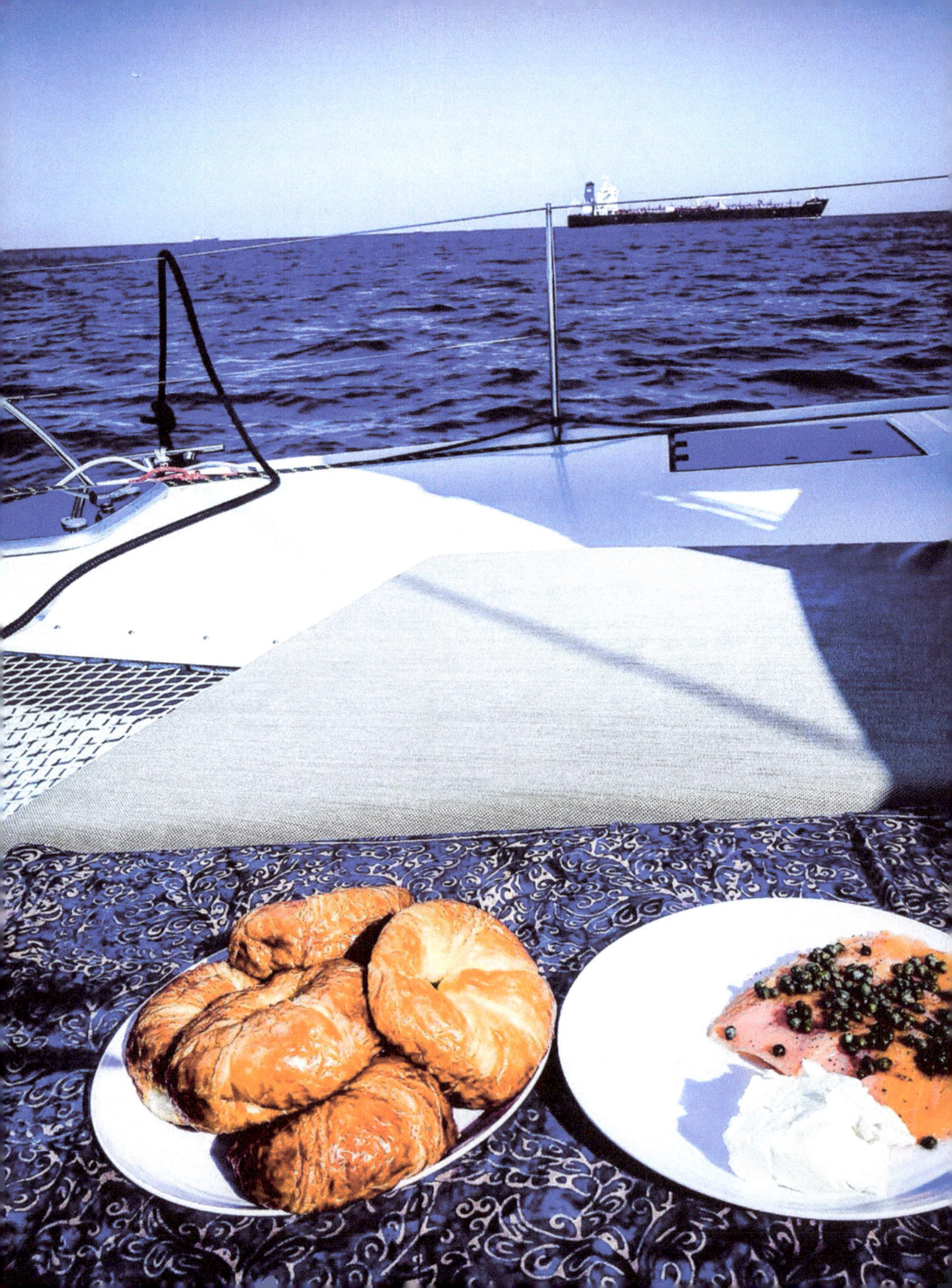

Aimé

What is love
Feeling of knowing
Without ever understating
The depth of life
Without love
Deep yearning
Need bearing
Our naked souls
Revealing as a whole
Humanity
In a continuity
Knowing to receive
Even better to give
These emotions
Certainty and passions
There are no equals
To a life lived in sequel
Finding the one true
To the story of who
Might complete
Our entire being, unite
Amazed, purified
Being love, intensified
Propelled in a fantasy
Perhaps met with reality
Together time stands still
Apart, eternity, if you will
Love

What is love
Find the one
Is the only way
To understand
Life's meaning, we may
Let's stand
Offer, receive
Protect and accept
The gift
To complete ourselves
Be part of a universe
One of love
Forgiveness
Truth, deepness
Real affections
Complete acceptance
Mistakes and imperfections
Of one's own humanity
Meanings of self reality
Will prove better
Even greater
Deeper, softer
Always intense
In amazing splendor
Forever, so tender

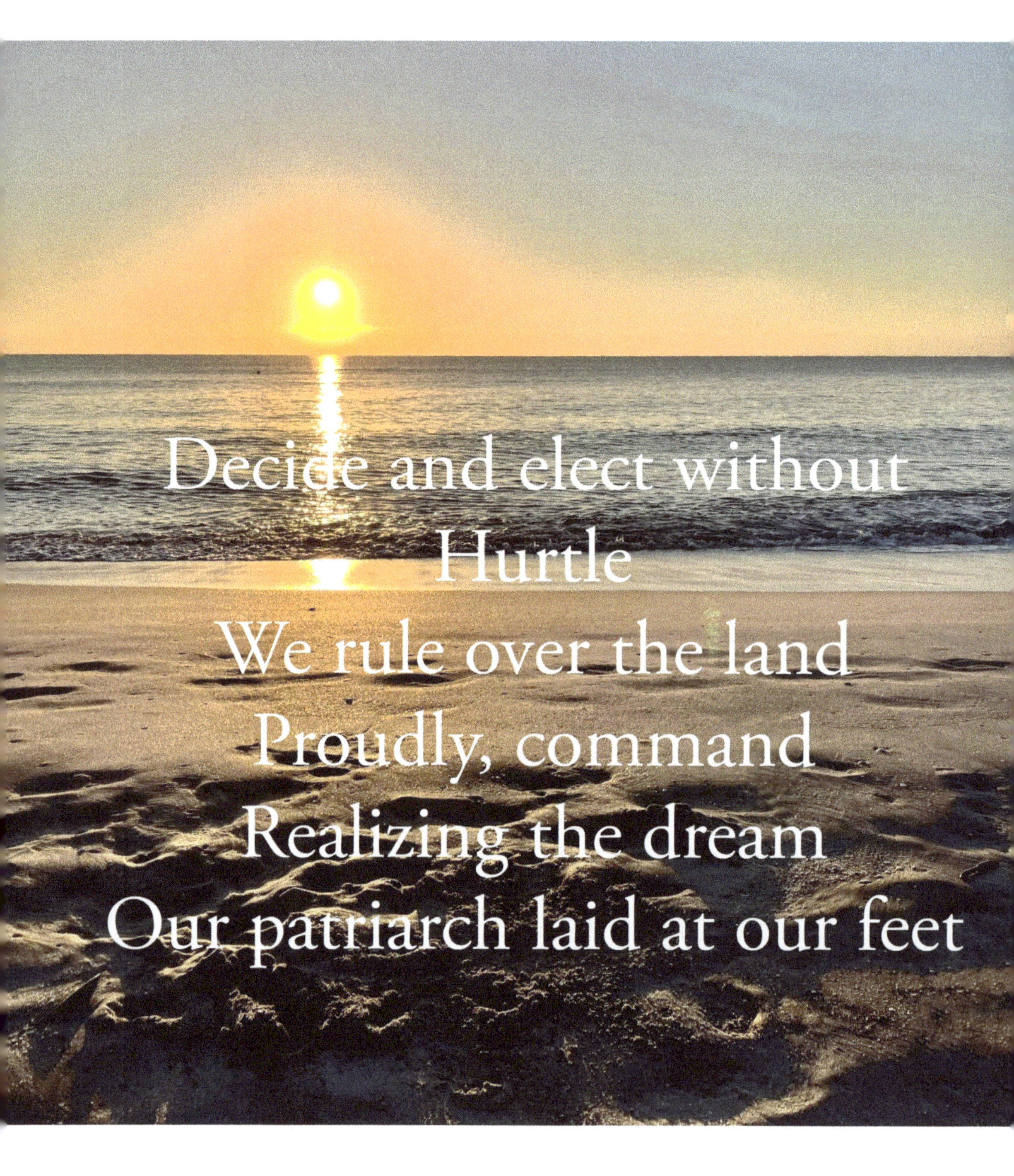

Decide and elect without
Hurtle
We rule over the land
Proudly, command
Realizing the dream
Our patriarch laid at our feet

RÊVER

Rêver d'aimer

Pire parfois rêver

D'être aimé

Peut parfois diminuer

Le besoin interdit

Par l'hypocrisie

De dire merci

Pourquoi inédit

Rest, admire the
simplicity
Of all this beauty
Enjoy and applaud
Remember to look
beyond
To say thank you

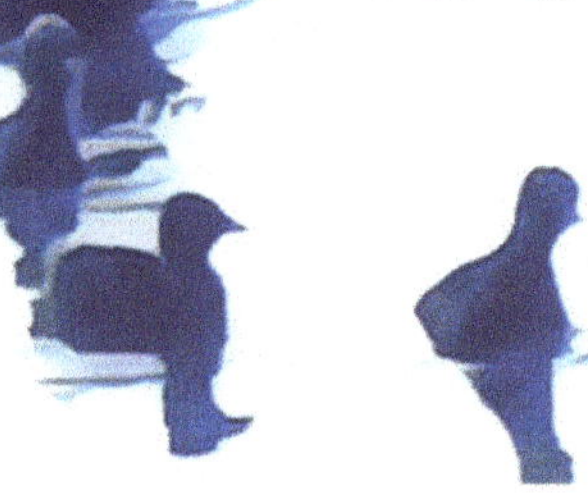

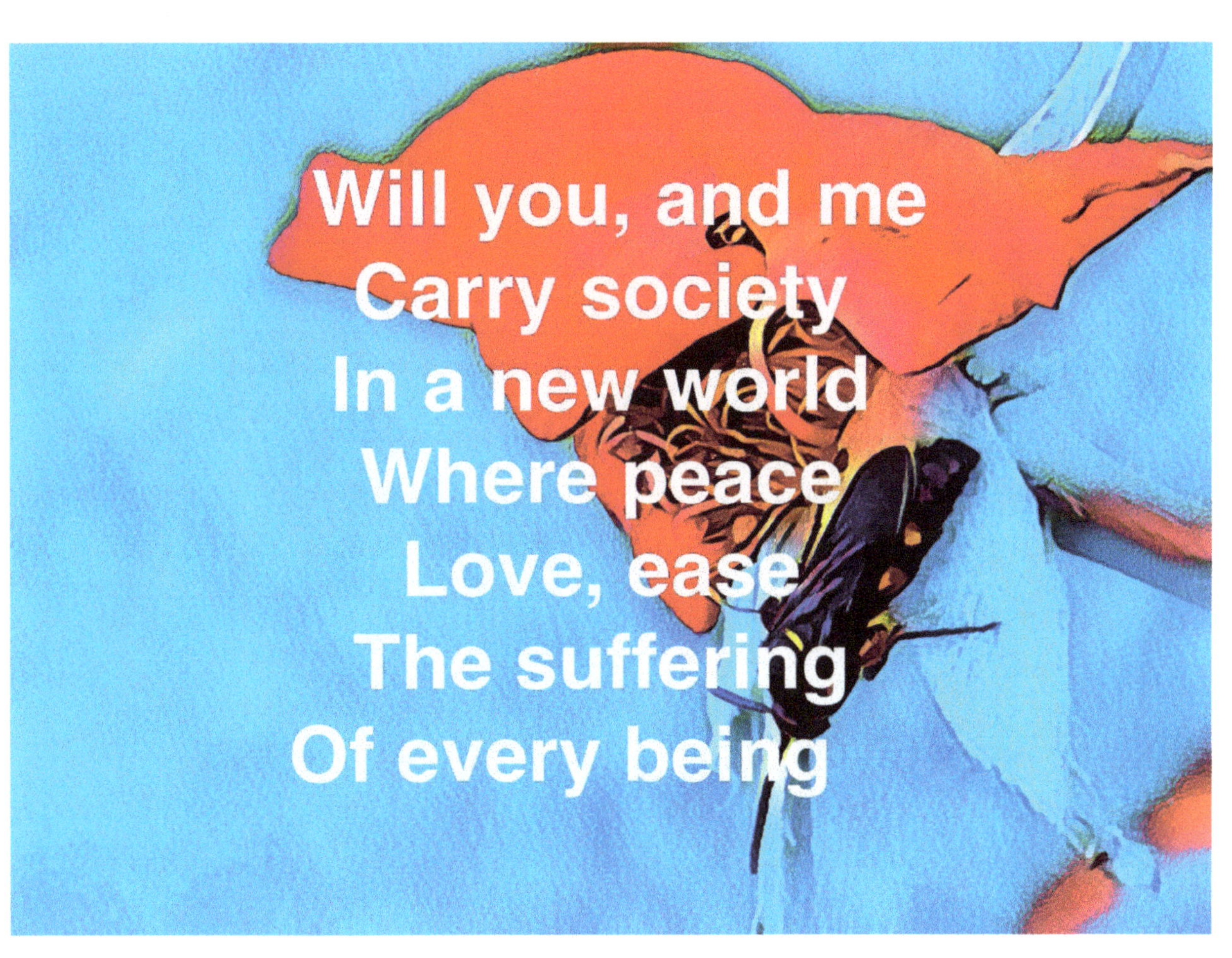

Will you, and me
Carry society
In a new world
Where peace
Love, ease
The suffering
Of every being

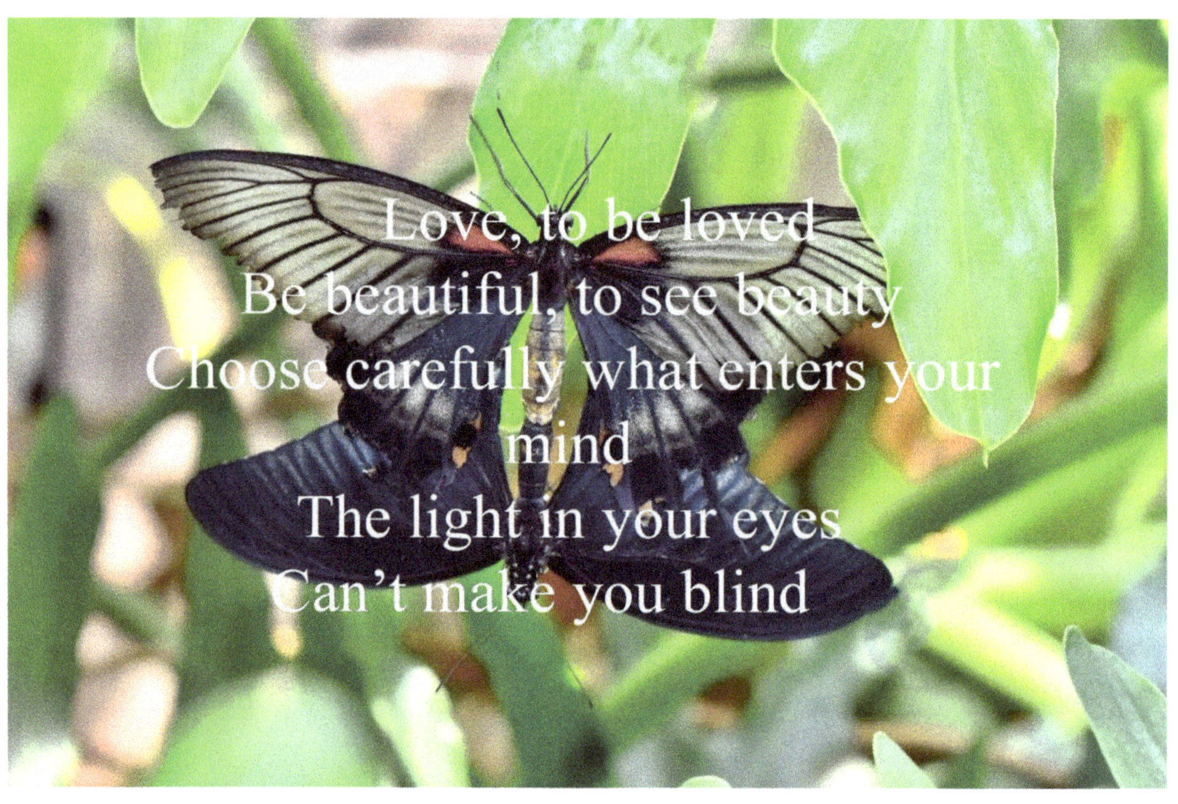

Love, to be loved
Be beautiful, to see beauty
Choose carefully what enters your
mind
The light in your eyes
Can't make you blind

Attention Awareness

Your attention
For two good reasons
Love and passions
Live your life, with this mission
Fulfill your dreams
Find peace
With ease
Let your hearts talk
To the beating sounds
Where love abounds
Enjoy simple moments
Be more present
Open your minds
Don't be blind
Let it be
For you to see
There is beauty
Complex uniformity
Trough out living entities
You will find communality
A liberation of self
Like anything else
Passion for our kind

Where you will find
A bright white light
In the dark foggy night
Stars, source, insight
The soul's ultimate flight
Bliss, enlightenment
Love and contentment
Imagine for an instant
The end of your torment
Rebirthed, like an infant
Rediscovering
The smells of the spring
The colors untamed and pure
The vitality of mother nature
The taste of a bright future
The touch of the wind murmur
Passion à tout les jours
Amour pour toujours
A fairy tale
A dream, everyday possible
Absolutely plausible
Love others deeply
Live your passion carelessly

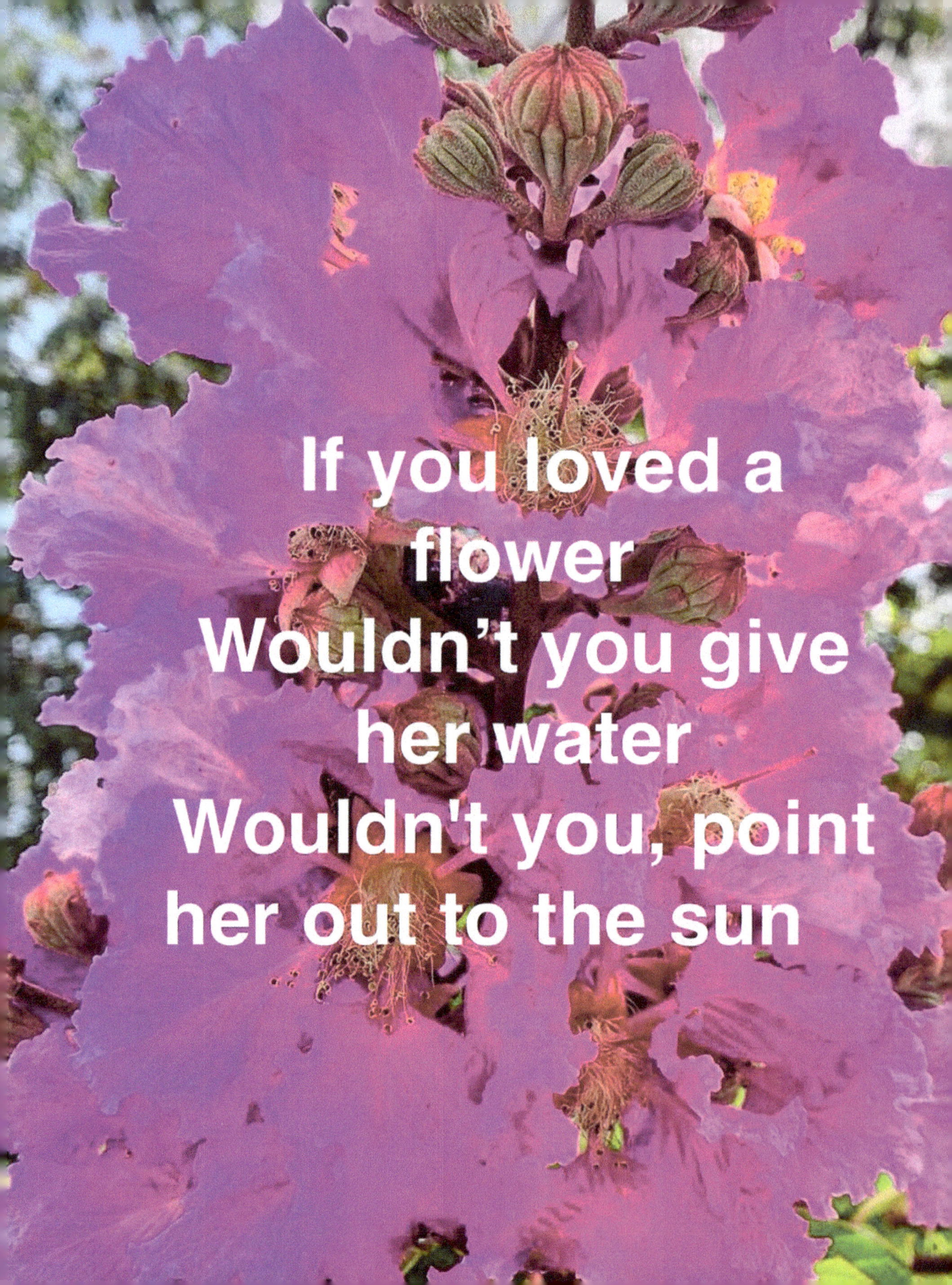

If you loved a
flower
Wouldn't you give
her water
Wouldn't you, point
her out to the sun

Autumn

It's autumn
Colors of yellow, orange, and red
Reminds me of sunrises
Except the sounds of the waves
Crashing on the beach
Replaced by the singing of the birds
In the trees
It all seems so out of reach
I often wonder
How far is the heart
How deep is too deep
Mother Nature
So kind and so pure
So beautiful
It's all there, it's here
Awake, understand
Open your eyes, comprehend
Life's last moments
Are met with sorrows
From those left behind
Life's first moments
Are met with sorrows
From you, who left behind
The creator.. for the creation
See and live your interpretation
Magical, colorful
So beautiful
Mother Nature
You are so pure
Why, do I wonder
Nothing is under
None is out of reach
The winds will teach
My heart in hands
Until I see the end
Birds are singing
The trees are living
Mother is so kind and so loving

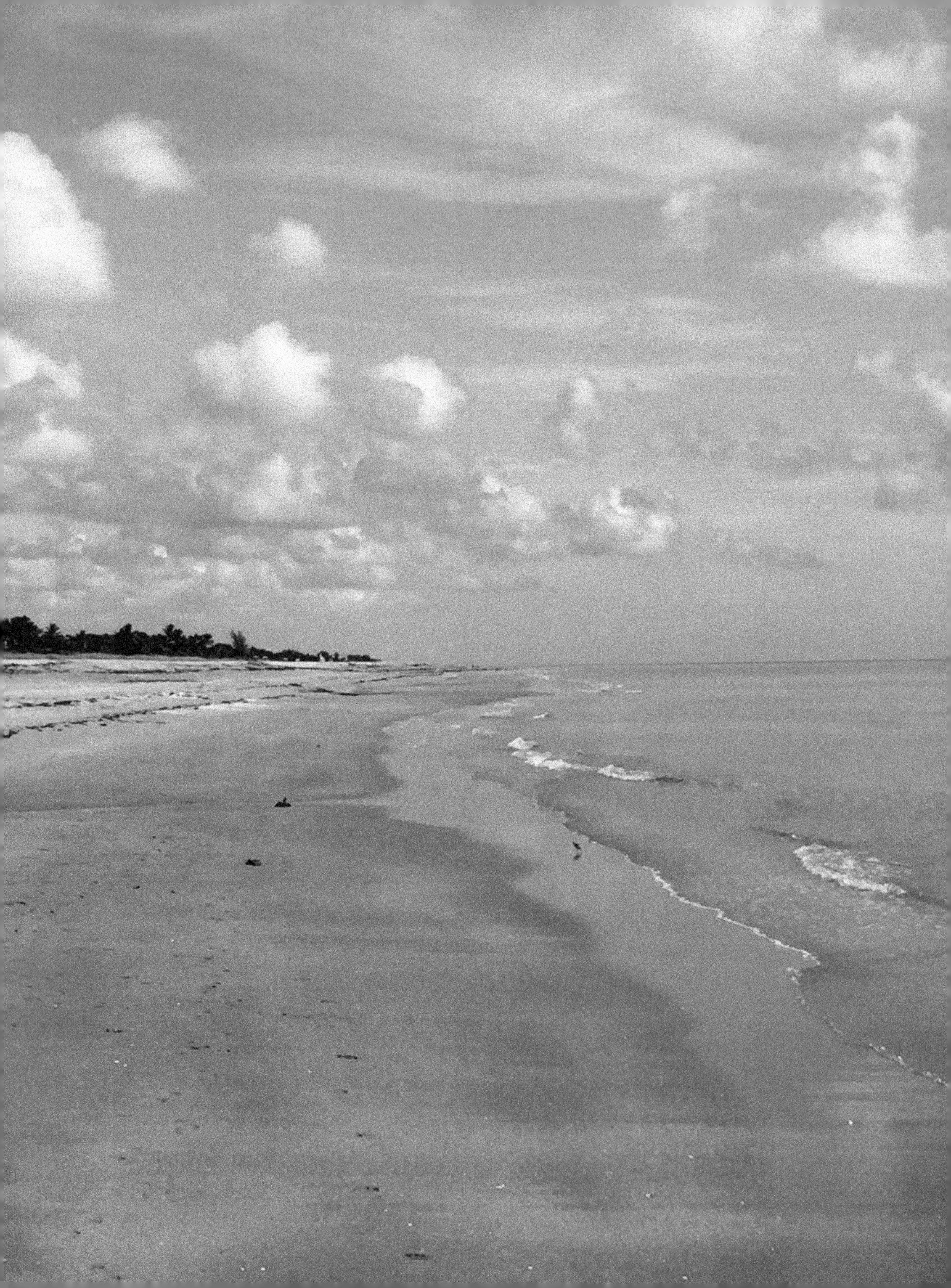

Beach

Today's a beautiful day
Innocent are laughing
Girls are blooming
Flowers representation
Of a perfect creation
Salt, ocean, smells
Sign odors can tell
Noise intoxication
Look for interaction
Waves breaking
Hearts pumping
Sand steaming
Souls searching
Today's a beautiful day
A lone observer
Quiet composer
Children's castles
Woman's marvels
Vast ocean
Be present

Wind blasts
Past went fast
Your future
Will be secure
Today's a beautiful day
Fresh oysters
Without her
Clouds' designs
Changing signs
Start conversation
Unknown conclusion
Euphoric atmosphere
Music cohere
Indulging crowds
Almost an overcrowd
Yet so lonely
Even amid so many
Today's a beautiful day
I have it all, lucky
Except she's not here with me

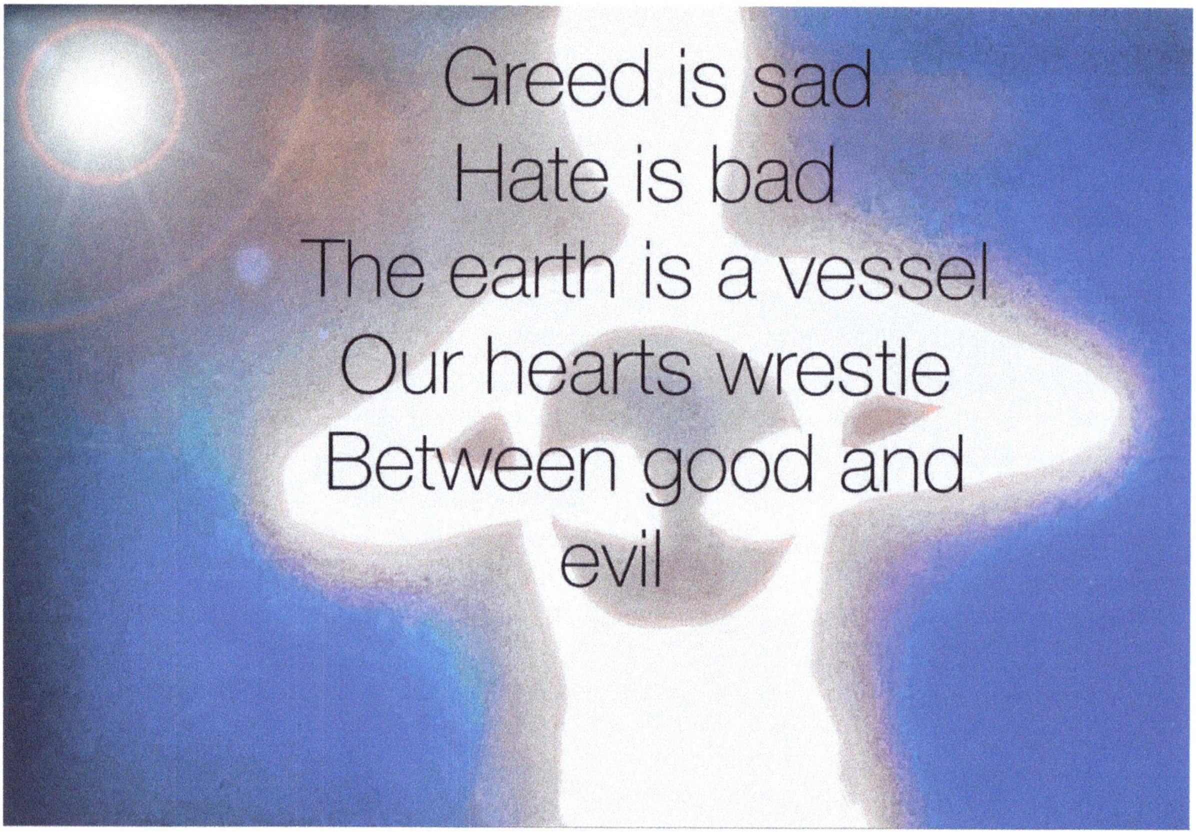

Greed is sad
Hate is bad
The earth is a vessel
Our hearts wrestle
Between good and
evil

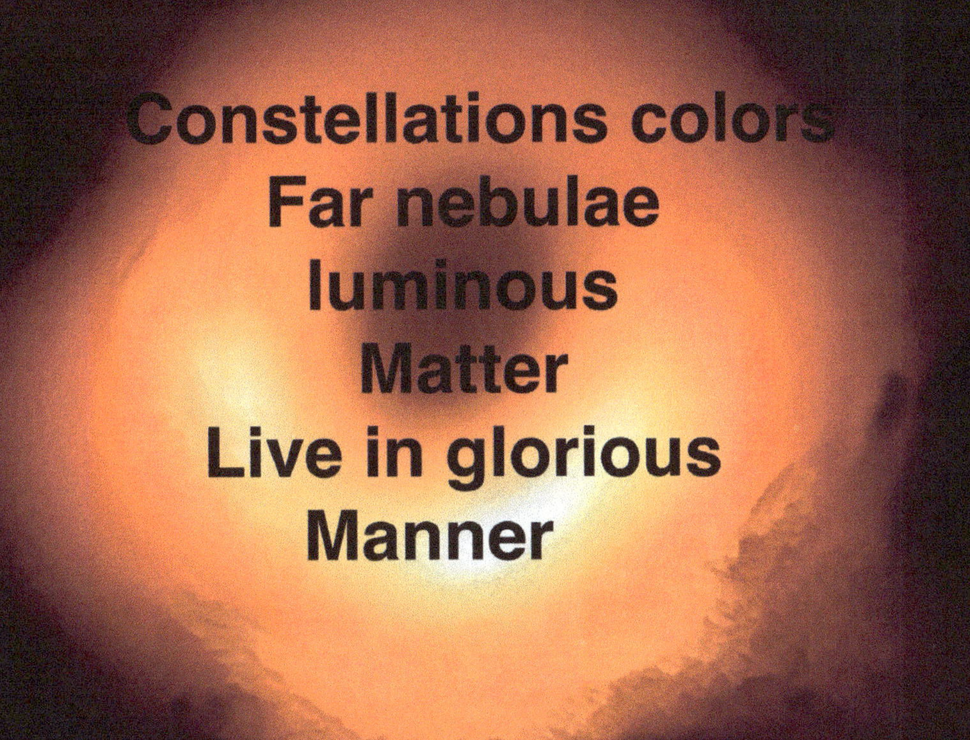

Constellations colors
Far nebulae
luminous
Matter
Live in glorious
Manner